BEYOND HINDU AND MUSLIM

Multiple Identity in Narratives from Village India

PETER GOTTSCHALK

UNIVERSITY PRESS
2000

OXFORD
UNIVERSITY PRESS

Oxford   New York
Athens   Auckland   Bangkok   Bogotá   Bombay   Buenos Aires
Calcutta   Cape Town   Dar es Salaam   Delhi   Florence   Hong Kong
Istanbul   Karachi   Kuala Lumpur   Madras   Madrid   Melbourne
Mexico City   Nairobi   Paris   Shanghai   Singapore   Taipei   Tokyo   Toronto

and associated companies in
Berlin   Ibadan

Copyright © 2000 by Peter Gottschalk

Published by Oxford University Press, Inc.
198 Madison Avenue, New York, New York 10016

Oxford is a registered trademark of Oxford University Press.

Library of Congress Cataloging-in-Publication Data
Gottschalk, Peter, 1963–
Beyond Hindu and Muslim : multiple identity in
narratives from village India / Peter Gottschalk.
p.   cm.
Includes bibliographical references and index.
ISBN 0-19-513514-8; 0-19-518915-9 (pbk.)
1. India—Ethnic relations.   2. Group identity—India.   3. Ethnicity—India.
4. Muslims—India.   5. Hindus—India.   6. Narration (Rhetoric)   I. Title.
DS430 .G66   2000
305.8'00954—dc21   99-046737

1 3 5 7 9 8 6 4 2

Printed in the United States of America
on acid-free paper

Dedicated, with deep gratitude, to the people of Bhabhua district,
who opened their lives
and their hearts
to me

हम सब दूसरों के लिए विदेशी हैं

("We are all foreign to each other.")
—Bhoju Ram Gopal

ادھر خاردار تاروں کے پیچھے ہندوستان تھا –
ادھر ویسے ہی تاروں کے پیچھے پاکستان –
درمیان میں زمین کے اس ٹکڑے پر جس کا
کوئی نام نہیں تھا ٹوبھ ٹیک سنگھ پڑا تھا –

("There, behind barbed wire, was India.
Over there, behind more barbed wire, was Pakistan.
In the middle, on a piece of ground which had no name, lay
Toba Tek Singh.")

—Saadat Hasan Manto,
"Toba Tek Singh"

Acknowledgments

The first note of thanks goes to the residents of the Arampur area, whose generosity and trust allowed me to share in so many dimensions of their selves. It is impossible for me to list everyone who made time and space for me. Special appreciation goes to Achutya Nand Singh, who guided me in Hindi, introduced me to his village, found me a home, and continually provided insightful interpretations. Jaideo Singh opened his house to me, and his family accepted me. His counsel guided me too often to remember. The Arampur Debate Society offered an endless supply of hot *chai* and warm friendship. In Banaras, Rakesh Ranjan shared his hospitality, personal insights, and expansive language expertise. Virendra Singh continued his long and patient tutoring of "Ram Iqbal" while Ramu Pandit offered his own unique perspective on the field and fieldworkers. Nita Kumar graciously accepted being my sponsor in India and provided administrative support, anthropological insights, and a scholastic model. The Centre for Studies in Social Sciences, Calcutta, kindly extended institutional affiliation for the project. Dr. Shailendra Tripathi provided a wonderful introduction to rural studies, finding room for me among fieldworkers in their jeeps and among his family in their home. Dr. Satyendra Tripathi, Director, extended the support of the Integrated Rural Development Program in Banaras Hindu University.

In the United States, my dissertation advisor, Wendy Doniger, provided constant support, insight, editing, and humor. This book represents the final fruition of a wonderful collaboration with Wendy, who has taught me much, molded me mightily, and set me "to go boldly. . . ." It would be impossible to note every feature of this text that benefited from our conversations and her suggestions and I am particularly indebted to her for her thoughtful foreword to this work. My dissertation readers, Steven Collins and Arjun Appadurai, unhesitatingly offered their expertise to shape this project and helped refine some of the many elements that it involved. Narayana Rao and Philip Lutgendorf offered their time to read drafts and make comments, many of which added significantly to my understanding. C. M. Naim has often acted as a touchstone to which I have returned for linguistic and other types of advice, and has generously reviewed some of my translations. McKim Marriot patiently offered invaluable insights into fieldwork and India through numerous conversations. Joe Elder continued to provide sage advice and practical insights. Ann Grodzins Gold shared her fieldwork experiences with me, as well as the quote from her collaborator, Bhoju Ram Gopal. Thanks, too, to the numerous colleagues who have listened to and commented on components of this project during conference and workshop presentations.

Among institutions, I appreciate the help that Southwestern University offered through Cullen faculty development stipends and the support of my new colleagues, especially the members of the Writers' Group who offered such useful feedback. Special thanks to Rich Pianka and Pat Ramsey of ITS who patiently aided me with my map-making. I am also very grateful to the University of Chicago, which financially supported my dissertation work abroad and in Chicago through the Divinity School, Committee on South Asian Studies, and advanced overseas dissertation research fellowship. There are too many faculty, administrators, and staff throughout the university for me to name whose help paved the way for this project. I thank the Government of India for the kind extension of a research visa. Special thanks to the American Institute of Indian Studies for its support for my visa application and to Director-General Dr. Pradeep Mehendiratta for its renewal. Oxford University Press has been particularly supportive of this project, and Cynthia Read wonderfully helpful. My thanks to John Bowen for his insightful comments as a reader.

Portions of Salman Rushdie's *Haroun and the Sea of Stories* are reproduced by permission of Penguin Books. The LaserURDU™ font used to print this work is available from Linguist's Software, Inc., PO Box 580, Edmonds, WA 98020-0580 USA tel (206) 775-1130.

Finally, and most emphatically, I want to thank the people closest to me for the support which abides so deeply and finds expression too rarely. My parents, Babette and Rudolf Gottschalk, come first of course. How can a tree adequately demonstrate appreciation for its roots? My brother and sisters also deserve a great note of thanks for their patience and support, as do my nephews and nieces, whose presence and love often helped me put my work in a larger context. Many colleagues from Chicago, especially Brian Bennett and Jeff Carter, gave invaluable input through the course of innumerable conversations. Friends like Bill, Steve, Christine, John, and Ken have given warm company, emotional support, and good humor throughout the course of this work. I continue to owe a debt to my teachers, who are too many to entirely mention but too important not to try: Sarah Wilde, Richard Wilde, Sylvia Campbell, Steve Marabeti, Clyde Pax, the late Theo von Laue, Frank Reynolds, and Bruce Lincoln. To Prem Kumar in India and Mat Schmalz in the United States: Darmok and Jilad on the Ocean. Finally, to my wife Deborah and my daughter Ariadne, who have lit my life with their fire and warmth: thank you, for evermore.

Contents

Photos follow page 64

Foreword

This study of the construction of Hindu, Muslim, and other identities in India has important implications for our understanding of interreligious cooperation and interreligious violence. It will contribute, in general, to our understanding of the various cultural logics which inform societies in conflict and, in particular, to our understanding of the Hindu-Muslim conflict in India. Gottschalk's work is about concepts of time and memory; he is searching for a constructive sense of history in the face of the formidable de(con)struction wrought by the Orientalist and subaltern critique. His study of India is informed by his previous work on the historiography and theology of Jewish approaches to the Holocaust; in both cases, he has delved deep into the emotional and cognitive problems of understanding a traumatic past. His particular contribution to the debates of historians is his subtle understanding of narrative, particularly religious narrative, and he puts his theories to a practical and constructive test in India. He writes beautifully and brings a quasi-novelistic sensitivity to his evocation of the settings in which real people come into real conflict. This brilliant and passionately conceived book is readable, moving, and timely; it changed my mind, entirely, about the ways in which Hindus and Muslims regard one another in India, and about the ways in which the concerns that bind one human being to another may override the political and economic forces that drive them apart.

—Wendy Doniger

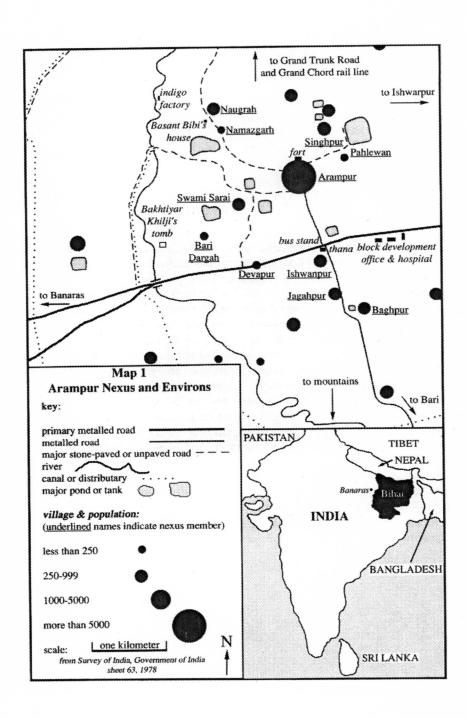

to Grand Trunk Road
and Grand Chord rail line

to Ishwarpur

indigo factory

Naugrah

Basant Bibi's house

Namazgarh

Singhpur

fort

Pahlewan

Arampur

Swami Sarai

Bakhtiyar Khilji's tomb

Bari Dargah

bus stand

thana block development office & hospital

Devapur

Ishwanpur

to Banaras

Jagahpur

Baghpur

to mountains

to Bari

Map 1
Arampur Nexus and Environs

key:

primary metalled road	─────
metalled road	─────
major stone-paved or unpaved road	– – –
river	∿∿∿
canal or distributary	·········
major pond or tank	▱ ▱

village & population:
(underlined names indicate nexus member)

less than 250 ●

250-999 ●

1000-5000 ●

more than 5000 ●

scale: |— one kilometer —|

from Survey of India, Government of India sheet 63, 1978

N

PAKISTAN

TIBET

NEPAL

Banaras

Bihar

INDIA

BANGLADESH

SRI LANKA

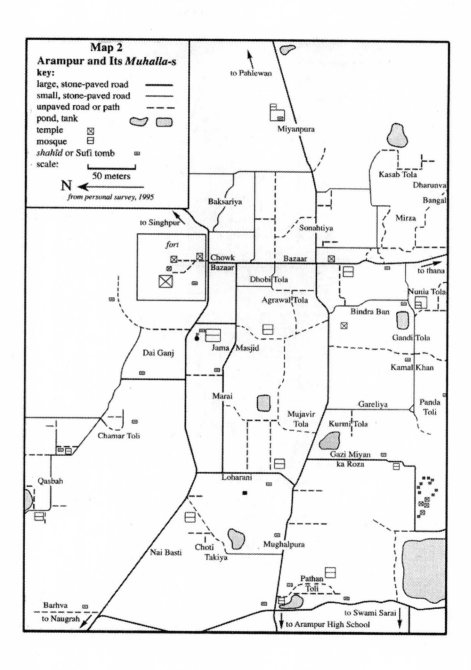

Map 2
Arampur and Its *Muhalla*-s
key:
large, stone-paved road
small, stone-paved road
unpaved road or path
pond, tank
temple
mosque
shahid or Sufi tomb
scale:
50 meters
N
from personal survey, 1995

to Pahlewan

Miyanpura

Kasab Tola

Dharunva

Bangal

Baksariya

Mirza

Sonahtiya

to Singhpur

fort

Chowk
Bazaar

Bazaar

to thana

Dhobi Tola

Nunia Tola

Agrawal Tola

Bindra Ban

Gandi Tola

Dai Ganj

Jama Masjid

Kamal Khan

Marai

Panda
Toli

Gareliya

Mujavir
Tola

Kurmi Tola

Chamar Toli

Gazi Miyan
ka Roza

Qasbah

Loharani

Mughalpura

Nai Basti

Choti
Takiya

Pathan
Toli

Barhva
to Naugrah

to Swami Sarai

to Arampur High School

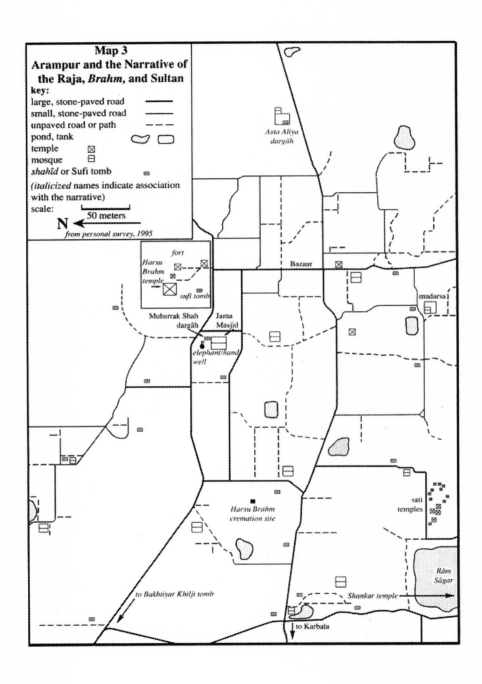

Map 3
Arampur and the Narrative of
the Raja, *Brahm*, and Sultan

key:
large, stone-paved road
small, stone-paved road
unpaved road or path
pond, tank
temple
mosque
shahīd or Sufi tomb

(italicized names indicate association
with the narrative)

scale:
50 meters

N

from personal survey, 1995

Asta Aliya
dargāh

Bazaar

madarsa

fort

Harsu
Brahm
temple

sufi tomb

Mubarrak Shah
dargāh

Jama
Masjid

elephant/hand/
well

Harsu Brahm
cremation site

sati
temples

Rām
Sāgar

to Bakhtiyar Khilji tomb

Shankar temple

to Karbala

Transliteration Guide

Scheme of Hindi and Bhojpuri Transliteration

Passages followed by "[H]" are transliterated according to the Hindi-to-English system below, which follows R. S. McGregor, *The Oxford Hindi-English Dictionary*:

अ	आ	इ	ई	उ	ऊ	ए	ऐ	ओ	औ	ऋ
a	ā	i	ī	u	ū	e	ai	o	au	r̥

क	ख	ग	घ	ङ		
k	kh	g	gh	ṅ		

च	छ	ज	झ	ञ		
c	ch	j	jh	ñ		

ट	ठ	ड	ढ	ण	.ड	.ढ
ṭ	ṭh	ḍ	ḍh	ṇ	r̥	r̥h

त	थ	द	ध	न		
t	th	d	dh	n		

प	फ	ब	भ	म		
p	ph	b	bh	m		

य	र	ल	ळ	व	श	ष	स	ह
y	r	l	ḷ	v	ś	ṣ	s	h

Scheme of Urdu Transliteration

Passages followed by "[U]" are transliterated according to the Urdu-to-English system below, which follows John Platts, *A Dictionary of Urdū, Classical Hindī and English*:

ا	اِ	اُ	آ
a	i	u	ā

اوُ	او	اوَ	اِي	اي	أي
ū	o	au	ī	e	ai

ب	پ	ت	ٹ	ث	ج	چ	ح	خ
b	p	t	ṭ	s̤	j	c	ḥ	kh

د	ڈ	ذ	ر	ڑ	ز	ژ
d	ḍ	z	r	ṛ	z	zh

س	ش	ص	ض
s	sh	ṣ	ẓ

ط	ظ	ع	غ	ف	ق
t̤	z̤	ʿ	g	f	q

ک	گ	ل	م	ن	و	ہ	ي
k	g	l	m	n	v/w	h	y

BEYOND HINDU AND MUSLIM

Introduction

One Territory,
Multiple Maps

A friend had just returned from India, and we sat having tea in my Chicago apartment. She spoke of the disillusionment caused by the divergence between her American university, book-based education of India and her first year's experience of living in India. One of the most difficult aspects of her life, she explained, was dealing with the communalism that increasingly simmered on the front burner of the 1996 national elections. Indian friends, whose opinions she thought she could predict, surprisingly began to echo the bigoted sentiments that bubbled and frothed in the heated climate of the elections. Her comments spurred my memories of uncomfortable moments I experienced occasionally in my rural research site—moments when a Muslim flamboyantly condemned Hindus or a Hindu harshly denigrated Muslims. Trying to camouflage my revulsion toward such talk without condoning these ideas with silence, I seldom responded to such situations with anything more than a halfhearted nod or a barely audible grunt. After all, I had come, in part, to explore such sentiments. Moreover, I knew that not only would any protest on my part be without good effect but also it would most likely make residents less forthcoming to me about such matters. Like my friend, I struggled with my feelings and lived with my frustration.

Despite my hesitancy to rebut publicly the expressions of communalism I experienced in India, I hope to address associated problems in American scholarship on South Asia. It was this hope which motivated my fieldwork in India and which informs this book. Western scholars of the Subcontinent rely too heavily on *Hindu* and *Muslim* as descriptive adjectives and analytic categories. Many defer too quickly to *Hinduism* and *Islam* as self-apparent terms for exclusive arenas of religious activity. In the end, too many students come away with the impression that South Asian cultures can best be viewed, de facto, through bifurcated glasses that discretely discern two halves of India—*Hindu* and *Muslim*—in time, space, and society.

I would suggest that such distinctions are not without their uses. But by privileging them to the degree that we often do, we create singular temporal,

3

spatial, and social maps which imply that communal divisions exist for all South Asians at all times. Instead, I would argue, we must continually problematize these maps with the awareness that other maps can overlap them, each alternately privileged according to context. It is true that any cultural study must accept its own limits. No matter how rigorous it attempts to be, a description can never produce a 1:1 scale map of any object of study. Jonathan Z. Smith aptly rephrases Alfred Korzybski's phrase, "'Map is not territory'—but maps are all we possess."[1] Yet, those of us who are scholars foreign to South Asia must somehow recognize the continually shifting cartography among South Asians and approach our studies with a set of maps that we shuffle occasionally according to the questions we ask of Subcontinental people and cultures. If we find that only one map is enough, then we should suspect ourselves of oversimplification. (For examples of the multiple maps possible for a single area, see maps 1 through 3.)

Perceiving the importance of religion in Indian society, many scholars erroneously conclude that this society can be described solely in terms of religious identity. Attempting to do so, these scholars overlook the nature of any individual as a conglomerate of various identities and fail to see the interests around which these identities form. By emphasizing only religious identity, scholars rarefy religions, removing them from the social milieu in which they develop. This environment involves economic, political, and other interests around which group identities form. These other interests may compete with or complement—but certainly influence—religious interests and the identities that they foster. Ironically, to understand better the religious identities of Hindus and Muslims in India, it becomes necessary to decentralize these identities as the sole locus of research and return them to a broader social context. A study of group identity in India demonstrates how religious interests inform and are informed by other concerns in Indian constructions of society, and how narratives told by Indians can reflect these interests.

"Muslim culture dominates everything done by the people of Naugrah" [H]. So Arampur area resident Ved Singh disapprovingly says as he finishes telling me a story that explained how many Hindus in his village and Muslims in the neighboring village of Naugrah descend from two brothers. The burgeoning religious identity of Muslims, he continues, has overshadowed the family connection that once linked the two groups. Singh gives voice to a sentiment held by many Hindus in India—that Muslims cannot really be Indian or share any identity with Hindus because Muslim religious values supersede all else. The singular identity ascribed to Muslims by Singh (and the equally two-dimensional religious identity of "Hindu" perceived by many Muslims) is unfortunate, yet revealing. Unfortunate, inasmuch as it allows for the essentializing and inflammatory language of contemporary communalist politics. Revealing, in that it demonstrates the significant convergence of narrative with notions of values and identity. An exploration of this convergence through indigenous narratives

1. Jonathan Z. Smith, *Map Is Not Territory*. Chicago: University of Chicago Press, 1978. p. 309.

demonstrates both the multiple group identities of any individual and the role of narrative in the formation and communication of these identities.

Naugrah and the village of Ved Singh adjoin one another in a constellation of villages centered on the large village of Arampur, the hub of my research site. Populated only by those who would religiously identify themselves as "Hindu" or "Muslim," this locale has witnessed intermittent moments of direct conflict between members of these two religious groups during long years of peaceful tension. After living in this area for fourteen months, from October 1994 to December 1995, I wrote a dissertation that attempts to problematize and clarify aspects of regional religious values and identity.[2] This book derives from that dissertation. In it, I contend that group memories reflect how other identities compete with or complement those of "Hindu" and "Muslim." I base this conclusion on the following five premises. First, groups build and reinforce their identity through the expression of shared interests. Second, the importance of the past is one such shared interest. Third, motivated by shared interests in the past, groups derive roughly consensual group memories from individual memories. Groups shape and reshape these memories intersubjectively through discourse and may communicate versions to successive generations. Fourth, villagers have interests other than religious interests. And fifth, individual villagers belong to various groups and share group memories with religious ones among them. An explanation of each premise, accompanied by examples of local voices, structures this book as it follows from chapter 1 (historical introduction to the problem and brief review of scholarship) and chapter 2 (description of project site and examination of territorial identities). These examples serve only an illustrative purpose; they are developed further in succeeding chapters.

My first premise is that group identity forms around common interests. Through the following story, Salman Khan, who describes himself as a Muslim, helps define a group identity held in common with the Hindu family of Ved Singh, from whom we heard earlier. "Two brothers came here with the Delhi sultan. They defeated the local raja and the sultan gave them all the land. The name of our village, Naugrah, means 'new house.' The other brother remained Hindu and settled in the next village. Our families remain close and we go to one another's weddings" [U]. Salman Khan defines a group identity— that incidentally includes Hindu and Muslim members—through the expression of values shared by both families. Paul Ricoeur theoretically describes this dynamic in his three-volume *Time and Narrative* (see chapter 3), wherein he argues that groups establish themselves around shared interests and express these interests through common narratives. Both Rājpūt and Paṭhān residents of the two neighboring villages often interpret Salman Khan's narrative as a lesson in intercommunal harmony. The familial identity among them overlaps and, at times, overshadows Hindu and Muslim identities. The narrative can also be

---

2. Peter Gottschalk, "*Multiple Pasts, Multiple Identities: The Role of Narrative among Hindus and Muslims in Some Villages in Bihar*. Ph.D. dissertation, University of Chicago, 1997.

interpreted as reinforcing a common class identity among the two groups through the expression of the shared interest in landownership. Although both Rājpūts and Paṭhāns often refer to their villages as though they are the sole inhabitants, in fact each village is comprised of several castes. The Rājpūts and Paṭhāns remain by far the largest landowners of their villages and economically and politically the most powerful inhabitants. Thus, the narrative reflects their sense of appropriation and ownership of the villages.

The second premise contends that among the interests which narratives express is the value of the past itself. Ricoeur maintains, in his book's central thesis, that humans inherently need to situate themselves in time. Therefore, the narratives shared by groups reflect, among other values, the value of the group's past. Salman Khan and Ved Singh separately explained how their family's story passed from parent to child over generations. Among the many members of their dual extended family whom I interviewed, all related this narrative in roughly the same form when asked how long their family has lived in their particular villages. Whereas an answer in number of years or generations would have sufficed, most residents gave, instead, a narrative as an answer. Calendars count years but narratives serve to describe the link between the past and the present. Among other things, the narratives of the Singh and Khan families relate their arrival in, settlement of, and economic domination of the area, as well as the peculiar familial relationship between their two groups.

As a third premise, I argue that the notion of group memory gives the observer a useful heuristic to analyze narratives in which groups express some of their common interests while bracketing issues of historical truth (see chapter 3). According to Ved Singh, "The local raja had a Brahman priest. The Brahman died due to an injustice done by the raja. So the ghost of the Brahman went to Delhi and told the sultan how to defeat the raja. The sultan sent the two brothers to attack the king" [H]. How does one describe such a narrative? History? Myth? Despite the efforts of some to expand and elaborate both notions, many scholars are likely to describe such a narrative in discipline-bound ways and words that imply a judgment of the factuality of the narrated event. The concept of group memory allows the observer to avoid the inference of veracity that these terms connote and helps reveal the interests that undergird the intent to narrate them.

Drawing on the work of Maurice Halbwachs and Paul Connerton, I argue that some narratives express group memories organized around shared group interests. The notion of group memory has found increasing currency among historians, anthropologists, and the mass media. The term conveys the dynamic aspect of narrative telling, which is never just a recollection but also the act of recollecting. This dynamic includes the process of individual remembering, group agreement or dissent, change in the narrative, and communication to others in the group, including younger generations. As group interests change, so can the narratives that reflect them. The notion of group memory agrees with concepts and terminology indigenous to the rural north Indian setting:

yād, *smṛtī*, and *memory* are all terms commonly used not only for individual recollection but also for what the group remembers.

To show the utility and robustness of the idea of group memory, I conduct a comparative analysis of four versions of the narrative concerning the raja, *brahm*, and sultan. One version comes from an oral telling by a low-caste Hindu woman and another from a pamphlet published by a local Brahman man. A member of another Brahman family provides a third narrative that criticizes the latter as not "historical" enough and draws on research of Western travelers and scholars found in a national library. Finally, the narrative as *not* found in the six-volume *Comprehensive History of Bihar* demonstrates the ways in which historiography—yet another form of group memory—operates through the qualification and disqualification of certain narratives. Rather than setting one narrative apart from another through the categories of "history" and "myth," I argue that all four examples depict types of expressions of group memories that vary, in part, according to specific strategies of authorization, verification, and transmission that are deliberately adopted to express particular interests.

Those more interested in the narrative expressions of multiple identity than in the theory of group memory can safely skip chapter 3. This chapter attempts to theorize a concept that has increasingly popular and useful applications and, then, comparatively portrays the dynamics of its expression. However, the very fact that the notion of group memory has become so widespread allows references to it in the last two chapters to be understandable without the clarification of theory.

My fourth premise is that villagers have interests which compete with and complement religious values (see chapters 4 and 5). "Will you write a history of the poor?" [H] Dalit Ram asks me. "The village name Naugrah means 'nine houses.' We had nine houses here before the Khans came and took our land." The "we" in this narrative refers to the Camārs[3] of Naugrah village. Through this narrative of past oppression, some Harijan residents express a notion of underclass solidarity in the face of current social and economic oppression. Although they occasionally define themselves as "Hindu" relative to their "Muslim" landlords, Naugrah's Harijans at other times distinguish themselves as *not* "Hindu" when middle- and upper-caste Hindus bar them from the *brahm*'s temple, force them to hold Kālī Pūjā a day before or after high-caste celebrations, and otherwise exclude them because of their caste. Thus, every narrative has a multiplicity of interpretations, any of which can come into play in certain contexts, reflecting the notions of identity predominant at that moment. Camārs of this village do not concern themselves solely with the re-

---

3. Currently in India, many members of the Hindu caste often associated with leather work prefer the caste name "Moci" instead of "Camar." Similarly, members of castes with the least social status prefer the term "Dalit" ("oppressed"; "crushed") to "Harijan" ("children of god"), as coined by Mohandas Gandhi. However, my terminology follows local practice of the caste members themselves.

ligious interests related in narratives such as the *Mahābhārat* and the *Ramāyan*, books considered "classic Hindu texts" by many Western and Indian scholars. Concerns for justice and social fairness figure prominently into the narratives of many Camārs, thus portraying an identity forged from the conditions of extreme economic and political vulnerability.

The fifth and final premise of my work asserts that villagers share identities other than those of "Hindu" and "Muslim." These include affiliations with class, caste, family, devotion, gender, and territory. "Indian" was among the most prevalent identities that my foreign presence aroused in those around me. Almost every area resident whom I asked, "Why is August fifteenth so important in India?" responded with the phrase, "We were slaves of the English and on August fifteenth, 1947, we obtained our freedom." Their narratives of British rule, Independence, and the Partition of India inevitably include the stories of freedom movement leaders such as Mohandas Gandhi, Jawaharlal Nehru, and Muhammad Ali Jinnah. The uniformity among these narratives is striking and underlines the strength of both individual memories and government-propagated versions of a nationalist narrative. By "strength" I do not refer to the accuracy of these narratives to relate what "actually" happened but, rather, to their capability to act as a locus of group identity within individual memory. For most local residents, the identity of "Indian" complements that of "Hindu," "Muslim," village resident, caste member, and so on. The national interests of political self-determination and economic self-reliance undergird the narratives of British rule. In turn, residents often use versions of this narrative to depict and interpret the new foreign "invasion" of their country made possible by current economic liberalization. The entries of the British East India Company quite some centuries ago and the Western power company Enron but a few years ago are often cast into the same narrative mold to express these interests shared by many Indians and played upon by nationalist political parties. These and other group memories reflect how other identities compete with and complement the identities and values of "Hindus" and "Muslims."

In a book that seeks to challenge the primacy of the Hindu-Muslim dichotomy, it might seem imprudent to even use these labels. Indeed, Bipan Chandra usefully cautions that

> many secular writers today, following in the footsteps of many of the earlier nationalist leaders, adopt or adapt the basic communal digits and assumptions and then proceed to reject the communal argument. This is to analyze communalism in terms of its own political practice and to fight it on its own terrain, to be its hostage.[4]

However, it would be erroneous to pretend that many, if not most, Indians understand themselves and their neighbors, in part, according to these labels. My attempt here is to explore and portray some of the many and diverse ele-

---

4. Bipan Chandra, *Communalism in Modern India*. New Delhi: Vikas, 1984. p. 12.

ments (religion included) found within individuals' identities that exist in dynamic tension with one another.

This project does not attempt to provide a comprehensive ethnohistory of any particular area. Nor does it strive to determine the historiographic accuracy of any narrative. Rather, it borrows certain examples of oral and written narratives to argue the point that there exists a spectrum of group memory that reflect group identities which, in varying contexts, alternately include and exclude religious identities.

Unfortunately, my research was limited mostly to the male population of the Arampur area because of the limited access to women that I had as a foreign man with fluency in Hindi and Urdu only. Upper-class women, who often have a Hindi- or Urdu-language education, are usually not allowed outside their homes and certainly not to talk to a foreigner. Lower-class women of the Arampur area, at greater liberty to move about publicly, speak Bhojpuri almost exclusively. This project could and should be replicated with more women as informants. In contrast to the men interviewed, who almost all still live in the villages of their birth, most women residents come from outside the nexus, marry into a new household, and learn new narratives and identities. How do women's views shift as they move across the highly localized landscape of family customs? What do they remember (or are allowed to remember) from their natal homes? How do their practices of domestic religion influence their notions of religious identity? These are but a few of the many questions that would rightly compel a project more devoted to women.[5] Had the current work aimed to provide a complete ethnography or ethnohistory of the Arampur nexus, instead of demonstrating the presence of multiple identities that both complement and conflict with religious identities, it would have been incomplete without this material.

All Hindi and Urdu words quoted are italicized and their English translations follow in parentheses. "[H]" or "[U]" after a phrase indicates that I have translated into English something said in either Hindi or Urdu, respectively. The designation reflects what the speaker identified as her or his mother language. No designation has been given for those speakers who did not declare their mother language. "[E]'" designates phrases spoken in English, and "[H/E]" or "[U/E]" denotes phrases spoken in a mixture of English and Hindi or Urdu. Transliteration follows R. S. McGregor, *The Oxford Hindi-English Dictionary*, unless the word is distinctly Urdu, in which case it follows John T. Platts, *A*

---

5. Excellent scholarship that considers these and related themes of South Asian women's lives includes Patricia Jeffery and Roger Jeffery, *Don't Marry Me to a Plowman! Women's Everyday Lives in Rural North India* (Boulder, Colo.: Westview, 1996); Susan Wadley, *Struggling with Destiny in Karimpur, 1925–1984* (Berkeley: University of California Press, 1994); Anita Weiss, *Walls within Walls: Life Histories of Working Women in the Old City of Lahore* (Boulder, Colo.: Westview, 1992); and many of the contributions to Lindsey Harlan and Paul Courtright, eds., *From the Margins of Hindu Marriage: Essays on Gender, Religion, and Culture* (New York: Oxford University Press, 1995).

Dictionary of Urdū, Classical Hindī and English.[6] Transliteration reflects local pronunciation when it is significantly different from either dictionary. Thus, the word for a school of Muslim learning is rendered in Hindi transliteration as *madarsā* but, in this work, is rendered following the Urdu transliteration: *madarsa.* Also, note that I chose this term, labeled "vulgar" by Platts, instead of the standard Urdu *madrasa* because this reflects the pronunciation of the larger number of nexus residents. Hindi and Urdu words in common usage in American English are not italicized.[7]

For the sake of the reading ease of nonspecialists, titles of books familiar to a general audience and proper names (whether for places, people, or deities) have not been written with diacritics. Specialized religious terminology (e.g., Kālī Pūjā), names of temporal markers (e.g., Muḥarram), and culturally unique terms (e.g., *bīṛī*) have been transliterated for the use of scholars of South Asia and religion. Finally, diacritics are used for the names of caste groups (e.g., Thākur) but not when they are used in personal names (e.g., Somavahan Thakur).

All names of residents and their villages have been changed out of respect for their privacy. The maps included are accurate in regard to the internal layout of villages and their geographical relation to one another but have been directionally skewed.

6. In the context of the contemporary debate regarding the distinctiveness of Hindi and Urdu and the historical debate regarding the term "Hindustani," it is interesting to note that Platts's original 1884 edition was entitled *A Dictionary, Hindūstánī and English.*

7. Common usage is here defined by inclusion in *The American Heritage Dictionary of the English Language,* third edition. New York: Houghton Mifflin, 1992.

1

Multiple Identities, Singular Representations

Modernity has proven to be an illusive animal to snare in the trap of description. This results, in part, from the manner in which its constituent elements serve as paradigms for understanding the world—paradigms so basic to Western interpretation that they are often as presumed as looking through one's eyes. Most Westerners, as children of the Enlightenment and the Protestant Reformation, unreflectively consider individualism, rationalism, secularism, and nationalism as prerequisite components of "modern" societies. Because they often adopt an idea of progress that posits the modern as the pinnacle of human cultural development, Westerners sometimes harshly judge cultures that fail to fulfill modern expectations, negatively labeling them as backward, medieval, or less developed. Absorbing and appropriating many of these paradigms and valuations through hundreds of years of Western cultural hegemony, many non-Westerners have come to share some of these views of modern Westerners and their critique of non-Western societies.

Secular ideals not only have blinded many American cultural observers concerning the prominence of religion in their own society's public life but also have misled them to depict many non-Western cultures as essentially religious. In the case of South Asia, some scholars have struggled against this oversimplification by denying the significance of religious identity in the public sphere before the advent of the British. Currently, scholarship has begun to appreciate better the multiple identities—including, for many, religious identities—by which an individual associates with any one of many groups according to social context. Through an examination of local narratives, this book aims to contribute to this effort by demonstrating the complex yet interrelated world among the various identities of family, class, caste, gender, territory, nation, and religion found among Arampur residents.

Rational Westerners and Religious Indians

A high school student in India once asked me about the Christian war against the Jews during the Second World War. Stunned by what seemed to me an unorthodox description of a familiar event, I fumbled to find the words for my own, previously unverbalized understanding that it wasn't a *Christian* war but a Nazi or German persecution of Jews. The differences in our frames of perspective compelled me to reflect on the ways I, as an American, conceptualize social conflict within my own culture and among others. Would an American historian depict the Vietnamese-American War as a conflict of Buddhists and atheists against Christians? How often do Americans portray the secessionist movement in Canada as a struggle of Catholics (in Catholic-dominated Quebec) against Protestants (in the Protestant-dominated remainder of the nation)? Then why are South Asian cultures so commonly described by Americans in terms of *Hindu* and *Muslim*? Following the lead of some Orientalist scholarship and of certain indigenous leaders who emphasize and, thus, exaggerate rifts between Hindus and Muslims, the tendency of many Western scholars is to rend the entire material of South Asian society down an arbitrary middle, dividing a singular Muslim identity from an equally singular Hindu identity. L. K. Sharma will recognize this very attitude when he protests the notion of a "Hindu bomb" in the passage quoted later.

Many Western scholars assume that modern Westerners act out of secular, rational concerns while South Asians (as well as Middle Easterners and inhabitants of other regions) act under a primary impulse of religious sentiment.[1] This is a particular feature of "Orientalist" thought.[2] Westerners, when considering the most morally repugnant of their number (Nazis, for instance), may portray them as diabolical and Machiavellian, but seldom irrational. Descriptions of Hitler as a "madman" or Nazis as "inhuman" are desperate outbursts from those who expect rational actors in European history and who have been cognitively overwhelmed by the evil propagated by fascist Germany.

Also, Westerners often presume that the identities of South Asians are predominantly, if not entirely, religious ones, in contrast with Europeans and Americans, who are nationalists first (except for the "fundamentalists" among them). A large part of Hitler's program to gain the support of Christian Germans in his war on the Jews was to deny the latter a national German identity and impose on them an exclusively religious identity. And, so, he contrasted "the Christian German" with "the Jew," not "the Jewish German." Yet, few historians today accede to Hitler's propaganda by describing Jewish Germans in this way. Historians commonly depict these religious themes as subordinate means serving political ends, seldom as ends in themselves. Thus, the Holocaust becomes a war of Nazis or Germans against a Jewish minority, not a war of Christendom versus Judaism—one between supposedly secular (thus, ra-

---

1. For further discussion of this topic, see Edward Said, *Orientalism* (New York: Vintage, 1978); Sam Keen, *Faces of the Enemy: Reflections of the Hostile Imagination* (San Francisco: Harper & Row, 1986); and Ronald Inden, *Imagining India* (Cambridge, Mass.: Blackwell, 1990).

2. Orientalism is a field of knowledge identified by Edward Said in the book by that name. Said argues that it offers essentialized romantic and exotic portrayals of "Orientals" in the service of European imperialism.

tional) cultural and political actors rather than one fueled by irrational religious sentiment and prejudice. Western scholarship of South Asia often creates an expectation that the objects of its inquiry (Hindus, Muslims, and Sikhs) will act according to the primary sources of their supposed identities (Hinduism, Islam, and Sikhism) since their religious identities far outweigh any other identity.

As a means of describing (and differentiating) those among them who publicly adopt a religious persona and politically express their religious doctrines and ethics, Westerners increasingly rely on the label "fundamentalist." This often ill-defined term becomes synonymous with "pre-Enlightenment" when applied to those who seem to want to return to an age (as imagined by some) when religious ideology weighed heavily in Western political discourse and public life, an age that preceded the definition of a secular, nonreligious public sphere and before the "emotionalism" of religion was relegated to the church, synagogue, and home only. Demonstrating this teleology of secular progress, the *New York Times* has frequently described society in Afghanistan as "medieval" and "backward" since the pervasive enforcement of a conservative interpretation of Islamic law by the Taliban in recent years.

Many Westerners categorize residents of the Subcontinent primarily according to their supposed religious identities that are juxtaposed, according to the implicit typology, to the seemingly secular identities of the West. Jonah Blank and Thomas Omestad inferred such types when they wrote about the 1998 nuclear testing standoff in South Asia.

> A stable "balance of terror" assumes that leaders will remain rational. . . . One million people were killed following the 1947 partition of the subcontinent, and this experience is seared in the collective memories of both societies. The antagonism is one not of cold ideology but of hot emotion.[3]

The writers imply that the Hindus and Sikhs who moved into the newly independent India and battled with Muslims immigrating to Pakistan reflect the population of India today—religiously Hindu or Sikh and blinded by anger. Unfortunately, professional scholars of South Asian civilization, the very sources who should most challenge such impressions, often reinforce them through their work. Contemporary scholarship has too often taken political communalist discourse as the point of departure in the study of communal tension when it should begin with an appreciation for the nature, depth, and pervasiveness of popular communalist sentiments.[4] This is not to say that scholars should dismiss political language. Indeed, as contemporary events have demonstrated all too tragically, political discourse often plays a critical role in shap-

---

3. Jonah Blank and Thomas Omestad, "Balance of Terror" in *U.S. News & World Report* (June 8, 1998), pp. 37–38.

4. In South Asia, the term "communal" usually connotes an extreme form of group exclusivity and discrimination usually centered around religious identities.

ing events at the grass roots of society. The war of words following the spate of nuclear tests at the turn of the century in South Asia demonstrates the deliberate deployment of communalist language by political leaders.[5]

On May 11, 1998, the Indian government detonated three nuclear weapons beneath the Rajasthan desert at Pokhran. Two days later, it exploded another two weapons that Pakistan's government followed with a series of a half-dozen similar tests some weeks later. Judging by the widespread celebrations in each nation following their respective detonations, many if not most Indians and Pakistanis proudly embraced the weapons as manifestations of their nations' perceived character—militarily strong, technologically advanced, and internationally unyielding. In an ironic twist, many Indians acclaimed their weapon as superior to Pakistan's because of its *swadeśī* ("nationally built") character, borrowing a notion from nationalist Mohandas Gandhi's[6] Independence-era rhetoric.

While enjoying for their political advantage the nationalist surge unleashed by their decisions to test, the prime ministers of both governments quickly rebuffed those who attached a religious dimension to the tests. India's Atal Bihari Vajpayee criticized those who depicted the situation as a standoff between India's "Hindu bomb" and Pakistan's "Islamic bomb" by pointing out that many of the participating scientists in his country's test were Muslim.[7] Later, Pakistan's Nawaz Sharif, responding to a question that asked if nuclear weapons represented an "Islamic bomb" that would be shared with other Muslim states, responded, "Do bombs have religion? We have never spoken of a 'Hindu' bomb."[8]

Protestations not withstanding, there was reason for some to conclude that the nuclear weapons of South Asia had religious associations, even long before the 1998 tests. In 1974, Indira Gandhi exploded India's first nuclear device on *Buddh Pūrṇimā*,[9] an auspicious day in the Hindu calendar celebrating the birth of the Buddha.[10] The prearranged message flashed to signal the test's success read simply, "The Buddha has smiled."[11] In an effort to counter domestic turmoil, Pakistan's prime minister at the time, Zulfiqar Ali Bhutto, responded to the test with a declaration that his nation would build an "Is-

5. For a brief overview of the Indian and Pakistani nuclear weapons development race, see the respective articles by Sumit Ganguly and Samina Ahmed in *International Security*, vol. 23, no. 4 (Spring 1999).

6. Mohandas Gandhi (1869–1948), Indian civil rights leader who became the key figurehead in the Independence movement. The Mahatma ("Great Soul") relied on nonviolent civil disobedience to champion the causes of the Indian National Congress.

7. Mahendra Ved, "Moratorium on Nuclear Tests Will Remain: PM" in *Sunday Times of India*, *Mumbai* (May 31, 1998), p. 1.

8. Harider Baweji, "Interview" in *India Today International* (June 15, 1998), p. 36.

9. Manoj Joshi, "Nuclear Shock Waves" in *India Today International* (May 25, 1998), p. 12.

10. The day is Vaiśākh śuklā fifteen. S. B. Singh, *Fairs and Festivals in Rural India: A Geospatial Study of Belief Systems*. Varanasi: Tara Book Agency, 1989, p. 48. Many Hindus consider Gautam Buddha as the eighth avatar of the god Shiv.

11. Joshi, p. 12.

lamic bomb."[12] Twenty-four years later, Vajpayee chose the same day on the Hindu calendar as had Indira Gandhi, whom he had once depicted as "Mother Durga," for the test he dubbed "Operation Shakti."[13]

The Sanskrit term *śakti* not only connotes power and strength but also refers to the energy of the Goddess. The Bhāratīya Janatā Party (Indian People's Party or BJP), the Hindu nationalist party that headed the current ruling coalition, organized mass celebrations for this *Śaurya Divas* (Day of Valor). Meanwhile, the Viśwa Hindū Pariṣad (World Hindu Council or VHP) announced plans for a *śaktipīṭh* (seat of Shakti) near Pokhran that would be consecrated with water from all of the nation's "religious places."[14] In Hinduism, a *pīṭh* can represent an altar or the seat of a deity. Senior VHP leader Acharya Giriraj Kishore declared that it would be modeled on the Bhārat Mātā Mandir (Mother India Temple) in Banaras[15] and that it "would be depicted by a *tāṇḍav nṛitya* (violent dance) image of Shiva and Durga."[16] Earlier, the BJP's chief executive in Rajasthan floated, then abandoned, the idea to carry the soil from the Pokhran site in multiple *yātrās* ("pilgrimages" or "journeys") throughout India[17] as echoes of previous VHP- and BJP-organized *yātrās*.[18] Another BJP leader explained, "The emotion behind the proposal to spread Pokhran sand was to spread the feeling of national self-confidence."[19]

Quite clearly, the Indian ruling party used the testing to promote a nationalist vision infused with a religious, specifically Hindu, focus. The BJP, along with the VHP and the Rāṣṭrīya Swayaṁsevak Saṅgh (Association of National Volunteers or RSS), the BJP and VHS's partner in the militant Hindu revivalist Sangh Parivar, celebrated the event as a national victory and memorialized it through Hindu rituals, beliefs, and symbols. They sought to suffuse an Indian nationalist identity with the pride of this achievement. Their program for doing so, however, radically departed from the paradigm established by

12. Lawrence Ziring, *Pakistan in the Twentieth Century: A Political History*. New York: Oxford University Press, 1997, p. 402.

13. Joshi, pp. 12–15.

14. Vinod Sharma, "BJP's 'Partisan Euphoria' Offsets Strategic Gains" in *Hindustan Times, New Delhi* (May 18, 1998), p. 1.

15. "VHP: No Going Back on Shaktipeeth Plan" in *Hindustan Times, New Delhi* (May 21, 1998), p. 7.

16. Saba Naqvi Bhaumik and Harish Gupta, "Jai Shri Bomb!" in *India Today International* (June 1, 1998), p. 17.

17. Tavleen Singh, "Beware the Nuclear Yogis" in *India Today International* (June 1, 1998), p. 25.

18. These included the Ektāmatā Yātrā ("Journey of the Unified Spiritual Essence") of 1983; the Rath Yātrā ("Chariot Journey"), Rām Jyoti Yātrā ("Journeys of the Light of Ram"), and Asti Kalaś Yātrās ("Journeys of the Urns") of 1990; the Ektā Yātrā ("Journey for Unity") of 1991–1992; and the Janadeś Yātrās ("Journeys to the People of the Country") of 1993. The Asti Kalaś Yātrā paraded urns containing the bones and ashes of Hindu militants killed during an early attempt to demolish the Babri Masjid in Ayodhya. Christophe Jaffrelot, *The Hindu Nationalist Movement in India*. New York: Columbia University Press, 1996 (1993), pp. 360–362, 416–419, 422, 450, 487.

19. Bhaumik and Gupta, p. 17.

Gandhi and Jawaharlal Nehru[20] at Independence. Although the latter two, at times, used language and pursued policies with Hindu themes (e.g., Gandhi's notion of Rām Rāj—rule of Ram—for India and Nehru's campaign for the Cow Protection Act), these independence leaders sought to establish a secular system of national government. The Sangh Parivar, however, defined a nationalist identity with a pungent sectarian quality. Ashok Chowgule, president of the VHP's Maharashtra unit, made this clear when he defended the planned *śaktipīṭh* against critics:

> Hinduism is a cultural and philosophical concept. . . . A Peeth is not so much a place of worship, but one where inspiration is sought. . . . It is true that rituals are undertaken at a Peeth. But . . . they do not have the same significance as in the Semitic religions.[21]

Chowgule made two rhetorical moves here. First, he dismissed concerns about the Hindu nature of the *śaktipīṭh* by arguing that it is Hindu only in "a cultural and philosophical" context, denying that it is religious at all. Second, after downplaying the (Hindu) ritual activity that will occur there, he conceded that such activity *will* happen and differ from "Semitic religions" (read: "Islam"). The subtext hints at a standard equation repeated in the Sangh: that to be Indian is to be Hindu and that non-Hindus are welcome to embrace their "true" Hindu identities and become "true" Indians, but if they do not, then they are forever suspect as "anti-national." Chowgule confirms this attitude when he explained that the VHP would pursue the construction as an issue of the nation, not just the Sangh, and that it was up to others to join in the effort.[22]

The members of the Sangh can be under little doubt that orthodox Muslims, who are repelled by the idea of more than one god and of depicting god in art, would think it repugnant to contribute to a national monument in the form of a Hindu temple centered on sculptures of a god and goddess.

Current American media attention on nuclear developments in India and Pakistan has very often accepted wholesale the rhetoric of communalist politicians who seek to convince potential constituents that they belong in distinct religious categories and that the politician, as a coreligionist, is their natural representative. Influenced by both Western academic and South Asian voices, the Western media have taken up this simplistic Hindu-Muslim portrayal. Bruce Auster in *U.S. News & World Report* suggested that Indian Muslims would not be celebrating their nation's tests because they had occurred at the order of a Hindu nationalist government—as though Muslims could not recognize that many preceding governments and Indians of all religions had con-

---

20. (1889–1964) Indian National Congress leader who played a prominent role in the Independence movement and became the first prime minister of India.

21. Ashok Chowgule, "Should a Temple Be Built at Pokhran?" in *Sunday Times of India, Mumbai* (May 31, 1998), p. 16.

22. Ibid., p. 16.

tributed to India's nuclear accomplishment, not just the BJP.[23] John Burns of the *New York Times*, writing a portrayal of A. P. J. Abdul Kalam, one of the leading scientists in India's nuclear program, focused almost exclusively on the issue of Kalam, a Muslim, serving a Hindu government. Without revealing who or how many so spoke, Burns stated that "some said Dr. Kalam's role meant the world now has an 'Islamic bomb,' but one that belongs to India—an India ruled by Hindu nationalists."[24] In saying so, he suggested that the identity of one of its designers confers a religious identity on the weapon that competes with the religious identity bequeathed by the ideology of the government.

Burns also plugs into the fears of many Americans (and Hindu Indians) with the buzz-phrase "Islamic bomb." In 1981, journalists Steve Weissman and Herbert Krosney wrote a book by that name published by the New York Times Book Company. The dust jacket described it as "the first complete story of the nuclear arms race in the Middle East" that "reveals the machinations of Iraq, Pakistan, Israel, India, Libya, and the Arab states and the complicity of France, Italy, Germany, Belgium, and other Western nations in the spread of death-dealing nuclear weapons." In a manner common to American journalism, the authors conflate "Islam" with "the Middle East." Although the book's text distinguished between South Asia and the Middle East, for the sake of attracting readers, the dust jacket highlighted the latter. "Islam" also becomes an undifferentiated group of "Muslims" who act in concert for the benefit of their religion. The book declared that, "*The Islamic Bomb* sums up the startling story of the Pakistani metallurgist, Dr. A. Q. Khan, and how he stole the bomb *for Islam* by penetrating a nuclear plant in Holland" (my emphasis).[25] Like Burns's portrayal of Kalam, the book depicted Khan as serving only his religion, not his nation. As a Muslim, he acted for all Muslims, including Iraq's Hussain, Libya's Qaddafi, and Iran's Khomeini. This is what makes an Islamic bomb so potentially alarming for readers in the United States and India. During the 1998 tests, both the *Times of India, Mumbai* and *India Today International* approvingly quoted from the book.[26] There are, however, Indians and Pakistanis who resist such singular representations. L. K. Sharma protested in a newspaper article, "The 'Hindu bomb' label may soon be acceptable to pseudo thinkers trained in the civilisational conflict mode of reasoning. Indian intellectuals who have a better understanding of Christianity never talk of a 'Christian bomb'"[27]—an important insight that echoes this chapter's initial argument.

23. Bruce Auster, "An Explosion of Indian Pride" in *U.S. News & World Report* (May 25, 1998), pp. 16–17.

24. John Burns, "Self-Made Bomb Maker" in the *New York Times* (May 20, 1998), p. A6.

25. Steve Weissman and Herbert Krosney, *The Islamic Bomb: The Nuclear Threat to Israel and the Middle East.* New York: Times Books, 1981.

26. "Gaddafi Had Offered India $8 b for N-Technology" in *Times of India, Mumbai* (June 13, 1998), p. 3. Manoj Joshi, "Priming an Old Fuse" in *India Today International* (June 15, 1998), p. 39.

27. L. K. Sharma, "'Have a Nuclear Bomb to End Conflict'" in *Sunday Times of India, Mumbai* (June 7, 1998), p. 13.

Although some people are sensitive to reductive identification, the widening infusion of religion and nationalism in the political discourse of South Asians increasingly threatens to replace the multiple identities that Indians and Pakistanis currently share with singular national identities. On a green-painted wall outside Lahore's Old City, the religious political party Jamā'at-ī-Islāmī (Party of Islam) has written the question in Urdu "What is the meaning of Pakistan?" and answered in Arabic "There is no God but God and Muhammad is his Prophet." Their use of the most fundamental affirmation of Muslim identity, the *shahāda*, to express Pakistan's meaning clearly equates Pakistan with Islam and, therefore, Pakistanis with Muslims. This undermines the secular state for Muslims and non-Muslims as envisioned by the nation's founding father, Muhammad Ali Jinnah,[28] and as symbolized by the adjoining fields of green and white on the national flag. Meanwhile, as we shall see, the secular ideals of Gandhi, Nehru, and the other Indian Independence leaders have also been threatened by the surging Hindu nationalist movement. Their slogan, "Hindi, Hindu, Hindustan," reduces India, and thus Indians, to only Hindi speakers and Hindus. Despite recent academic attention to this dynamic, scholarship has historically often promoted a bifurcated vision of South Asia as socially divided between "Hindus" and "Muslims," overlooking shared identities. This chapter demonstrates this perspective, examines its historical development, and demonstrates the need for a more nuanced understanding of identity in India that comprehends the complexities of grassroots social dynamics. We continue by asking, What has been the nature of religious self-identification in South Asia, and how has it changed historically?

Religious Self-Identification and Exclusion in Historical South Asia

Unfortunately, the history of South Asian religious identities and community interrelations suffers for lack of historiographic sources for the period preceding European imperialism. The sources available generally describe large, elite institutions rather than local, popular expressions. For this reason, most scholars attempting to explore precolonial and early colonial religiosity commonly turn to the records of governments (such as official reports or unofficial memoirs) or organizations (such as Sufi brotherhoods or *sadhu* orders) and attempt the difficult task of discerning broader religious sentiment. Amplifying this problem is the focus of many contemporary scholars of South Asia on social conflict that has often overlooked how the interests and identities of Hindus and Muslims may intersect and overlap in certain contexts. Here we review some salient issues in the history of religious self-

---

28. (1876–1948) Muslim League president who became the leading figure in the creation of a Muslim state partitioned from an independent India. Referred to in Pakistan as "Qaid-i-Azam" (Great Leader).

identification and exclusion in South Asia—without attempting to portray that history completely—for the sake of showing some of the underlying issues and complexities involved at present.

Many scholars maintain that self-identification, exclusion, and tensions among religious groups on the Subcontinent derived solely from the colonial encounter. Such arguments, however, ignore evidence from a variety of sources that demonstrates that Western imperialism only aggravated and gave modern shape to religious discrimination that existed long before. In the late ninth century, the Saffarid dynasty of eastern Persia recorded its victories in the "infidel country of *al-Hind*."[29] They used a name for a territory first identified as *Hindush* by the Persian emperor Darius I (d. 486 B.C.E.) and described by the Greek ethnographer Herodotus.[30] A century later, al-Masudi reflected the respect of many contemporaries for Sanskrit philosophy when he wrote in his *Murūj adh-dhahab* that some Sasanid Persians believed wisdom to have derived originally from *al-Hind*.[31] In the eleventh century, the traveler al-Buruni wrote his *Kitāb al-Hind* (Book of India) in an effort to describe Hindu customs, cosmologies, and philosophies. He referred to the contemporary rulers of Kabul as *Hindu shāhīya* (Hindu kings),[32] distinguished between Hindus and Buddhists, and described Hindus as "our religious antagonists." In contrast, he described his co-religionists (we-Muslims) as "followers of the truth."[33]

Meanwhile, the Brahman Kalhana in his mid-twelfth-century Kashmiri chronicle *Rājataraṅgiṇī* (Ocean of the Rivers of Kings) used the Sanskrit word *Turuṣka* (Turk) as an ethnic label that implied a chauvinistic, if not iconoclastic, Muslim identity, although he was aware that many Turks in the region were Buddhist and Hindu.[34] So, for instance, Kalhana described the Kashmiri Kṣatriya[35] ruler Harsha (1089–1101) as "the Turk king" because, like the stereotypical Muslim/Turk of today, he "left not one temple . . . not despoiled of its images."[36] Although he never used the term *Hindu* anywhere in his chronicle, Kalhana implied his understanding of a people to whom he belonged that he defined as adhering to a particular set of religious beliefs and behaviors. He clearly distinguished Buddhists and Turks from a group that included the devotees of Shiva, Vishnu, Shakti, and other deities. The latter group included at least Brahmans and Kṣatriyas and excluded *Śvapāka*s (low-castes) from

29. André Wink, *Al-Hind: The Making of the Indo-Islamic World*, vol. 1. Delhi: Oxford University Press, 1990, pp. 124.

30. Ibid., p. 190. The name refers to the area "beyond" (i.e., eastward from a Persian perspective) the river known today as the Sindhu or Indus.

31. Ibid., pp. 19–20.

32. Ibid., p. 125.

33. Ainslie Embree, ed., *Alberuni's India*, Edward C. Sachau, trans. New York: W. W. Norton, 1971, p. 7.

34. Kalhana, *Rājataraṅgiṇī: The Saga of the Kings of Kaśmīr*, Ranjit Sitaram Pandit, trans. New Delhi: Sahitya Akademi, 1990 (1935), pp. xxxiv–xxxv.

35. The warrior-king division or *varṇa* of the classical Indian social model.

36. Kalhana, p. 352.

temples.[37] Furthermore, Kalhana implied a shared identity among those of "this country" in juxtaposition to invaders as he explained that, "When overrun by the impious Dards, Bhauttas [Ladakhis] and Mlecchas [Huns] this country had lost religion, [King Bhairava] had promulgated the observance of religious conduct by settling the people from the land of the Aryas . . . [*sic*]"[38] These examples from Middle Period authors show the ways in which South and West Asians applied the categories of *Hindu* and *Turk/Muslim* in their identifications of themselves and others long before the arrival of Europeans in South Asia. These terms conflated relationships between territory, ethnicity, and religious belief and behavior.

The poetry of Kabir, the Banarasi *bhakt* (devotional) poet whose birth preceded the East India Company's charter by two centuries, demonstrates how some Middle Period South Asians saw not only exclusive religious identities but also inclusive ones that could include members of groups between which conflict occasionally happened.[39]

> The Hindu says Ram is the Beloved.
> the Turk says Rahim.
> Then they kill each other.[40]

Kabir clearly intended to juxtapose Hindu and Muslim beliefs, practices, and identities, though not for the sake of championing one above the other. Rather, he sought to demonstrate how his nameless devotionalism circumvented these diverse traditions and led to a single reality.

> Hindus died worshipping idols,
> Turks died bowing heads.
> They burn, these bury—
> neither learned Your reality.[41]

Kabir often named this reality Ram but his *nirguṇ bhakti* (devotion to a deity attributed with no qualities) clearly did not owe allegiance to the narrow characterization of the god by that name that such current groups as the RSS and VHP promote. Kabir's Ram existed as an oceanic reality accessible to anyone

---

37. "In this realm gods of dread supernatural power did not surely reside at that time, otherwise how could a *Śvapāka* woman have entered their temples!" Ibid., p. 219.

38. Ibid., p. 42. For a superb exploration of the nuances of identity—including religious, ethnic, and linguistic identities—from the fourteenth century to the seventeenth century, see Cynthia Talbot, "Inscribing the other, inscribing the self: Hindu-Muslim identities in South India" in *Society for Comparative Study of Society and History*, vol. 37, no. 4 (1995), pp. 692–772.

39. There is debate regarding the dates of Kabir's life. Linda Hess gives a birth year of 1398, while David Lorenzen opts for a death date of 1518. Linda Hess, trans. *The Bījak of Kabir.* Delhi: Motilal Banarsidass, 1986 (1983), p. 5. David N. Lorenzen, *Kabir Legends and Ananta-das's Kabir Parachai.* Albany: State University of New York Press, 1991, p. 18.

40. Hess, p. 42.

41. Nirmal Dass, trans. *Songs of Kabir from the Adi Granth.* Albany: State University of New York Press, 1991, p. 155.

through heartfelt devotion. The experience of this inner existential reality demonstrated the insignificance of external religious association.

> Kabir says, plunge into Ram!
> There: no Hindu. No Turk.[42]

Further, Kabir used his typically outrageous language aggressively to kick out the very props by which some "Hindus" and "Turks" sought to set up their platform of exclusivist truth claims, whether texts, beliefs, or practices.

> It's a heavy confusion.
> Veda, Koran, holiness, hell—
> who's man? who's woman?
> A clay pot shot with sperm.
> When the pot falls apart, what do you call it?
> Numskull! You've missed the point.

Kabir also applied his crass depiction of the physical baseness of all humans to undermine caste distinctions based on purity.

> It's all one skin and bone,
> one piss and shit,
> one blood, one meat.
> From one drop, a universe.
> Who's Brahmin? Who's Shudra?[43]

Clearly, then, Kabir both recognized the distinctions and conflicts between Hindu and Turk identities of his day (as well as between caste identities) *and* attempted to substitute a common devotional identity in their stead.

Kabir's imagined common devotional identity found a realization in some of the movements that considered him a *sant* (an especially pious person) and that included both Hindus and Muslims. The oral and written biographies that his followers propagated demonstrate tendencies toward both common and exclusive identities. The popular story of Kabir's death depicts the debate between his Hindu and Muslim devotees over whether his corpse should be burned or buried, according to Hindu and Muslim custom, respectively. In the end, the argument proves empty because the corpse disappears entirely. Like the *sant*'s poetry, this narrative begins with communal distinction and ends with an affirmation of a noncommunal identity devoted to a reality that transcends (literally) religious and caste differences. Nevertheless, some devotees turn the narrative stream once again toward a camp of communal identification, as in the versions which depict Shiv, Vishnu, Brahma, and Indra greeting Kabir upon his postmortem arrival in heaven.[44]

---

42. Hess, p. 67. The following Kabir passages continue from this page.
43. The lowest ranked of the four divisions or *varna*s in the classical Indian social model.
44. Lorenzen, pp. 40–42.

Among the numerous precolonial religious institutions in South Asia, the Kabir Panth and other *nirguṇ bhakti* groups were more likely to foster inclusive devotional practices through their imageless devotions, while other organizations promoted more exclusive communities.[45] The *panth* (path or sect) in various *sant* traditions inherently involved mechanisms to authenticate and verify religious identity in accord with that tradition. These included the development of lineages connected to a great *sant*, the establishment of a fixed scripture, and the practice of particular rituals in conscious self-distinction from other *sant* panths.[46] Even Guru Nanak (b. 1469), who, as first guru of Sikhism, is commonly assumed to have favored a synthesis of Islam and Hinduism, clearly distinguished himself from the *qāzīs*, mullahs, and Sufis of his day whom he condemned and, like Kabir, promoted a devotional identity that transcended those of Muslim and Hindu.[47]

Meanwhile, orders of militant *sadhus*[48] played an instrumental role in the definition of broader, yet still exclusive, religious identities. Peter van der Veer describes their development: "The first half of the second millennium A.D. witnessed the expansion of ascetic orders, along with the cults of their gods, throughout the Indian subcontinent, as well as the development of temple worship, mostly with Brahman officiants."[49] These orders combined trade with military duty and allied their economic ascent with an expansion of their cults across South Asia, establishing a comprehensive binding of Shaivite and Vaishnavite worship for many of the myriad, previously loose pages of local religious beliefs and practices.[50] Precolonial political efforts to form a single organization of Hindus soon followed and provided the basis for the discourse of communalism taken up by the imperial British and fostered by current religious chauvinists.[51]

Among Muslims, many Sufi[52] devotional sites and practices played an integrative role parallel to that of *nirguṇ bhakti* groups. Richard Eaton has argued convincingly for the integrative nature of many Sufi institutions in Mughal-era Bengal. Mosques and shrines acted as loci of religious, social, economic, and political forces that expanded human settlement into hitherto jungle areas without the coerced conversions commonly assumed to be associated with

45. Peter van der Veer, *Religious Nationalism: Hindus and Muslims in India.* Berkeley: University of California Press, 1994, p. 52.

46. Daniel Gold, "Clan and Lineage among the Sants: Seed, Service, Substance" in *The Sants: Studies in a Devotional Tradition*, Karine Schomer and W. H. McLeod, eds. Delhi: Motilal Banarsidass, 1987, pp. 305–328.

47. W. H. McLeod, *Gurū Nānak and the Sikh Religion.* Delhi: Oxford University Press, 1996 (1968), pp. 158, 161.

48. A Hindu renunciant who lives an ascetic life in pursuit of release from the cycle of rebirth.

49. Van der Veer, pp. 45–46.

50. Ibid., p. 50.

51. Ibid., p. 25. For an in-depth examination of these efforts in Banaras, see Vasudha Dalmia. *The Nationalization of Hindu Traditions: Bhāratendu Harischandra and Nineteenth-Century Banaras.* Calcutta: Oxford University Press, 1997.

52. A Muslim mystic who may or may not belong to a lineage of spiritual teachers.

the advances made by Muslim military leaders. Through what Eaton calls "creative adaption," recently introduced Islamic paradigms met and merged with previously existing religious paradigms. At times and for some, this process advanced to displace entirely the preexisting worldview and its associated deities.[53] Gyanendra Pandey shows the integrative effect of Sufi veneration in a late-nineteenth-century Urdu manuscript from the *qasba* neighborhood of a North Indian town that describes Hindus and Muslims jointly contributing to the repair of a Sufi shrine, among other buildings.[54] The theme of founder and civilizer can be found in the devotion to the Sufi Asta Auliya in Arampur, who is credited by some of his Hindu and Muslim devotees with clearing the jungle, settling the village, and converting the local "uncivilized" people (see chapter 4).

However, van der Veer makes the crucial observation that the devotional inclusivity of the Sufi tomb stands in stark contrast to the communal exclusivity of the mosque, wherein *only* Muslims perform their *namāz*.[55] This is certainly in evidence today at the larger *dargāh*s,[56] where only Muslims perform *namāz* at the commonly attached mosque (though anyone can perform devotional acts at the tomb itself). So, long before the arrival of Europeans on the Subcontinent, some rituals had physically defined the (at least, male) Muslim social body, and others allowed a religious identity associated with a shared devotional community without regard to communal identity. Some Sufi orders, meanwhile, pursued exclusivist agendas, at times providing *gāzī*s (Muslim warriors against infidels) for the expansion of *Dār al-Islām* ("the abode of peace") in South Asia.[57]

Another case of devotional inclusivity that integrates the socially distinct without completely erasing their differences can be found in Sandria Freitag's analysis of the annual Rām Līlā performances—a "Hindu" event in many scholars' eyes:

> The emphasis in Tulsidas's version of the *Rāmāyan* on devotion over orthodoxy, on shared brotherhood over community and caste divisions, enabled the [local] dynasty to use this event to express the integrative nature of the kingdom, encompassing even Muslim weavers. Indeed, as participants in Banaras's dominant Hindu culture—processionists representing an influential patron, or makers of ceremonial decorations, costumes, and pilgrims' souvenirs—members of the lower classes became integrated through the world of Banarsi public areas, regardless of their other forms of identity.[58]

53. Richard Eaton, *The Rise of Islam and the Bengal Frontier, 1204–1760*. Delhi: Oxford University Press, 1994, pp. 265–269.

54. Gyanendra Pandey, *The Construction of Communalism in Colonial North India*. Delhi: Oxford University Press, 1990, p. 128.

55. Van der Veer, p. 37. *Namāz* is the ritualized Muslim prayer performed five times daily.

56. "Place within"; shrine or tomb to a Muslim saint or Sufi.

57. Ibid., p. 34.

58. Sandria B. Freitag, *Collective Action and Community: Public Arena and the Emergence of Communalism in North India*. New Delhi: Oxford University Press, 1984, p. 31.

In this way, the political elite (i.e., the ruling raja who patronized the event and associated his rule with that of the avatar Ram) and the nonelite (Hindus and Muslims, high and low castes and classes) can be seen to have shared identities in a way unexpected in the bifurcated vision of most modern communalists and many contemporary scholars.

This handful of examples of communally divisive elements and religiously deliberate self-identification in precolonial South Asian societies is not intended to negate the argued role of British imperialism in the formation of *Hindu* and *Muslim* identities. Rather, it shows how preexisting realms of religious exclusionism fostered identities from which later colonial and postcolonial communalist discourse could, and would, borrow. This is not to say that the Hindu and Muslim (and Sikh and Buddhist) religious nationalisms currently extant in South Asia exist as unchanged "continuities" from precolonial times but, rather, that they, like all social formations, have evolved (in a nonteleological sense) as a few of the diverse responses of preexisting traditions to changing social, economic, political, and religious conditions.

British imperial rule of South Asia unconsciously and consciously agitated extant communal dynamics in South Asia through four mutually interacting factors: ethnography, historiography, the census, and representational politics. To exploit South Asian markets, as well as raw and human resources to their fullest, the British government had a vested interest in maintaining social stability while altering the political and economic situation to their advantage. It was, therefore, no paradox that the East India Company and the initial British Indian government prohibited the entrance of Christian missionaries, whom they saw as a threat to social harmony, while actively interfering in indigenous political and economic institutions. However, to preserve the social status quo, the British first had to determine what that was, and so they attempted to discern and depict this through three forms of knowledge: historiography, ethnography, and statistics.

In his "Preliminary Discourse," with which he inaugurated in 1784 the Asiatic Society that he helped to found, Sir William Jones demonstrated his personal sense of subjectivity when he explained that

> if it be necessary or convenient, that a short name or epithet be given to our society, in order to distinguish it in the world, that of *Asiatic* appears both classical and proper, whether we consider the place or the object of the institution, and preferable to *Oriental*, which is in truth a word merely relative, and though commonly used in *Europe*, conveys no very distinct idea.[59]

Despite such ideals of objectivity by scholars as recognized as Jones, the Orientalists who interpreted South Asian relics, texts, and oral literature for British interests (even if unwittingly) did so having carried shiploads of intellectual

---

59. *Asiatic Researches; or, Transactions of the Society, Instituted in Bengal, for Inquiring into the History and Antiquities, the Arts, Sciences, and Literature of Asia*, vol. 1. Varanasi: Bharat-Bharati, 1972 (1884), p. ix.

baggage from Europe. Ethnographers and geographers—such as Francis Buchanan and William Crooke—canvassed cities and countryside, describing lifestyles, economies, and topography that roving artists, like Thomas Daniell and his nephew William, illustrated through the contemporary lens of Romanticism. These artists created images that complemented the narratives established by historiographers, who projected Western historical patterns forged in the Renaissance and tempered in the Enlightenment. In spite of Jones's efforts to convey a "distinct idea" for Asia through the use of a nonrelative term, many members of his Asiatic Society created expectations in the minds of Europeans that Asian cultures would reflect premodern European social conditions in which religion supposedly played a very public, socially divisive, and developmentally retardant role.

Just as the Renaissance "discovered" in the crumbling relics of Rome and Athens evidence of root European civilizations with defunct pantheons of gods, many Orientalists "discovered" (and catalogued, restored, and maintained through the Archaeological Survey of India) throughout South Asia remains of a similarly "classic" civilization defined by its supposedly monolithic religion, Hinduism. Historiographers projected the narrative forward to this civilization's demise beneath the weight of "Islam," which rolled like a wave out of the mountains of Afghanistan across the northern plains of South Asia, as Orientalist James Tod portrayed it:

> In A.H. 365 (A.D. 975) he [Motawekel] carried his arms across the Indus, forcing the inhabitants to abandon the religion of their ancestors, and to read the Koran from the altars of Bal and Crishna. Towards the end of the century he made his last invasion, accompanied by his son, the celebrated Mahmood, destined to be the scourge of the Hindu race, who early imbibed the paternal lesson inculcating the extirpation of infidels. Twelve several visitations did Mahmood make with his Tatar hordes, sweeping India of her riches, destroying her temples and architectural remains, and leaving the country plunged in poverty and ignorance. From the effect of the incursions she never recovered; for though she had a respite of a century between Mahmood and the final conquest, it was too short to repair what it had cost ages to rear: the temples of Somnat'h, of Cheetore, and Girnar are but types of the magnificence of past times. [60]

Elsewhere he described the invading Muslims as "barbarous, bigoted, and exasperated foes."[61] These images not only depicted the imagined Hindu classic period but also reflected an enduring European anxiety concerning the Muslim states of the eastern and southern Mediterranean with which they had often competed economically, battled politically, and debated religiously in the previous centuries. This narrative of the zealotry and destructiveness of "religious"

60. James Tod, *Annals and Antiquities of Rajasthan or the Central and Western Rajput States of India*, vol. 1. William Crooke, ed. London: Oxford University Press, 1920 (1829–32), pp. 199–200.
61. Ibid., p. xiv.

conquerors also revealed a post-Enlightenment critique of religion and its disturbing consequences when too influential in the public order.

Although disagreeing with the idea of a Hindu "civilization," Utilitarian philosopher James Mill reflected this post-Enlightenment view in *The History of British India*, a six-volume account begun in 1806 and very influential in Britain until the later nineteenth century. Not an Orientalist and relying on less qualified and competent accounts (often from Christian missionaries and evangelicals) than those of the Sanskritists whom he criticized,[62] Mill chastised Jones for his cultural tolerance by questioning the legitimacy of Jones's claims that civilization in South Asia existed before the arrival of the British: "It was unfortunate that a mind so pure, so warm in the pursuit of truth, and so devoted to oriental learning, as that of Sir William Jones, should have adopted the hypothesis of a high state of civilization in the principle countries of Asia."[63] He went on to explain his objection to the argument for a Hindu civilization on the grounds of the perceived evils of despotism and priestcraft.

> We have already seen, in reviewing the Hindu form of government, that despotism, in one of its simplest and least artificial shapes, was established in Hindustan, and confirmed by laws of Divine authority. We have seen likewise, that by the division of the people into castes, and the prejudices which the detestable views of the Brahmins raised to separate them, a degrading and pernicious system of subordination was established among the Hindus, and that the vices of such a system were there carried to a more destructive height than among any other people. And we have seen that by a system of priestcraft, built upon the enormous and tormenting superstition that ever harassed and degraded any portion of mankind, their minds were enchained more intolerably than their bodies; in short that, despotism and priestcraft taken together, the Hindus, in mind and body, were the most enslaved portion of the human race.[64]

Of course, he saw the "Turks" as little better, despite the supposed legal limitations on political rulers and religious leaders: "But has all this prevented the Turkish despotism and priestcraft from being the scourge of human nature; the source of barbarity and desolation?"[65]

Despite the attention that they lavished on *yuga*s, *kalpa*s, and other indigenous South Asian patterns of time, the Orientalists and other British scholars seem to have failed to notice that they had projected the European triple temporal schema onto South Asia. The Hindu, Muslim, and modern (European) civilizations that they imagined for South Asia replicated classical, medieval, and modern periods of Europe. Mill begins his *History* with an account of the

---

62. C. H. Philips, "James Mill, Mounstuart Elphinstone, and the History of India" in *Historians of India, Pakistan and Ceylon*, C. H. Philips, ed. New York: Oxford University Press, 1962 (1961), pp. 220–222.

63. James Mill, *The History of British India*. Chicago: The University of Chicago Press, 1975, p. 227.

64. Ibid., pp. 236–237.

65. Ibid., pp. 237–238.

yug system, yet his table of contents and text clearly demonstrates that he organizes his narrative around descriptions of both the cultural attributes and political history of successive Hindu, "Mohammedan," and British periods. Following Mill by a century, former Indian Civil Service employee Vincent Smith published his *Oxford History of India* (1919), which became very successful (there were four editions), particularly as a standard textbook in Indian education systems.[66] Again, the table of contents reflects a tripartite division of time (and society): "Ancient and Hindu India," "India in the Muslim Period," and "India in the British Period."[67] These British Orientalists simply followed contemporary Western conventions for European history with the threefold partition of time devised by Petrarch in the fourteenth century. However, whereas Petrarch's system characterized three ages according to the quality of contemporary civilization (i.e., "classic," "dark," and "enlightened"), the system as applied to South Asia focuses on the supposedly ascendant religious and/or civilizational identity of Subcontinental rulers: predominantly Hindu rulers in ancient times, predominantly Muslim rulers in middle times, and predominantly modern (note, not Christian) rulers in modern times. The enduring impact of this temporal division can be seen today not only in Western and Indian scholarship but also in the history textbooks used in Bihar schools. Children study "ancient" (*prācīn*), "middle period" (*madhya kālīn*), and "modern" (*ādhunik*) Indian history in standards VI, VII, and VIII, respectively. The textbook *Sabhyatā kā Itihās* (History of Civilization) which the students study in standards IX and X reflect this time frame on a global level (see Appendix).

The British used religion as a primary criterion for the categorization not only of time but also of society. The decadal Census of India, initiated in 1872, sought to delineate South Asian societies principally via categories of caste and religion.[68] Rajendra Lal Mitra, the eminent Sanskrit scholar consulted about the listing and ranking of castes for the 1881 census, hinted at just how interrelated the historiographical, ethnographic, and statistical epistemologies were when he declared, "Its [the census's] duty is clearly to follow the textbooks of the Hindus and not decide on particular claims."[69] The statistical description of (caste) Hinduism, then, would derive, in part, from the historiographical definition of the religion based not on contemporary and "particular claims" but on a supposedly authoritative Hindu textual "canon" (i.e., they have always read these texts), which, in turn, devolved from ethnographic surveys (i.e., when asked, they told us they read these texts). The British Orientalists of South

66. A. L. Basham, "Modern Historians of Ancient India" in *Historians of India, Pakistan and Ceylon*, C. H. Philips, ed., pp. 266–267.

67. Vincent Smith, *The Oxford History of India.* Karachi: Oxford University Press, 1981 (1919).

68. For a wide-ranging examination of the enumeration strategies of the British in South Asia, see Arjun Appadurai, "Number in the Colonial Imagination" in *Modernity at Large: Cultural Dimensions of Globalization*. Minneapolis: University of Minnesota Press, 1996, pp. 114–135.

69. Bernard Cohn, *An Anthropologist among the Historians and Other Essays.* New York: Oxford University Press, 1990 (1987), pp. 243, 245.

Asia paid far more attention to Hinduism, opting to rely on their Middle East-ern–assigned colleagues to describe Islam from the supposed heartland. But the first census demolished previous colonial assumptions regarding the size of the Muslim population, which they had seriously underestimated.

As representational politics became a reality, the size of this population and other groups described and enumerated by the census data became even more significant because it now reflected a possible pool of constituents (the current term is "vote bank").[70] Events in Banaras and much of Uttar Pradesh depicted this shift when religious discourse, in league with ritual space and activity, no longer simply acted as the stage and props for local community relations, as in the eighteenth and early nineteenth centuries, but became a tool for translocal political mobilization by the twentieth.[71] In pursuit of constituents, indigenous political leaders worked to determine and service these blocs of voters by es-tablishing exclusive group identities and defining their particular interests. Some strove to subsume groups within their own to expand their power base. Gandhi sought to include Untouchable castes into the "Hindu majority," while others attempted to do the same with the often unwilling Sikhs.[72]

The Congress Party's success with this electoral logic in such campaigns as for the Cow Protection Act and their resistance to constitutional safeguards for the "Muslim minority" prompted Jinnah to use the All-India Muslim League initially to threaten tactically and then to pursue reluctantly the par-tition of Pakistan and India.[73] As Muslims, Hindus, and Sikhs were enumer-ated, classified, and expected to act politically as discrete blocs, many of their leaders associated these constituent groups with particular languages—"Urdu for Muslims; Hindi for Hindus; and Punjabi for Sikhs."[74] Language became a locus of political turmoil in the nineteenth century as the British created language policies that determined the official language of local governments and educational instruction while indigenous political parties, recognizing the possible political and economic benefits, campaigned for the adoption of the language of "their community."[75] This resulted, for example, in Muslims in Punjab who grew up with Punjabi as their mother language de-claring themselves to be primarily Urdu speakers and demanding, as a mea-sure of their political power, that the government rule and schools teach in Urdu.[76]

70. Van der Veer, p. 27.

71. Freitag, pp. 95–96.

72. Van der Veer, p. 26.

73. Ayesha Jalal, *Democracy and Authoritarianism in South Asia: A Comparative and Historical Perspective.* New York: Cambridge University Press, 1995, pp. 14–15. See also the author's *The Sole Spokesman: Jinnah, the Muslim League and the Demand for Pakistan*, Cambridge: Cambridge University Press, 1985.

74. Fariq Rahman, *Language and Politics in Pakistan.* Karachi: Oxford University Press, 1996, p. 195.

75. Ibid., pp. 58–78.

76. Ibid., p. 195.

The social division of India via categories of religion also resulted in spatial divisions. As mentioned earlier, many Western historiographies preface the decline of the "ancient Hindu civilization" with the invasion of Central Asians into natively defended territories—in other words, Muslims attacking Hindus. This reinforces the portrayal of Muslims as the perennial outsiders/invaders of South Asian societies. Historians often describe "Muslim kingdoms" besieging "Hindu kingdoms" during the "Muslim middle period" until "Hindu India" succumbed to a "Muslim India." This original bifurcation of space ("Hindu Subcontinent" and "Muslim Central Asia") leads to an erasure of the fact that Hindus and Muslims share social space. In this way, the "Muslim kingdom" of Bijapur struggles with the "Hindu kingdom" of Vijayanagara. Were Hindus resident in Bijapur? Muslims in Vijayanagara? Certainly, but Western historiography often identifies each kingdom according to the religious tradition of its politically ruling dynasty. The religious lives of one family supposedly determined the character of a kingdom and the space that it inhabits. The spatial division of South Asia according to religious identifications culminated ultimately in the actual partition of the Subcontinent into India and Pakistan by the retreating British in 1947. The borders of the two independent nations were determined by two boundary commissions, both led by an English barrister who had never previously visited South Asia.[77] He established the borders primarily to run between areas dominated by Muslims and by non-Muslims, as determined by statistical census data.[78] This left Jinnah complaining of a "moth-eaten" Pakistan with its two "wings" geographically discontiguous and deprived of the Gangetic heartland of South Asian Muslim culture.

Thus, the British intellectually constructed their view of South Asia based on observations that they interpreted according to their preconceptions and agendas and recorded categorically in historiography, ethnography, and statistics. After that, South Asian political leaders adopted many of the results of these epistemologies to their own ends.

The limitations of British constructions must be recognized alongside their influences. Like its political hegemony, British epistemological imperialism was uneven in effectiveness, and South Asian responses ranged from willing participation and grudging acceptance to unconscious absorption and active antagonism. The variety of perspectives embodied in religious reform groups demonstrates the plurality of responses to the Western presence and other contemporary issues. Of course, the *bhakti* and Naqshbandhi movements of the Middle Period reveal that debate among South Asians regarding religious self-definition was a continuing process of transformation that long preceded the European arrival.

A series of riots in Banaras demonstrated the multiplicity of identities among Banarsis and the British state's limited ability to determine identity. In 1809,

---

77. Ziring, p. 57.

78. S. M. Burke and Salim Al-Din Quraishi, *The British Raj in India: An Historical Review.* New York: Oxford University Press, 1996, p. 507.

riots that stemmed from a dispute involving an area encompassing both a Hindu relic and a Muslim *imāmbārā* (a space specifically used during the Muslim commemoration of Muḥarram) pitted Muslim weavers and butchers on one side against Hindu Rājpūts, Gosains, Marāṭhas, Brahmans, and mendicants on the other. Later, some of these groups demonstrated their communal self-definition when they represented themselves as "Muslims" and "we, the Hindus" on judicial petitions.[79] Yet, in riots the next year, various city residents identified themselves as "Banarsi" in united opposition to the British state. Freitag quotes Acting Magistrate R. M. Bird, who referred to a variety of participating Hindu and Muslim castes when he reported that "The Lohars, the Mistrees, the Jolahirs, the Hujams, the Durzees, the Kahars, the Bearers, every class of workmen engaged unanimously in the conspiracy. . . ."[80]

Be this as it may, large reform movements in the colonial and post-Independence period have all had to respond in some way to Western critiques and epistemologies. The Deobandi, Arya Samaj, and Brahmo Samaj are among the many movements begun in the nineteenth century that combined a response to the West with an effort of religious self-identification. In the twentieth century, the RSS, Jamā'at-ī-Islāmī, and VHP have developed as similar reform movements, albeit with more stridently political and exclusivist messages. These, in part, rely on the epistemologies introduced by the Western culture that each attacks so fiercely.[81] Overall, then, on the one hand many local forms of knowledge and behavior successfully resisted change since they could be displaced no more easily by British systems of knowledge than by later religious nationalist ideologies. On the other hand, many South Asians sought to serve their communities through accommodation with Western ideas, as Sir Sayyid Ali Khan demonstrated with his application of European education methods in his Aligarh Anglo-Muhammadan College.[82] Like the bridges, roads, and other elements of the physical and administrative infrastructure, the epistemological infrastructure, to a great degree, remains in the service of, and has been expanded by, both the state and special interest groups.

Independence and Partition, of course, radically altered the entire political situation in South Asia with reshaped and sharpened communalism. Successive Indian and Pakistani national governments cast one another as implacable foes. The logic of political communalism reached its ultimate end with both the actual division of South Asia into independent Muslim-majority and Hindu-majority nation-states and their essentialization in reductionist rhetoric as simply "Muslim" and "Hindu" governments. In 1989, a large billboard stood on Lahore's busy Circular Road. Intending to promote then–Prime Minister Benazir Bhutto's Pakistan People's Party, it depicted a painted scene

---

79. Freitag, pp. 40–41.

80. Ibid., p. 46.

81. For a useful overview of the rise of these movements, see van der Veer, pp. 56–73.

82. For a careful, if socially narrow, study of personal and group identity among the first students at Aligarh, consult David Lelyveld, *Aligarh's First Generation: Muslim Solidarity in British India.* Delhi: Oxford University Press, 1996 (1978).

of carnage as Sikh and Hindu men slaughter Muslim men, women, and children beneath the Urdu legend "Martyrs of Pakistan's independence." In relief against the orange rage of a ravenous fire, a Sikh holds a pike with the impaled body of an infant. While a portrait of Jinnah oversees this scene from one corner, the portrait of Bhutto in another implies her protective vigilance against any contemporary repetition of this slaughter.

The politics of language reflects this dynamic of national stereotyping well. Before Partition, the Indian Constituent Assembly gave serious attention to Hindi, Urdu, and Hindustani in the debate about a successor to English as the official national language. One can visualize Hindi and Urdu at opposite ends of a spectrum of north Indian vernacular languages with Devanagari script and Sanskrit vocabulary roots at one end and Perso-Arabic script and Persian and Arabic vocabulary borrowings at the other. Between them, Hindustani existed as an extensively used vernacular written in both scripts.[83] Gandhi, Nehru, and S. C. Bose had favored Hindustani as a pan-Indian language.[84] However, Partition ended any broad interest in making linguistic accommodations to Muslims in India and the language associated with them: Urdu. Hindi alone moved onto center stage of the national language controversy, joining rather than replacing English. Urdu also lost its preexisting position as official language in many states.[85] Popular identification with this linguistic middle ground rapidly diminished as those identifying Hindustani as their mother tongue declined 99.99% between 1951 and 1961.[86] Conversely in Pakistan, Urdu quickly became the official national language as Bengali, the primary language of East Pakistanis, faced severe prejudice from the West Wing–dominated national government. Many West Pakistanis viewed Bengali culture with suspicion as "too Hindu." Meanwhile, the Sanskrit-derived Gurumukhi script all but disappeared from use in Pakistan's West Punjab, completing a decline that began with British efforts in the nineteenth century to standardize languages in the Punjab.[87]

However, the communal identification of Hindi with Hindus faded quickly after Partition, especially in Bihar. Just as the polarization of Hindi and Urdu had signaled earlier the communalization of language, now the rising identification with regional languages reflected resistance to centralization. Between 1951 and 1961, the percentage of Bihar residents who identified their mother language as Hindi fell from 81% to 44%. This was offset by a precipitous rise in the percentage of self-declared speakers of "Bihari"—a category of languages identified by G. A. Grierson in his *Linguistic Survey of India* (1903–1928) that includes Bhojpuri, Maithili, and Magahi. In the same period, the percentage

83. Paul Brass, *The Politics of India since Independence.* New Delhi: Cambridge University Press, 1994 (1990), pp. 158–179.

84. Jalal, p. 225.

85. Brass, *Politics*, pp. 158–179.

86. Lachman M. Khubchandani, *Plural Languages, Plural Cultures: Communication, Identity, and Sociopolitical Change in Contemporary India.* Honolulu: University of Hawaii Press, 1983, p. 90.

87. Rahman, p. 194.

for Bhojpuri speakers rose from .05% to 17% for an overall gain of 412,674%! Self-identified Urdu speakers rose from 7% of the total Bihar population in 1951 to 9% in 1961. The district that Arampur belonged to at that time led in Bhojpuri identification, with 85% of the population declaring it their mother tongue in 1961.[88]

These language politics have figured into the historiographical, ethnographic, and statistical strategies that contemporary religious nationalists have eagerly seized on to promote their agendas. A case in point is the promotion by the RSS of the formula *Hindi, Hindu, Hindustan*, with accompanying histories and surveys to define an "Indian" identity through the correlation of language, religion, and territory.[89] Some groups use statistical data to play on fears that the Muslim minority will soon become the majority in India and outnumber and overwhelm Hindus. Thus, there has been an effort to bolster Hindu numbers through the "uplift" of Untouchables and tribals[90] and protest against the occasional mass conversions to Islam, Buddhism, or Christianity. Defensive Muslim groups have responded, at times, through their own essentialized notions of the Hindu majority.

These factors have all combined to produce a current upsurge in communal rhetoric and conflict not seen since Partition. Recent events such as the Sikh massacres following Indira Gandhi's assassination, the Muslim massacres following the destruction of the Babri Mosque, and the subsequent Bombay bombings that targeted Hindus are all too well known to need recounting here.[91] Although contemporary events have fortunately not nearly approached the quantity of bloodletting occasioned by Partition, corrosive communalist rhetoric seems to have become more pervasive throughout India. Parts of the country, such as Hyderabad, that had known little communal violence even in the time of Partition, have been shaken recently by tremors, if not earthquakes, of conflict.

Eleven people died when bombs exploded on their trains in South India. The three bombs of December 6, 1997, injured another fifty-four passengers. A note found by police on one of the trains explained that the "Islamic Defense Force" had caused the explosions in protest against the government of India for failing to prosecute the leaders of the Hindu crowd that destroyed the Babri Mosque in Ayodhya five years before to the day of the bombings.

88. Paul Brass, *Language, Religion and Politics in North India.* Delhi: Vikas, 1974, pp. 65, 88.

89. For an excellent examination of the history of Hindi, Urdu, and their political uses, see Amrit Rai, *A House Divided: The Origin and Development of Hindi/Hindavi.* Delhi: Oxford University Press, 1984.

90. Van der Veer, p. 28.

91. Foremost among riot chroniclers and analysts stands Ashgar Ali Engineer. Among his publications is *Communal Riots in Post-Independence India,* New Delhi: Sangam Books, 1991 (1984). A useful overview of the Ayodhya issue can be found in Sarvepalli Gopal, ed., *Anatomy of a Confrontation: The Babri Masjid–Ram Janmabhumi Issue.* New Delhi: Penguin, 1991 (1990). For analysis based on studies of the Hindu nationalist movement, see Jaffrelot's *Hindu Nationalist Movement in India.* The perspectives of Indian Muslims are examined in Mushirul Hasan, *Legacy of a Divided Nation: India's Muslims since Independence.* Boulder, Colo.: Westview, 1997.

Doubting the coincidence of a previously unknown Muslim militant group so forcefully demonstrating itself, many Indian Muslims wondered immediately whether this might be a ploy by Hindu nationalist parties to shore up support for themselves in the previously unconvinced South just months before parliamentary elections in February 1998. Other Indians assumed that some Muslims remain violently disturbed by the events in Ayodhya half a decade earlier. Whatever the truth might be, it is obvious that some Indians murdered innocent citizens without regard for their religious affiliations to arouse the memory of December 6, 1992.[92]

The significance of the worst communal violence since Partition has not dissipated by the turn of the millennium. Although India seems to have recovered after the Ayodhya devastation and the subsequent riots in India and bombings in Bombay, it would be a serious misperception to confuse the end of large-scale violence with the dissipation of communal tensions. Muslims in many parts of the country remain wary of their position in India, while many other Indians fear that political parties will exploit these tensions by stirring anger and anxiety in regard to past injustices, whether committed by a seventeenth-century Mughal or twentieth-century Marathi. The very recent demise of the Congress Party that frequently touted such "noncommunal" figures as Mahatma Gandhi (a Hindu shot dead by another Hindu for "placating" the Muslims) and Indira Gandhi (a Hindu, married to a Parsi, assassinated by her Sikh bodyguard that she retained as a symbol of her trust after her 1984 debacle in Amritsar) has further opened the way for religious chauvinism to become a political centerpiece for national elections as parties promote themselves.

This expansion of conflict has begun to overtake previously less volatile rural regions. Residents of the Arampur nexus in Bihar where I did my fieldwork recall very few Muslims emigrating to Pakistan from their area. Yet they now tell of increasing local communal conflicts that often center on controversies regarding religious activity in contested spaces such as the processions of the *ta'ziya*s (replicas of Husain's tomb at Karbala) during Muḥarram or the *devīmūrti* (image of the goddess) during Durgā Pūjā.[93] Many residents recognize a definite increase in communal polarization, especially, again, as demonstrated in religious performance.

Clearly, changing attitudes and participation show three dynamics at work. In the first, residents are increasingly viewing these ritual performances as singular in character: more of an expression of religious identity *alone* and less of local affiliation *among others*. Although Arampur Hindus may express pride

92. John Burns, "Train Bombings Kill 11 in India, Fanning Fear of Vote Violence" in the *New York Times* (December 7, 1997), p 16.

93. A dynamic considered by a variety of scholars concerned with different South Asian periods and contexts and who often describe these conflicts in theatrical terms. See Freitag, *Public Arenas;* Nita Kumar, "Work and Leisure in the Formation of Identity: Muslim Weavers in a Hindu City" in *Culture and Power in Banaras: Community, Performance, and Environment, 1800–1980* (Berkeley: University of California Press, 1992 [1989]), pp. 147–170; and Sudhir Kakar, *The Colors of Violence: Cultural Identities, Religion, and Conflict* (Chicago: University of Chicago Press, 1996).

still in the *ta'ziya* of their *muhalla* ("neighborhood"), they no longer participate with their Muslim neighbors in its procession as fellow members of that
muhalla because the procession has become solely a "Muslim event." Undoubtedly this results, in part, from religiopolitical efforts by the RSS, VHP, and
the BJP, all of which have some kind of presence in the Arampur area (most
notably an RSS *sākhā* [branch] that performs athletic exercises atop the Arampur
fort every morning in the winter). Meanwhile, some Muslims have stopped
participating with their neighbors in the Muḥarram procession for reasons of
Muslim identity—for them, the procession is "un-Islamic." This attests to both
the multiple dimensions of Muslim identity and the impact of Islamic revival
movements (such as the Deobandi School), many of which have contributed
to the divergence of the two religious communities by condemning "Hindu"
accretions to Islamic ritual and belief, let alone the participation of Muslims
in Hindu rituals.

Second, many Indians increasingly see one another as singular in identity,
particularly religious identity. In 1995, Kashmiri Muslim separatists bombed
pilgrims on their annual journey into the Himalayas. A Bihari villager happily
approved of a rumored threat by Bal Thackeray, leader of the Hindu chauvinist political party Śiv Senā, that any further attacks on Hindus would result in
his party's stopping Indian Muslims on their pilgrimage to Mecca. The fact
that the bombers represented a minority of Muslim separatists in Kashmir while
the Mecca-bound travelers originated from throughout India made as little
difference to him as the non-Kashmiri origin of the Himalayan-bound pilgrims
mattered to their attackers. His logic seemed clear enough: Muslims stop Hindus on pilgrimage so Hindus should stop Muslims on pilgrimage. Them and
us. "They" are entirely undifferentiated: not Kashmiri and Bihari, not secessionist and citizen. And "they" have nothing in common with "us."

Despite these realities, a third dynamic must not be overlooked during our
focus on communalist forces. That is, despite changes, Hindus and Muslims
have interacted and continue to interrelate in private and public arenas—even
those identified as "religious" by participants—sharing identities beyond their
religious ones. This review of religious exclusionism in South Asia has empha-
sized the political dimension in recognition of the increasingly apparent role
of political agents in the communalization of India. But Peter van der Veer
makes a crucial observation when he writes, "I would argue that the formation
of religious communities is certainly affected by state formation but cannot be
reduced to it."[94] It would be a mistake to pretend that political agents have
full responsibility for contemporary religious identities and conflicts. To do
so is to deny the agency and self-awareness of political nonelites and to overlook the inherent potential for disagreement between groups with different or
even conflicting notions and practices of belief, ritual, purity, and the past.

No doubt, significant tensions have existed and exist in South Asia between
those who would identify certain conflicts as religious. Undoubtedly, too, some

---

94. Van der Veer, p. 30.

South Asian leaders have purposely promoted religious conflict in pursuit of personal political advantage: the notion that one can participate in a god's fight or in the defense of one's belief and/or practice makes for powerful invective with which to incite others to one's cause. Yet rhetoric and temporary support should not be confused with more actualized and enduring conditions. As a whole, Western scholars are far more willing to accept a universalized construction for South Asia of a religious divide projected and wielded by particular political and cultural leaders than they would for Europe or the United States. In so doing, they become unwitting (if not, as in some instances, more conscious) accomplices with the communalist objectives of Hindu and Muslim chauvinist groups.

The Problem of Multiple Identity in Scholarship

Western and South Asian scholarship has taken four different approaches to the issue of religious identity in the Subcontinent. Each contributes to our understanding of identity and religion in India in its own way. Although many authors do not explicitly tackle issues of identity, their works about Indian religions and communities imply assumptions about the topic. First, some authors imagine discrete and singular realms of religious life detached from broader patterns of social, economic, or ritual interrelation. They describe the ritual lives of Hindus and Muslims, for instance, as neatly contained within exclusive spheres of temple and mosque. Second, following the mounting communal violence and the rise to political power of Hindu nationalist parties in the past decade, a great surge of scholarship has focused on Hindu and Muslim identity and communal interaction. Works of this type usually focus exclusively on the friction and occasional violence between these two communal identities. Third, some scholars explore how Hindu, Muslim, and other group identities are constructed historically, with a focus on the impact of large-scale political and bureaucratic forces on Indian society. Fourth and finally, some scholars consider religious identity as one element among others within a particular group's larger sense of identity. To demonstrate the need for another, complementary approach to the issue of religious identity, it will be useful to provide some further description and show the limitations of each of these approaches.

The Singular Identity Approach

This path to the study of religious identity in South Asia can often be found among scholars who wish to restrict their studies to a particular religious tradition. In so doing, they often imagine the "tradition" as something akin to a self-contained river that originates in some source that imparts a particular character to the water, winds its way across the historical landscape, and remains fairly self-contained despite occasional influences or impediments of significant religious and political movements. In this view, Hinduism and Islam derive from quite different sources, with origins in Aryans, Dravidians, Sanskrit, and the Vedas on the one hand and in Arabs, Arabic, the Prophet Muhammad, and the Quran on the other. The singular identity view portrays the two traditions as having had quite different histories in South Asia, as Hinduism imparted its qualities to the ancient period until the floodwaters of an expanding Islam washed across the landscape, sweeping away this Hindu civilization with a Muslim one and ushering in a new period.

The exclusivist approach divides the Subcontinent along religious lines temporally, spatially, politically, and socially, as discussed earlier. Civilizational identities for Hindus and Muslims are expected to be synonymous with a religious identity, while the British colonial government is characterized by its modernity, not its Christianity (at least, not explicitly). In the eighteenth and nineteenth centuries, British historiography focused principally on the political events and actors of the largest political units, and their typology of time reflected this. Yet why do contemporary scholars, who long ago retired the supremacy of political narrative from the discipline of history, complementing it with social and economic narratives, still rely on such a simplistic temporal schema that is also elitist? This schema partitions time with the understanding that Hindu rulers (and, by inference, all Hindus) share an identity that inherently distinguishes them from and opposes them to Muslims.

As noted previously, such singular identity scholarship commonly divides South Asia spatially, too. At times, space is ascribed an inherent religious association. For instance, singular identity scholars often describe Banaras as a "Hindu city." Although such a characterization might be understandable in light of the tremendous importance of the city for many Hindus throughout the world and the great significance of Hindu pilgrimage activity to the city's economy, it ignores both Muslim religious life in Banaras that has developed during the last seven centuries and the quarter of the present city's population that is Muslim. Beyond the oversimplification of this treatment of social space, such exclusionary depictions fail to achieve their goals—an accurate portrayal of the religious lives of Hindus. Often scholars imply that Muslim contact with the Hindu space of Banaras—or of South Asia itself—dimmed its Hindu character and, thus, its essence. But, in fact, Hindus participate in Muslim (and other, including Christian) functions such as 'urs celebrations and charismatic healings. Although perhaps less likely to frequent Hindu religious sites and celebrations, Muslims play an integral role in the Hindu pilgrimage economy of the city, fashioning decorations, making saris, crafting amulets, supplying sacrificial animals, and driving special *tongas* and rickshaws.[95]

Scholars who rely on a singular identity model commonly describe groups and individuals by Hindu or Muslim affiliations first, by regional location or caste second, and then by other qualifications. Thus, they ignore the identities that Hindus and Muslims may share despite their differing religious identities, such

95. Personal conversations with Ramu Pandit and Virendra Singh, June and July 1997.

as those based on living in a shared neighborhood, village, state, or nation. And they also miss the possibility of shared religious identities, such as those that result from the mélange of devotional traditions, including Sufism and *bhakti*, that have influenced one another in north India at various times. Kabir, one of Banaras's most famous sons, and many of his devotees dissociated themselves from Hindu and Muslim identities in search of a nameless devotionalism.

The Conflict Approach

The last dozen years have witnessed a frightening increase in the public rhetoric and violence of communal hatred in India. This began with the 1984 communal slaughter resulting from the assassination of Indira Gandhi, was followed by the 1992 destruction of the Babri Mosque and the subsequent riots, and culminated with the meteoric ascent of Hindu chauvinist parties (principally the BJP and Śiv Senā) to political power. In response, much recent scholarship has turned to issues of Hindu and Muslim identity as formulated and expressed in periods of conflict. Among the most important authors of this perspective are Ashgar Ali Engineer, [96] Sudhir Kakar, and Ashis Nandy.[97] These scholars concern themselves primarily with the important effort to portray various conflicts and provide an insight into the motivating factors of participants. Focusing as they do on the didactic rhetoric and violent behavior accompanying severe communalism, many of these scholars use the terms *Hindu* and *Muslim* in ways that reflect the oppositional discourse of the communalists they study. Those who do question the labels of communal identity usually limit their critique to an observation that such terms cannot relate to monolithic identities because Hindus and Muslims are divided into subgroups. So, for instance, psychoanalyst Kakar usefully notes the nested subidentities of culture (e.g., Persian, Arab), caste (e.g., Kayāsth, Brahman), and class (e.g., elite, lower) among Hindus and Muslims in Hyderabad.[98]

The Historical Approach

In contrast with the conflict approach, the historical approach attempts to examine communalism with an emphasis on the long view. Authors such as Bipan Chandra,[99] Gyanendra Pandey,[100] Sandria Freitag, and Peter van der

---

96. See Ashgar Ali Engineer, *Lifting the Veil: Communal Violence and Communal Harmony in Contemporary India.* New Delhi: Sangam, 1995; and his edited anthology, *Communal Riots in Post-Independence India.* New Delhi: Sangam, 1991 (1984).

97. Ashis Nandy, "The Politics of Secularism and the Recovery of Religious Tolerance" in *Mirrors of Violence: Communities, Riots and Survivors in South Asia*, Veena Das, ed. Oxford: Oxford University Press, 1990.

98. Kakar, *The Colors of Violence*, pp. 9–10.

99. Bipan Chandra, *Communalism in Modern India.* New Delhi: Vikas, 1984.

100. Gyanendra Pandey, *The Construction of Communalism in Colonial North India.* Delhi: Oxford University Press, 1990.

Veer locate the roots of current Indian religious conflict in the colonial or precolonial past. Some, like Chandra and Pandey, consider communalism to be the direct result of British policies and ideologies applied to South Asia. Others, such as Freitag and van der Veer, see religious conflict as a continuation, albeit transformed by the colonial encounter, of dynamics extant before the European impact. They neither deny the impact of the British nor relegate to them complete responsibility for the current communal situation, preferring to recognize the agency of South Asians even as imperial subjects. Most of these scholars recognize the alternative identities beyond the religious that groups have, whether class-, territory-, or politics-based. For instance, although Chandra's attention is on the class conflict inherent in communalism, he also recognizes that caste, *muhalla*, village, and extended family acted as "traditional social institutions" that provided a sense of identity before the impact of capitalist development. As a result of this development, he argues, communalism has become "an alternative focus of unity and solidarity."[101]

The Composite Identity Approach

Finally, some scholars portray religious identity as one component of some broader group identity. Susana Devalle and Nita Kumar typify this approach within their work. Devalle argues for an awareness of what she calls "composite identities":

> For some communities, religion—the central category to define fundamentalism—may serve, together with other elements (mostly a consciousness of historical permanence, language and often territory), as one of the pillars of ethnocultural identity. The case of Sikhs in Punjab, of Muslims in Kashmir and other ethno-regional assertions reveal varied (historico-cultural) dimensions of composite identities.[102]

The composite approach attempts to set religious identity within a larger social context. Kumar accomplishes this with her portrayal of a particular group of weavers in Banaras, who identify themselves as a specific caste, as artisans, as Muslims, and as Banarsis. Although they may share any one of these identities with others outside their group, they combine into a single, unique group identity.[103] Devalle, Kumar, and others of the composite approach focus on a specific group identity (in which *Hindu* or *Muslim* fit as one compositional unit) that is singular in contrast to some groups although possibly fragmented within and to itself.

---

101. Chandra, pp. 312–315.
102. Susana C. C. Devalle, "Social Identities, Hindu Fundamentalism, and Politics in India" in *Bhakti Religion in North India: Community Identity and Political Action.* Albany: State University of New York Press, 1995, p. 311.
103. Nita Kumar, "Work and Leisure," pp. 147–170.

A Case for Multiple Group Identities

Throughout this review of scholarship on Indian communalism, the primary issue that has concerned us is the fact that many reporters of South Asian culture—both indigenous and foreign—erase common identities through the exclusive emphasis on religious community and, thus, religious division. As mentioned earlier, this erasure is intensified with the common scholastic focus on social conflict instead of cooperation. In keeping with the object of their studies, scholars of religions necessarily forefront religious belief, activity, products, and identity in their works, even as they challenge the monolithic stereotypes attributed to those identities by demonstrating how each divides into subgroups. It becomes perhaps even more imperative for scholars who work in cultures as stereotypically "religious" as South Asia's to show the greatest caution by setting religious identity in its broader social context. Yet, those who do focus on a specific group and explore the various facets of their identity often say little about the possibility of multiple identities among individual members, some of which may not be shared by all in the group. Because individuals seldom belong to just one group, they must somehow integrate multiple group identities into their individual identity. The narratives that they relate about their homeland, their families, and themselves reflect the variety of group identities that form their personal identity like the atoms of a molecule. Like molecules, individuals adapt to changing environments by changing their internal arrangement, allowing them to bond with one set of molecules at one moment and another set at another moment without ever losing their internal consistency.

This pattern reveals a weakness in the notion of *communal identity* because the term implies that Hindus and Muslims identify only with a community of other Hindus and Muslims. Although some Indians may embrace and propagate such an identity, few Indians live with such a singular self-understanding. Overreliance on the communal notion is akin to examining identity with a very narrow view—recognizing the importance of one aspect of an individual's identity but ignoring many other possible social bonds. At the same time, the term *religious identity* also has its shortcomings because, in a secular perspective, it suggests an identity that develops in a community of common practices and beliefs devoted to one or more superhuman agents. However, as we will see, many Hindus and Muslims do not live within discrete and distinct religious worlds but practice faith lives that obscure clear identity boundaries. Furthermore, many Hindus and Muslims (and Jews and Christians) associate themselves with those labels because they perceive a community of people who not only worship in the same way but also draw from similar, broad cultural traditions. Even if they do not believe in any god, many Hindus and Muslims identify themselves as such, based on their self-awareness of sharing something that may be part of their family identity, ethnic identity, and/or cultural identity. Lacking any better terminology, we use here the terms *communal* and *religious identity* hesitantly, reluctantly, and with due caution.

The present project attempts to extend previous scholarship through a local demonstration of some alternative group identities available to individuals in a particular rural setting—identities that complement and compete with *Hindu* and *Muslim*. The next chapter describes the geographic, social, economic, and political dimensions of that setting while noting the importance of territory in many local understandings of identity.

2

The Village Nexus

The ethnographic research for this book took place among the residents of a group of villages situated in the western Bihar district of Bhabhua.[1] An understanding of this region and its socioeconomic situation is necessary not only to comprehend the conditions of the people from whom the research material derives but also because of the importance of territory to many forms of identity. The chapter concludes with a historical overview of religious self-identification and exclusion in South Asia.

Residents of the study area identify themselves with a concentric set of territories: household, *muhalla* (neighborhood), village, village nexus, district, state, and nation. The nexus is comprised of individual villages, villages of *muhalla*s, *muhalla*s of households, and so on. A description of the physical, social, and economic environment surrounding the residents of the Arampur nexus also demonstrates how residents may associate themselves with any or all of these nested sets of territory.[2] That they characterize themselves according to territorial, as well as social, aspects of the region is evidenced in the common phrase, *Jaisa pānī, vaisa ādmī* (As the water, so the person), which expresses the understanding that the localized qualities of water influence the qualities of local residents. On a broader scale, the popular conception of regional variation and identity is expressed with the adage,

Kos, kos par pānī	Different water every single *kos*,
Car kos par bānī.	a different language every four *kos*.[3]

---

1. Bhabhua district came into existence in 1991 with the division in two of Rohtas district, which itself was the result of the division of the erstwhile Shahabad district into Rohtas and Bhojpur districts more than a decade earlier. Manosi Lahiri, *The Bihar Geographic Information System*. Bombay: Popular Prakashan, 1993, p. 35.

2. Some seemingly nonterritorial identities (e.g., family, caste, class) may have territorial associations. For instance, a family may identify itself both with those blood relations living in a household and with members scattered in surrounding villages or states.

3. A *kos* is the rough equivalent of 2 miles.

41

Thus, the association of the physical and socioeconomic setting of a large area with a range of local identities would seem natural to many nexus residents.

I initially envisioned a project based on the inhabitants of a single village. However, it soon became apparent that local residents from a number of demographically different, neighboring villages shared, at times, a sense of identity based on their mutual association with a constellation of villages. They expressed this identity through their social associations, economic activities, references to themselves, and attitudes to outsiders. Yet, at other times the same residents asserted identities that undermined the seeming unity of a broader identification, such as when a disparaging comment was made about a particular village by someone who, only the day before, had mentioned the social unity of the area (see chapter 4 for examples). Rather than take these expressions as contradictory, I prefer to see them as demonstrative of a set of identities in each person which shifts—temporarily foregrounding one before others—according to context. In this way, the variety of both complementing and competing identities can be seen to exist in one person. By taking the constellation, or nexus, of villages as the locus of the study, I hope to portray some of the varieties of personal identification possible among and within villages of different demographic compositions. The variance of religious populations between nexus villages offers also an opportunity to examine the variables at play in communal identification.

My notion of nested territories derives from Satadal Dasgupta's *Caste, Kinship and Community*, in which he examines the social structure of a Bengali caste. Earlier work by Eric Miller on the Malabar coast demonstrated how caste associations exist within a nested set of political units (e.g., village and chiefdom), which are limited by various geographic features (e.g., the Kora River).[4] Dasgupta gives a broader vision of territorial affinity as he attempts to delineate the internal and external relations of this caste through an analysis of the interrelated categories of caste structure, kinship structure, and community structure. The last he conceives as being comprised of five, territorially based levels of social integration for the caste. The size of the territory determines the spatial proximity of caste members and the degree of their unity.[5] Dasgupta sees five such levels: *ghar* (household), *para* (cluster of households), *gram* (village), *tallat* (cluster of villages), and *thana* (the largest nonabstractly cognized region for caste members).[6] Because my project does not investigate the social structures of Dasgupta's Bengali caste but, rather, explores the nodes of identity in a constellation of villages in western Bihar, the nested territories to be examined here (household, neighborhood, village, nexus, district, state, and nation) vary from his. This study finds its sources among the resi-

4. Eric J. Miller, "Caste and Territory in Malabar" in *American Anthropologist*, vol. 56, no. 3 (1954), pp. 410–420.

5. Satadal Dasgupta, *Caste, Kinship and Community: Social System of a Bengali Caste*. Hyderabad: Universities Press, 1993 (1986), pp. 9–16.

6. Ibid., pp. 16–21. N.B.: Dasgupta does not provide diacritics with these transliterations.

dents of a particular constellation of villages, and there we begin our examination of nested territories, their socioeconomic character, and the identities associated with them.

The Arampur Nexus

Despite the wide variety of official designations for various local territories, residents selectively use only some and identify themselves with even fewer. Community development block, election commissionary, and *taluk* are among the administrative territorial demarcations with which residents have little or no personal affinity. For example, the local community development block (the smallest administrative region) and *thānā* (police district) take their names from Arampur. Yet, residents seldom refer to the actual area designated as *thānā* or "block." Rather, they usually reserve these terms to denote only the immediate vicinities surrounding—and the buildings housing—the police station and the block development office. The territory associated with the administrative meaning of these terms includes many villages with which residents rarely associate. For instance, while walking to a temple situated 30 meters opposite the police station, a resident will say that she is going to the "Hanuman temple at *thānā*," distinguishing it from the other Hanuman temples of the area. But she will probably not refer to any corporate group as *thānā*, which would ostensibly include all the residents within the official *thānā* boundaries.

When asked by a visitor where they come from, many area residents answer "Arampur," even when they do not reside within the official limits of that village but come from certain surrounding villages. Even those who live within Arampur proper are likely to refer to others of the area as being from Arampur also. This reflects, in part, the corporate identity associated with the constellation of villages, which makes Arampur village its social and economic center. I refer to this constellation as a village nexus because residents cognize the individual villages as forming a group centered on the large village of Arampur. There is no official or informal equivalent to "nexus"; residents refer generally to this area as Arampur. To clarify local usage, in this book I refer to the village itself as Arampur and to the constellation of villages as the Arampur nexus.

Geographically, the Arampur nexus sits with its back against a low, forest-draped range of mountains—the northern edge of the Central Indian plateau. From west to east stretches the Gangetic River Valley, with the Grand Chord rail line and the Grand Trunk highway not far to the north, aortas among the many transportation arteries that run along the length of the valley. The nexus includes an important crossroads at which a north-south road intersects a critical east-west road. The latter leads, in one direction, to the nearest town (Kendra, some 20 kilometers away); and, via the Grand Trunk, onward to Banaras (less than 100 kilometers away, see map 1). The north-south road links many of the nexus villages. Emerging from the large village of Bari to the south, the north-south road first meets the nexus as it runs through the twin villages of

Baghpur (population 931) and Jagahpur (pop. 455).[7] It continues onward to bisect the east-west access road at the village of Devapur (pop. 383), with its accompanying bus stand, before continuing northward until it terminates in Arampur itself (pop. 6,366). Its northerly passage obstructed by Arampur fort, the road forks east and west—east toward the midsize village of Singhpur (pop. 1,187) and west to the somewhat larger Naugrah (pop. 1,439).[8] Swami Sarai (pop. 857) borders Arampur to the west. Along with these seven villages (from which the bulk of my informants came and, thus, which represent the locus of my study's focus), perhaps another four villages comprise the nexus centered on the very large village of Arampur.

Agriculture dominates nearly every aspect of life in the nexus. Situated higher than the low-lying alluvial plain that conducts the Ganges River eastward, the nexus rests on a more flood-resistant flatland. Although little local land benefits from the few irrigation canals available, the general area gains from the natural drainage of the abutting mountain range.[9] Landowners cultivate nearly all of the surrounding land,[10] using electric pumps to draw on the relatively shallow water table[11] when there is insufficient rainfall or canal water available. Their natural fertility supplemented by the widespread use of artificial fertilizer, fields support at least two but often three annual crops, usually a mix of wet rice, wheat, barley, lentils, and mustard. Sugar cane is a common crop as well. Tractors are used to plow as commonly as oxen, and a group of particularly wealthy landlords may occasionally rent a harvester together. Few pastoralists graze their animals in the immediate vicinity, but families keep for household use an assortment of cows, water buffalo, oxen, goats, and/or chickens, according to their financial means. Only some cultivators grow fruit or vegetables other than for domestic use. Under government encouragement, several landowners have built large, lucrative fish reservoirs recently. Only a few of the lower-caste residents rely on the one meandering river for fish, although many boys each try dauntlessly in the rainy season with a small bamboo pole, a length of line, and a rusty hook.

Most residents earn their livelihood through agriculture. Among the eleven villages that roughly comprise the nexus, an average of about 11% of the 13,385 residents declare themselves as cultivators (0.4% of women, 20% of men) and 12% as agricultural laborers (4% of women, 19% of men), while 2% say they

---

7. Many residents consider these two villages as one, referring to them collectively as "Jagahpur," although the two residential areas are 50 yards apart. Like Naugrah and its satellite village of Namazgah, the differences in the village are caste and class based, with particular groups comprising the population of the smaller satellite while the wealthier landowners live in the larger village.

8. All unreferenced population figures derive from Office of the Registrar General, India. *1991 Census of India: Compressed PCA for Bihar (01–09)* diskette. New Delhi: Census Publications, 1991.

9. P. C. Roy Chaudhury, *Bihar District Gazetteers: Shahabad*. Patna: Superintendent Secretariat Press, 1966, pp. 2–3.

10. Only 17.4% of the area in Arampur development block is uncultivated.

11. *Census of India 1981, Series 4—Bihar, District Census Handbook—Rohtas District, Parts XIII—A & B, Village and Town Directory*. Patna: Government of Bihar, 1985, p. 4.

are occasionally employed (3% of women, 1% of men) and 71% are officially "unemployed" (93% of women, 51% of men). Obviously, government census data, on which these figures rely, are concerned with participants in a public economy and, therefore, do not take into account the considerable domestic and child-rearing labor of women.

Despite the aggressive Zamindari Abolition Act (more aggressive in its wording than its execution), a minority of landowners control the majority of land. Although some nonlanded residents may attempt to challenge the zamindars, who remain in all but name, the police at the local *thānā* are likely to enforce the status quo, siding with the zamindars, who can afford to out-bribe their competition. "Naxalite" members of the MCC (Marxist Communist Centre) and upper- and middle-caste and class landowners with their private armies have long struggled violently against one another in central Bihar over the issue of land redistribution. Yet, such conflict is rare in Bhabhua district. Perhaps as a harbinger of future strife, provocative graffiti for the *Mazdur Kisān Samgrāmī Pārisad* (Laborer Farmer Fighting Assembly) could be seen near the time of my departure in the nexus area for the first time during my stay. The zamindars have their weapons ready.

About one in twenty of the nexus population engages in other types of work (0.6% of women, 9% of men), including 1% as manufacturers and processors in household industry (0.4% of women, 2% of men) and 1% as involved in trade and commerce (0.1% of women, 2% of men). Carpet making had been on the rise in the past dozen years until falling foreign demand closed a number of local looms. Still, this business continues to employ, year-round, scores of men and boys throughout the nexus. Meanwhile, the dull red sandstone quarried in Bihar since the age of the Mauryas[12] provides many jobs. Workmen earning 25 rupees (U.S. 71 cents) a day cut the sandstone out of nearby mountain faces and chisel it by hand into loose gravel or transportable blocks. The industrialization that entered western Bihar in the 1920s[13] has found little obvious manifestation in the nexus. The only smokestacks are those rising above the temporary brick kilns established in surrounding areas.

The production of *bīrī*s employs the largest number of household workers. Men and women sit all day in or outside their homes rolling chopped tobacco in tobacco leaves. They earn 25 rupees for every thousand made (a very good day's production). The tobacco comes from state forests in the neighboring mountains, where middlemen purchase harvest lots from the government, hire members of the scheduled tribes who dwell in the hills to harvest it, and then pay nexus residents to make the *bīrī*s before selling them to distributors. Of course, most women who work in *bīrī* production or as agricultural laborers are responsible, as well, for the domestic work of cooking, cleaning, and raising children in their own homes. Despite their proximity to and economic

---

12. Frederick Asher, *The Art of Eastern India: 300–800*. Minneapolis: University of Minneapolis Press, 1980, p. 29.

13. Chaudhury, p. 407.

reliance on the mountains, nexus dwellers consider this as an area apart. Residents often speak of the mountains as the abode of criminals and tribals, and only one nexus family admitted to having contracted a marriage with anyone living in the mountains.

The Villages

Each component village of the nexus varies in area, population, and composition. The villages of the nexus under particular attention here have a total of 13,305 residents, of whom only 47% are female, suggesting gender-discriminating health care and/or female infanticide.[14] Yet, among that portion of the population (23%) under age 7, 50% are female. Nearly half of men are literate but only one in five women. Of residents, 13% are of scheduled castes and 2% are of scheduled tribes. Under the heading "Religion by Head of Household," the 1981 census reported that among the 89,803 residents in the whole of Arampur block, 86% declared themselves Hindu and 14% Muslim (aside from the single Christian reported).[15] Within the nexus, the religious composition varies as widely by village as any other factor, with most having no Muslims (Jagahpur, Baghpur, Swami Sarai, and Singhpur), while Naugrah and Arampur have nearly an even split of Hindus and Muslims. The overall population of Arampur block increased by a quarter in the decade preceding 1991 (up from 18% for 1971–1981),[16] an increase higher than that of Bihar but lower than that of India as a whole.[17]

A variety of social, economic, and religious conditions make Arampur the center of the nexus area. For one, it is the site of the largest bazaar in a 10-kilometer radius. Although individual villages have small shops from which people can buy sugar or soap, it is necessary to shop in Arampur for most clothing, food, and other merchandise. Set along the north-south road leading from the bus stop and halving Arampur's large collection of flat, concrete-roofed *pakkā* and peaked, tile-roofed *kacchā* houses, this bazaar provides a home not only for stores but also for a dozen or so tea stalls and *pān* shops.[18] Men from the nexus come regularly to Arampur expressly to socialize with others from neighboring villages at any of these or other shops on the roads leading east and west out of Arampur from the Bazaar. Arampur also houses a number of grain buyers who act as middlemen between cultivators in the area and mills in nearby cities. Leaving their harvested fields in the surrounding villages, well-

14. Figures for Bhagwanpur have been extrapolated from 1981 figures by using the average decadal increase in population from the rest of the core.

15. B. B. Lal, *Census of India, 1981. Series 4: Bihar. Paper 1 of 1985: Household Population by Religion of Head of Household.* Patna: Bihar Secretariat Press, 1985, pp. 54–57.

16. Ibid., p. 14.

17. In 1991, the decadal increase for Bihar was 24% and 27% for India.

18. Following popular reference to the main bazaar as simply "bazaar" and to differentiate it from the handful of other, smaller bazaars in Arampur, I will refer to Arampur's central bazaar as "Bazaar."

to-do cultivators on belching tractors pull trailerloads of grain to these buyers, while their less wealthy counterparts arrive balancing their heavy burlap sacks on worn bicycles. They may join friends for a drink in tea stalls or at the toddy plantation once they receive the money for their grain.

Activity surrounding the temple atop Arampur's defunct fort also centralizes the village within the nexus. For at least a century, pilgrims from across north India have traveled to Arampur village for the sake of worshiping the ghost of a dead Brahman ensconced there. Today this temple draws many local residents for daily or weekly *pūjā* (worship service). It also attracts pilgrims (mostly Hindu, but some Muslim and Christian as well) from Bihar and neighboring Uttar Pradesh. Many of these devotees and supplicants hope that the power of the *brahm* will exorcise *bhūt*s or *pret*s (ghosts and spirits) afflicting family members (see chapter 5). The daily traffic of both local devotees and pilgrims follow the local roads from the south, east, and west that all meet and terminate at a vast sandstone gate. Residents claim that this gate stands as one of the few remnants of the mighty fort of the locally famous raja. Past this gate and atop the eroding mound it guards—the remains of Arampur fort—towers the tall steeple of the *brahm*'s temple. The roads below lead travelers through Arampur's main bazaar—its busiest commercial and public socializing space. Devotional traffic and business multiply during the temple festivals of January, March, and October, when direct buses run from Banaras to the Arampur bus stop. Residents of villages neighboring Arampur take advantage of this traffic to ply their trades of leatherwork, fruit selling, or bicycle repair along the road from the bus stand to the temple.

Arampur is also the site of a number of Sufi tombs that attract varying numbers of daily devotees and seasonal pilgrims—both Hindu and Muslim. At its annual *'urs*—the celebration of a Muslim mystic's death and ultimate union with God—each of the myriad local tombs lures devotees from the village, the nexus, or beyond, according to the notoriety of the saint. Certainly, the most important of these is the tomb of Mubarak Shah. Tended by the descendants of this ascetic Muslim intellectual, the onion-domed tomb stands at the corner of Arampur's large Jama' Masjid (mosque of the [Friday] gathering). Devotees, Hindu and Muslim, frequent this site throughout the year, offering prayers and making requests. They celebrate Mubarak Shah's *'urs* on the thirteenth of Jumāda's-sānī in the Muslim calendar, coming from as far as neighboring states. Those emigrant workers from the area who can leave their faraway workplaces at this time do so to celebrate with nexus family and friends. Selling fruit to socializing adults and candy to excited children, pushcart merchants roll their livelihoods near the tomb's gates, while itinerant traders unwrap their cloth sacks and squat by carefully placed piles of multicolored combs, plastic toys, and devotional items. On another night, a pair of dueling *qawwālī*[19] troupes match wits until near dawn in a field behind the fort with an audience of hundreds of nexus dwellers.

---

19. A tradition of Islamic devotional music unique to South Asia.

A less dramatic, yet no less important, feature of Sufi tombs that helps centralize Arampur is their constant availability to devotees seeking special favors from a saint. The tomb of Asta Auliya, the second most frequented in Arampur, rests on a raised platform surrounded by whitewashed walls in the middle of a large, well-swept courtyard. A small open mosque stands along its eastern perimeter wall. Drooping strings of twine and yarn tied to the tree overhanging the tomb and the withering flower garlands attest to previous visits of supplicants, some of whom tie ribbons on the tree in the hopes that *bābā* (respected person) will help stir life in their wombs. Every day, devotees approach the tomb barefoot, pray with bowed head and lit incense, touch their hands to the tomb and then to their foreheads, offer some coins, and walk away backward so as not to turn their backs disrespectfully to the saint's grave. Both Hindus and Muslims describe their prayer as *du 'ā*, a form of personal prayer derived from Islamic traditions. Occasionally, devotees leave bottles or pots of water for an hour or a night alongside the tomb, expecting that some of the Sufi's power will charge the water with healing abilities. More rarely, a family brings a relative before *bābā* in the hope that the holy man's presence can exorcise some marauding *pret* or *bhūt* which, having seized the member, has forced him or her to act abnormally and unpredictably (see chapter 5). The large number of *shahīds* (Muslim martyrs) and Sufi tombs in Arampur and these services they provide—significantly enough, with neither the need nor the cost of a Brahman priest—make that village an important center for Hindus and Muslims alike.

Less obvious than its status as a center of religious activity is Arampur's position as a hub for education. Most surrounding villages have their own primary and middle schools. Although the regional high school is named after Arampur, it is actually situated in the nearby village of Swami Sarai. However, Arampur is home to two of the three local private schools and the only nearby *madarsa* (Islamic school). In the last few years, these private primary and middle schools have grown with the local middle class, who want an alternative to the sporadically staffed government schools. Thus, they act as magnets for upper-class children from all the nexus villages. The children of those who both can afford to spare their teenagers from work and consider higher education to be worthwhile attend the locally initiated yet public high school. Not wanting his children to repeat his experience of having to travel 15 kilometers to the nearest high school, Baba Singh founded a school on land his landlord family donated in 1956. Today, this low, flat-topped, brick school that the state has since assumed under its control acts as a key unifying force among the wealthier (and some of the less wealthy) children of the nexus. Kids, who would otherwise grow up with more of an affinity for their individual villages, meet here daily, socialize, support the school cricket team, and make friendships and associations across village, caste, and (to a lesser extent) class lines. This demonstrates the obvious point that distance defines the nexus: villages farther away from Arampur will be less willing to send their children to school (or their men for tea). The less they circulate in and out of Arampur, the less they will identify with the villagers who do and the nexus at large.

Other elements, not centered on or situated immediately in Arampur, also reinforce nexus cohesion and association. Particular types of religious activity promote a nexus identity through the integration of an individual and his or her family into a general map of religious devotional spaces that includes an *ʿīdgāh*, [20] temples, and the tombs of saints. The religious activities that most prominently serve this end are the Muslim holidays of Baqar ʿĪd and ʿĪdu'l fiṭr. During these important days of religious observance, Muslims from across the area, including some from outside the nexus, come to the vicinity's only *ʿīdgah*, situated in Naugrah, for the prescribed community prayers. Afterward, friends—Hindu and Muslim both—visit Muslim households in their own and other villages. Similarly, the Vishvakarma temple bordering Swami Sarai acts as a center for public celebrations of the biannual Viśvakarma Pūjā. [21] Artisans from throughout the nexus gather to observe and participate in devotions to the patron god of their livelihood at this temple, which their contributions helped construct decades earlier.

Besides those in Arampur mentioned previously, other tombs of *shahīd*s and saints play additional roles in reinforcing a nexus identity, as the devotion of Sitaram Sharma's family to the tomb of a *shahīd* outside their native Arampur demonstrates. Although he works as a primary organizer of the local RSS *śākā* (branch) and is never reluctant to criticize Muslims, Sitaram Sharma joins his family at the side of a saint's tomb near Singhpur one day. There they place a garland of orange flowers atop the half-dozen embroidered *cādar*s (sheets) draped on the concrete-surfaced barrow of the tomb. Most of the twenty-five adults and children present are Sitaram Sharma's family members. They stand facing the edge of the raised brick platform on which the barrow rests. One of the elder family members explains that, although they did not know the name of the saint, his family does this *pūjā* once a year in honor of this man who once helped them. He identifies Rashiduddin Shah, the man who performs the ritual, as the *pujārī* (sacrificer) and "Muhammedan by caste" before describing the family member who technically sponsors the ritual as "Hindu" by caste. As members of the Lohar caste, Sitaram Sharma and some of his family regularly join the other artisans of the nexus in celebrations at the Viśvakarma temple on the other side of the nexus in Swami Sarai. In this way, their devotional lives inscribe the nexus area with meaningful places, shared at particular times with other members of their family, caste, and/or other nexus residents, and superimposed on the familiar map of their everyday economic and social lives.

The residents of the villages that comprise Arampur nexus identify themselves not only with the nexus but also with their individual home villages. They express and reinforced this in myriad ways. As Dasgupta observes,

> The political solidarity of the village is best expressed in times of rivalry and dispute with another village, when the villagers belonging to different castes and

---

20. A large courtyard set aside specifically for ʿĪd prayers.

21. Residents observe Viśvakarma Pūjā on the government-designated holiday in the month of Āśvin (September-October) as well as at another date.

religious groups join together even if it means taking a stand against their own caste-mates residing in the other village. The relative unity of the village, in other words, is expressed in its territorial contiguity and identity, a sense of ritual integrity, political solidarity against external influences and a degree of economic self-sufficiency.[22]

As we shall see, this village solidarity always carries the germs of division, as crosscurrents of caste, class, and religious interest may under various circumstances come to the surface and submerge notions of village unity. An example of the ritual integrity (and disintegration) of a village occurs during the annual Kālī Pūjā, which Hindus of every village celebrate in June and July. Various villages celebrate in different ways, yet common features in the Arampur nexus include a small ritual within the inhabited village, followed by the circumambulation of the village's fields, and ending with the sacrifice of animals (either through slaughter or release) at the village Kali shrine or temple on the eastern boundary of the village. Participants explain that the ritual helps protect their village, its inhabitants, and the fields for another year. The women, men, and children who participate in this ritual under the hammering summer sun come from all castes and classes *except* the lowest castes and Muslims. Harijans, isolated spatially in separate *camṭols* (Camār quarter) in some villages, are also often removed ritually as well. They may perform their own Kālī Pūjā with the same rituals and circumambulations, but only on another day.

Muslims have their own ritual ways of delineating the territory of their villages and affirming their identity with their villages, as demonstrated during Muharram. In the first days of this 10-day commemoration of the martyrdom of the Prophet Muhammad's grandson Husain in 680 C.E., a horseshoe reputedly from Husain's steed is removed from its storage in the tomb of Mubarak Shah and held aloft by a specially trained bearer. A crowd of Muslim men and boys from Arampur stands anxiously by, waiting until the power of the Sufi directs the horseshoe (and its bearer) to dart off in a seemingly random direction. However, the direction is anything but random. The bearer visits nearly every Sufi and *shahīd* tomb—large and small—in the village, pausing momentarily to allow the *naʿl* (horseshoe)[23] to touch the tomb before darting off once more across fields and through alleyways. In this way, the *naʿl* maps the village according to the tombs of martyrs and saints while a predominantly youthful crowd follows, making mental note of and having bodily interaction with each place. When the *naʿl* completes its saint-inspired passage through Arampur, it shoots off down one of the main roads to the tombs and/or mosques

<hr />

22. Dasgupta, p. 212. For an insightful analysis of the British imperial influence in the construction of village identities as well as examples of the unified expression of village identity, see Michael Katten, *Category Creation in the Colonial Setting: Identity Formation in 19th Century Telugu-Speaking India*. Ph.D. dissertation, University of California, Berkeley, 1998.

23. *Naʿl* is also the Arabic word for *sandal*, a fact which many pilgrims come to know when they perform the *hajj* in Mecca (see Malcolm X, *The Autobiography of Malcolm X*. New York: Ballantine, 1993 [1964], p. 330).

of Bari or the nearest town, thereby contrasting the mapping of all the sacred spaces "within" with the mapping of some of those "without." The procession continues for a couple days, always beginning in the morning at the tomb of Mubarak Shah and ending in the evening wherever the *na'l* has led it.

Local residents describe the contemporary erosion of common identities overlapping religious identities when they reflect that in earlier decades both Hindus and Muslims participated in the Durgā Pūjā and Muḥarram processions. Some residents express regret that such cross-participation seldom occurs nowadays and blame the current environment of communalist politics for the change. Undoubtedly and not without connection, contemporary Islamic revivalist ideas have influenced many local Muslims to avoid "un-Islamic" activities, including Muḥarram processions, while groups like the RSS revile "non-Indian" (read: "Muslim") celebrations. Nevertheless, the Muḥarram processions provide an example not only of village identity but also of *muhalla* identity.

Muhallas

Each village is comprised of *muhallas* (neighborhoods) defined, usually, by caste (see map 2). Often the *muhalla* name indicates the nature of the residents; for example, low-caste Hindus live in Chamar Toli and butchers live in Kasab Tola.[24] In other instances, the name refers to a group reputed to have once lived there. Although no one does gold work in modern Arampur, residents claim that members of the Sonār caste once lived and worked in the neighborhood of Sonahitya. Whatever the *muhalla*'s name, it is likely to be inhabited by one or a few castes that claim the same religious affiliation and, at times, express a neighborhood unity and identity. During Muḥarram, *muhallas* in Arampur design and build their own *ta'ziya* (a transportable replica of Husain's tomb at Karbala), then process with it around their neighborhoods until reaching the Bazaar, where they meet the procession from the other two groups of *muhallas*.[25] The number of *ta'ziyas* is limited by the police, who issue permits for only these three processions in Arampur in an effort to reduce the chances of conflict. Although this restriction requires some *muhallas* to share in the creation and parading of their *ta'ziya*, residents express their unique *muhalla* identities by creating *choṭī ta'ziya* (small *ta'ziyas*). The procession is organized to pass through each participating neighborhood so that the *ta'ziya* can be shown to all residents—male and female, old and young—and set momentarily next to the smaller, nonmobile, local one. Although they will not usually process with the *ta'ziya*, Hindu residents may join in the lighthearted expression of neighborhood pride and village competition regarding whose *ta'ziya*

24. *Ṭolī* and *ṭolā* mean "quarter of a town or city."
25. Note must be made that, as in many parts of South Asia, many local Muslims observe Muḥarram, which commemorates the death of the Shii Imam Husain, although they are all Sunni.

is best.[26] Another expression of *muhalla* solidarity occurs during certain *'urs,* when separate neighborhoods, whether Hindu or Muslim, donate one or more *cādar*s to important saints at their tombs and make a show of their parade from their neighborhood to the celebrated tomb. We shall examine this event in greater detail in chapter 5.

Bhabhua District, Banaras City, and Points Beyond

The crossroads of the local north-south and interstate east-west roads acts not only as a social magnet within the nexus but also as the gateway to other regions and states. As the center for access to Kendra, the nearest town (about 20 kilometers distant), and faraway Banaras (about 100 kilometers), the crossroads conduct social as well as vehicular traffic. Under the Arampur police *thānā*'s watchful presence, bee-haunted sweet stalls, inventory-packed small shops, cramped barber shops, and stilt-legged *pān* booths line both sides of the main road near the intersection, taking advantage of the bus stop that the whole nexus relies on for travel elsewhere. From before sunrise to long after sunset, men sporadically line the rough benches of the handful of teashops as they await buses or simply kill time with friends and acquaintances. The occasional female traveler stands detached from the bustle, usually with luggage, children, and a male relative. Shoe repairmen squat without shelter along the usually busy thoroughfare, bent over a broken strap with needle in hand, at their side a small charcoal brazier used to heat tools that mend broken plastic shoes. Drivers lounge on their colorful, chrome-plated rickshaws awaiting prospective passengers from buses that stop at the crossroads to discharge and take up passengers before clattering their way farther north, east, and west. As an alternate route to Banaras, the sporadically maintained east-west road becomes particularly useful when traffic on the Grand Trunk coagulates at the occasionally staffed inspection post on the Uttar Pradesh–Bihar border.

---

26. This intercommunal dimension of the Arampur *muhalla*s' Muharram processions contrasts with potentially confrontational processions that occur throughout north India. Muharram and various Hindu *pūjā*s have at times, even annually, become the locus of considerable friction between Muslim and Hindu groups that occasionally clash violently. Arampur residents still remember when local processions almost gave way to open conflict in the cases of the Arampur Muharram commemoration and a nearby village's *pūjā* procession. In the former, great anxiety arose in regard to a limb of a Bo tree, sacred to many Hindus, that obstructed the passage of the *ta'ziya*. In the latter case, a *devīmūrti* being carried from a nearby village to its immersion site passed through a predominantly Muslim village. A confrontation developed, and the image was jostled and dropped. For a challenging interpretation of such standoffs, see Nita Kumar, "Work and Leisure in the Formation of Identity: Muslim Weavers in a Hindu City" in *Culture and Power in Banaras: Community, Performance, and Environment, 1800–1980,* Sandria B. Freitag, ed. Berkeley: University of California Press, 1992 (1989), pp. 156–163. The author likens the communal standoffs to a "local drama" acted out so that "its tension, intensity, and accompanying fun are very localized." Instead of seeing only the divisiveness of the violent and tragic confrontations that occasionally accompany Muharram processions, Kumar discovers a theater of interaction.

The traffic passing from the area through this crossroads demonstrates how the nexus, although in Bihar, gravitates toward two centers—Banaras and Patna—much as a planet might rotate around two suns.

One resident explained that, unlike other districts in Bihar, Bhabhua district had not been affected by *bihārīkaraṇ* ("Biharization"), by which he meant a slide into the poverty, corruption, and violence by which many Indians characterize the state.[27] Educationally and commercially, he said, the district was part of Uttar Pradesh. Another explained that Bhabhua district suffered less from the violent crime endemic in many parts of Bihar because it was close to and associated with Uttar Pradesh and Banaras. Sandria Freitag has aptly described why Banaras is at the center of that gravitational pull westward. It is, she writes, the "largest urban center in the eastern Gangetic plain" and "the center of the Bhojpuri cultural region"—"a focal point for a vernacularly based culture that encompassed what is now eastern U.P. (Uttar Pradesh) and western Bihar."[28] Obviously, Banaras acts as an important religious center as well.

From time to time, a Jeep leaves the village nexus with an enshrouded corpse strapped to the roof atop a bamboo stretcher. On the long, bouncy trip to the burning ghats of Banaras, mourners chant *Rām nām satya hai* (The name of Ram is truth). Almost all nexus Hindus transport their dead there, entrusting cremation to the practiced hands and large pockets of the low-caste funerary workers, the *Doms*.[29] Some relatives take their terminally ill elderly to charitable homes such as Mukti Bhavan ("Liberation House"), situated off the city's Nai Sarak, whose manager told me that more clients come from Bhabhua than from any other district.[30] In the effort to secure for them the liberating boon of dying within the precincts of Banaras, their relatives care for them at the *bhavan* during their final days. The poorest of Arampur's lower castes, who do not have the resources to transport their dead, burn the corpses themselves

27. By some indicators, Bhabhua district fares better than most of the rest of Bihar. In 1991, the district of which Arampur *thānā* was then a part had the sixth highest population of any in Bihar yet was ranked twenty-seventh of forty-two districts in population growth rate (*Census of India 1991, Series 5 Bihar, Paper 1 of 1991 Provisional Population Totals*. Patna: Secretariat Press, 1991, pp. 27–29). The district's literacy rate was 45% (27% of females, 61% of males) against Bihar's overall 38% (*Census of India 1991, Paper 2 of 1992*, pp. 210, 231), and 50 to 75% of villages were electrified by 1986, better than most of Bihar (Lahiri, p. 127). However, the ratio of females to males of 892 per 1,000 (*Census of India 1991, Paper 1 of 1991*, p. 29) compared poorly with a Bihar average of 911 per 1,000 (*Census of India 1991, Paper 2 of 1992*, p. 46). The district has less than one-tenth the number of schools for girls than for boys at all levels of education as well as one of the worst teacher-student ratios, at many levels, for all of Bihar (Lahiri, p. 122).

28. Sandria Freitag, "Introduction: The History and Political Economy of Banaras" in *Culture and Power in Banaras: Community, Performance, and Environment, 1800–1980*, Sandria Freitag, ed. Berkeley: University of California Press, 1992 (1989), p. 1.

29. Jonathan Parry provides a detailed account of the religious, social, and economic interactions of life, death, cremation, and afterlife in his *Death in Banaras*. New York: Cambridge University Press, 1994.

30. For a thorough description of life and death at Mukti Bhavan, see Christopher Justice, *Dying the Good Death: The Pilgrimage to Die in India's Holy City*. Albany: State University of New York Press, 1997.

outside their villages under a heaped pile of dried cow dung, a small portion of precious wood, and, perhaps, a worn car or tractor tire. Death is but the last occasion to visit Banaras for many Hindus of the Arampur nexus. Some go for a purifying morning bath at specific times, such as during the transition from winter to summer. Others go in fulfillment of a vow or to visit Banaras's famous temples.

Although Muslims do not view Banaras as the important ritual center that it is to most Hindus, many do frequent the important *madarsa*s and religious book stores of the city's Muslim neighborhoods. The stores offer Hindi and Urdu books on Islamic topics, as well as Muslim wall calendars and pocket almanacs that depict the Islamic lunar year and accompanying religious holidays. Only a very few deeply religious Muslim families of the nexus send their children to *madarsa*s in Banaras, although a number of nexus residents have found teaching positions in these schools. Area Muslims consider Banaras the best location for the *qawwāl*s who are occasionally hired for events. Far from singing the purely devotional *qawwālī* found throughout north Indian and Pakistani Sufi *dargāh*s,[31] these *qawwāl*s commonly complement their devotional songs with entertaining competitions between troupes, engaging in mutually mocking ridicule and barely disguised innuendo.

From sunrise to after dusk, a steady stream of brawny buses in various states of repair roar up and down the east-west road between the nexus and Uttar Pradesh. Merchants squeeze into the usually packed passenger cabin, protecting the hidden rolls of cash they carry to purchase merchandise in the city of their ultimate destination. Since long before the era of Mughal rule, western Bihar's road and riverway systems have played an important commercial role. They carried the pilgrim traffic that facilitated the development of many Bihari Hindu and Muslim pilgrimage centers into towns.[32] The impressive ruined architecture remaining from the era of the conqueror Sher Shah Suri (mid-sixteenth century) and British ethnographer William Crooke's comments about the worship of the *brahm*[33] evidence the past significance of the nexus area as both pilgrimage and administrative center. Some of the oral narratives of Arampur residents about their village also portray a considerable town that later went into decline. Indeed, the Bhabhua area remained fairly unaffected by the commercial boom at the end of last century because of its remoteness from both rail and canal systems.[34] Although (and, perhaps, because) the expansion

31. Background and performance analysis of devotional *qawwālī* can be found in Regula Burckhardt Qureshi, *Sufi Music of India and Pakistan: Sound, Context and Meaning in Qawwali.* Chicago: University of Chicago Press, 1995 (1986).

32. Chaudhury, p. 104.

33. W. Crooke, *The Popular Religion and Folklore of Northern India*, vol. 1. Delhi: Munshiram Manoharlal, 1968 (1896).

34. F. H. Barrow, "Report on the Census of Shahabad," letter no. 103.C (18 June 1881) in Census of Bengal, 1881, District Report, Patna Division, p. 100. For a detailed description and analysis of commerce and markets in Bihar, see Anand A. Yang, *Bazaar India: Markets, Society, and the Colonial State in Bihar.* Berkeley: University of California Press, 1998.

of railroads during this period ushered in a vast increase in the transport of passengers and goods in the area immediately to the north, Bhabua saw little benefit.[35] However, the mid-twentieth-century rise of truck transportation—which doomed the slow-paced river and canal steamers—furthered the quick access of people to more distant and remote places and markets,[36] including Arampur. Nexus merchants now roam the length of the Gangetic Plain to order merchandise for sale in Arampur: cloth from Allahabad, shoes from Delhi. Meanwhile, carpet loom owners bring their unfinished products to Badoi, a major carpet-making center near Banaras, and return with the raw materials for more carpets, which may ultimately cover American and European floors. Those without their own vehicles—the vast majority—rely on the frequent buses.

Migrant workers from the area, having visited their wives and families on the short break they get but once or twice a year, may abandon efforts to get inside a bus. Instead, they climb the ladder to the roof, pushing up their luggage ahead of them. Furloughed soldiers and paramilitary police, using their practiced authority to bully a seat inside, head for the bus door. Both groups go to Banaras to connect with further transportation back to their duties in Dhanbad, Calcutta, Bombay, or Kashmir. They travel to one of Banaras's three train stations or many bus stands or, perhaps, to the large rail hub at Mughal Sarai. In general, the region has long been a source of migrant labor.

Through the British Empire, Bhojpuri-speaking laborers scattered across the ocean from the Maldives to Guyana. As early as the 1790s, certain Britishers exclaimed the useful qualities they imagined of the residents from whom they drew some of their top sepoys. Thomas Twining, serving the East India Company in Bihar at that time, wrote that they were "eminently martial people, easily inflamed, and impatient of control, but with management and firmness, their subordination is easily secured."[37] P. C. Chaudhury, author of the 1966 district gazetteer for the government of Bihar, shared a similarly grandiose image of the area population when he wrote:

> The people of this district are very hardy, brave, adventurous and military-minded. As they are not satisfied with the quiet life of the farmer and take delight in courting dangers, they generally prefer military or pseudo-military life. Hence they generally form the bulk of the constabulatory not only in the districts of Bihar but also in the neighboring State of Bengal. They generally get themselves [sic] recruited in the army. This is the main reason for emigration from this district.[38]

Additional considerations for emigration probably include the high population density and growth of the region and the accompanying economic difficulties.

---

35. Chaudhury, p. 366.
36. Ibid., pp. 366–367.
37. Mildred Archer, *Early Views of India: The Picturesque Journeys of Thomas and William Daniell, 1786—1794*. London: Thames and Hudson, 1980, p. 128.
38. Chaudhury, pp. 94–95.

Students from the Arampur nexus also board the bus to Banaras. The burgeoning middle class and landowning elite often school their children in the city's multitude of schools, *madarsa*s, and colleges, as well as in the three universities there. The children reside in residential halls or with extended family who have settled in the city. The wealthiest nexus residents may drive their children into the city with their own motorcycles, cars, or Jeeps, combining the chore with urban shopping and entertainment. Beginning in the 1960s, the Green Revolution has significantly increased the profitability of cultivation (although the final cost, in terms of land exhaustion and environmental impact, has yet to be reckoned). Landowners have invested much of their new capital in local businesses and used the returns to pay for expensive education and buy luxury items like Jeeps.[39] Their children acquire costly tastes over the course of their urban education and introduce a new consumerism back home in keeping with the rising conspicuous consumption that has followed the central government's plan of national economic liberalization during the 1990s. Many upper-class families in the nexus have bought or plan to buy a second home in Banaras.

Besides roads, other communication links connect the nexus to Banaras and the rest of India. The broadcasts of Akashvani (government-run radio) and Doordarshan (government-run television) to which residents turn for entertainment and news originate from the huge, steel-and-concrete broadcast tower in Banaras. Patna is too distant for its broadcasts to be heard, and the CNN, BBC, and MTV cable revolution has not yet reached the area, although some residents tune in to BBC and Voice of America on their shortwave radios. The introduction of telephones into parts of the nexus in 1994 serves to strengthen ties to family members and college friends in Banaras.

Just as the traffic in and out of the nexus demonstrates the religious, economic, and educational centrality of Banaras, local newspaper subscriptions reflect the area's political orbit around Patna and the local penchant for political news. Of the 78 daily newspapers to which nexus residents subscribe, 66 are published in Patna, and only 12 are Banaras editions.[40] Magazine subscriptions taken through the sole local news agent include *Saras Salil* (a women's magazine, 100 subscriptions), *Nandan* (children's monthly, 10), *Māyā* (political weekly, 10), *India Today* (political biweekly, 10), and *Manohama* ("ladies'" magazine, 5). A number of residents independently obtain *Pañcayanya*, published by the RSS. Magazines of Islamic content commonly circulate among residents who have borrowed them from neighbors returning from one of Banaras's Muslim bookshops. The town nearest the nexus provides film entertainment with two movie theaters and several video stores. Home VCRs

---

39. Basu, Tapan, Pradip Datta, et al., *Khaki Shorts and Saffron Flags: A Critique of the Hindu Right.* New Delhi: Orient Longman, 1993, p. 112.

40. Newspaper subscription figures break down as follows: Patna editions—*Hindustān* (Hindi, 40 subscriptions), *Āryāvart* (Hindi, 10), *Āj* (Hindi, 10), *Sangam* (Urdu, 2), *The Hindustan Times* (English, 2), *Indian Nation* (English, 2); Banaras editions—*Āj* (Hindi, 12).

allow the wealthy to supplement the movies shown on Doordarshan. Occasionally, they lend their equipment to the village community for religious holidays. Organizers set the television and VCR in front of a crowd of children sitting impatiently outside, anxiously anticipating a video about a Hindu hero or a Bombay gangster.

Biharis and Bhojpuri Speakers

The fairly easy and common access to Banaras by the middle and upper classes and the sojourning further abroad by emigrant workers and traveling merchants provide a context in which residents situate themselves as Bhojpuri speakers and Biharis. Residents are well aware that many other Indians consider Bihar as the most impoverished, backward, and crime-ridden state in the nation. Some, like Arampur resident Nasiruddin Khan of Arampur, agree. "This is the worst region within India," he says as he reflects on his experiences as a 24–year veteran carpetmaker who had spent half that time working in Uttar Pradesh. He talks of being a Bihari outside the state: "Go to U.P. (Uttar Pradesh) or M.P. (Madhya Pradesh) and people will ask, 'Where do you come from?' They think that you are a *badmāsh* (ruffian)" [U]. Demonstrating the attitudes of others to Biharis, a lawyer in Banaras explained to a foreign scholar that a man he knew had a particularly difficult *bhūt* owing to the fact that it was from Bihar.[41] Meanwhile, a charismatic Catholic healer described a village in Bihar as "Sodom and Gomorra" on account of the sexual sins ascribed to its emigrant, bonded labor.[42] Likewise, the phrase "to go to Bihar" in Hindi can be understood in Banaras to mean "to have gay sex."[43]

Statistically, Bihar seems barely less dire than many of its stereotypes. The state's per capita domestic product in 1986–1987 was the poorest in India at less than Rs. 500.[44] In an index of economic development with an all-India average of 100, Bihar scored only 54 points in 1989.[45] Between 1981 and 1991, the state population increased 23% to 86,374,465,[46] of whom only 38% were literate (23% of females, 53% of males).[47] Among other states in India, Bihar ranked second in population and third in density,[48] sixteenth in the ratio of

41. Mathew N. Schmalz, "Slave of Christ: Portrait of an Indian Charismatic Healer." Paper presented at the annual Conference on South Asia, Madison, October 1996, p. 8.

42. Mathew N. Schmalz, "Sins and Somatologies: Sexual Transgression and the Body in Indian Charismatic Healing." Paper presented at annual American Academy of Religion conference, San Francisco, November 1997.

43. Personal Conversation with Ramu Pandit, November 1994.

44. *An Atlas of India*. New York: Oxford University Press, 1990, p. 14.

45. Ibid., p. 40.

46. *Census of India 1991, Series 1 India, Paper 1 of 1992, Volume I, Final Population Totals*. New Delhi: Government of India Press, 1993, p. 16.

47. *Census of India 1991, Series 1 India, Final Population Totals: Brief Analysis of Primary Census Abstract, Paper 2 of 1992*, pp. 46, 53.

48. Ibid., pp. 83–84.

females to males,[49] eighteenth in electrification,[50] and last in literacy.[51] Among other states, only Madhya Pradesh had fewer hospital beds for its population.[52] Yet, statistics notwithstanding, nexus residents often proudly identify themselves with Bihar, especially in conversation about other states. Aware of the deprecations of its critics, some Arampur residents rally to their home state's defense. One explained, "People think that Bihar is full of goons and thieves but this isn't true—U.P. is like that. Bihar is so *śarīf* (civilized)" [H]. Similarly, Mirnan Ansari adroitly acclaimed Bihar while counterattacking its detractors. He explained that people in Uttar Pradesh feared Biharis and, when asked why that was, answered that it was due to the criminals in Bihar's mountains who actually come from U.P.! After an inquiry as to where she lived previously, Lakshmi Devi responded resolutely, while serving customers at her tea shop, "I was born here, I was married here, I do not know anything more than here." When asked if her family came from outside Bihar, she replied forcefully, "I'm not from Hindustan or Pakistan—I'm from here. *Ham log bihārī hai*" (We people are Bihari) [H]. Similarly, Devapur resident Balaram Singh quoted approvingly some Krishna Consciousness devotees he knew who said, "Hindustan is heaven, and Bihar is its gate."

Further evidence of Bihari pride and identity comes from the helpful recommendations residents gave me as an outsider who should visit the region's noteworthy places. They suggested tourist sites based on their association with territorial identity, not nearness to the nexus. So residents commonly exhorted me to visit Rohtas Fort in Bihar but seldom the equidistant Chunar Fort in Uttar Pradesh, sometimes the Buddhist center at Nalanda but never the much closer Sarnath. Undoubtedly, some of these associations develop through education. Both government and private schools use the same textbooks published by the state government, such as the readers in *itihās* (history) that highlight and underline Bihar's place in an Indian nationalist narrative. Additionally, Hindi, Urdu, and English primers include essays on Bihar and its famous sons and daughters (such as India's first president, Dr. Rajendra Prasad).

Bhojpuri plays its own role in the sense of common identity among western Biharis. Emigrant laborers in non-Bhojpuri speaking areas no doubt learn to appreciate the unifying nature of Bhojpuri that resident nexus dwellers take for granted. Of the 125 residents asked about their mother language, nearly all gave "Hindi" as their answer. Some (all Muslim) replied "Urdu," but scarcely more than one in ten said Bhojpuri. Then, when I prodded the informants to say what other languages they knew, their answers included "Sanskrit," "Arabic," "Persian," "Bengali," "Devanagari," and "English." Few added "Bhojpuri." Finally, when at last I asked if they could speak Bhojpuri, more than half laughed and said, "Of course." Hindi and Urdu may be the languages of edu-

---

49. Ibid., p. 46. The gender ratio being 911:1,000 for Bihar against 927:1,000 for all of India.
50. Lahiri, p. 48. Less than 60% of villages are electrified.
51. *Census of India 1991, Paper 2 of 1992*, p. 53.
52. Lahiri, p. 48. Bihar has less than 50 hospital beds per 100,000 population.

cation and commerce, but Bhojpuri is the social medium, so common as to be taken for granted. Through his review of census data, Lachman Khubchandani comes to a striking conclusion:

> In many urban and border regions in South Asia, one often notices a citizen iden-
> tifying his language with caste or class or original (ancestral) regional affiliations,
> and not so much with the actual speech he uses as a native speaker. According to
> the 1961 Indian census, Bihari was identified as mother tongue by fifteen thou-
> sand individuals from twenty states and Union territories, but not a single indi-
> vidual from Bihar claimed Bihari as his mother tongue.[53]

It is useful to balance Freitag's earlier comment, that Banaras acts as a center because it is the largest cultural center in the Bhojpuri-speaking territory, with the preceding maxim that language varies every few miles. In this way, popular understandings of Bhojpuri can create a sense of broad regional identity in one context while, in another, foster a much more constricted western Bihari identity. In yet another context, Bhojpuri can serve a very narrowly defined notion of a very local identity. One Arampur resident went so far as to say that each *muhalla* of his village had a different *bolī* (manner of speech).

Yet, issues of identity reach beyond simply the use of a language and include its culture and politics. Khubchandani notes that even those who speak nothing but Bhojpuri, who do not know the basics of Hindi, claim the latter as their mother language because they identify themselves with the Hindi "tradition."[54] Meanwhile, of the 74 Muslim area residents questioned about their mother language, 49 identified Urdu, 12 declared Hindi, 8 Bhojpuri, 5 Hindi-Urdu, and 1 Devanagari. Speakers take care not only in how they identify themselves with a language group but also in how others identify them. A young man demonstrated this one day after he said that he was Muslim. I then asked him his mother language. "Urdu," replied a young bystander, who identified himself as Hindu and a Hindi speaker. The Muslim man quickly corrected him with an answer spoken with defiant finality, "Hindi."

The importance that so many attach to language identity seems to stem more from self-perception than from linguistic practice. Despite the certainty with which many residents identify and distinguish themselves through an association with either Hindi or Urdu, differences in oral practice seem far less absolute. Self-proclaimed Urdu speakers commonly use Sanskrit-derived terms such as *parivār* (family), *dharm* (religion), *deś* (country), *karṇa* (cause), and *atithi* (guest), and self-identified Hindi speakers often use the Persian- or Arabic-derived equivalent of these words: *khāndān*, *mazhab*, *mulk*, *waja*, and *mehmān*. Although one might conclude that Hindi speakers have a *tendency* to borrow from a Sanskrit-derived vocabulary and Urdu speakers have a *tendency* to borrow from an Persian- or Arabic-derived vocabulary, this reasoning still obscures

53. Lachman M. Khubchandani, *Plural Languages, Plural Cultures: Communication, Identity, and Sociopolitical Change in Contemporary India*. Honolulu: University of Hawaii Press, 1983, pp. 46.
54. Ibid., p. 47.

the vast shared lexicon (not to mention the nearly identical grammars) of these sister languages. When asked whether they could understand speakers of the other language group, few residents replied in the negative. (Some Hindi speakers, however, did admit to not being able to understand Hindi speakers who inordinately replace "Hindustani"[55] terms with Sanskrit equivalents.) In written language, almost all literate Urdu speakers can read Hindi because of the national mandate that Indians learn this, the official national language. Only a very few literate Hindi speakers can read Urdu.

As with many identities, language identity has altered over time as part of broader social changes. As we shall see later, there has been an increasing identification of Muslims with Urdu in north India. However, Khubchandani makes the important note that these changes may more likely reflect shifts in social identification than actual changes in speech practices.[56] While the claims to Hindustani as a mother language dropped precipitously between 1951 and 1961, the number of Biharis declaring their mother tongue as Bhojpuri jumped from 1,900 to 7,842,700 in the same period—a gain of 412,674%. This slowed to an 80% rise between 1961 and 1971. These trends reflect the assertion of regional identities in the state during this period and the counterpull of an association with what Khubchandani calls "prestigious language labels," such as Urdu and Hindi.[57]

Indian

The final identity associated with territory to be examined here is Indian. As a conspicuous outsider, I became an obvious *other* to residents who often asserted nationalist notions of an Indian *us* as a foil to notions of a foreign *them*. My presence acted as a magnet for expressions of national identity (among others), attracting positive, negative, and neutral attitudes about India, being Indian, and the non-Indian world. Described by residents as an *aṁgrez* (English person), an American, and a *gorā* (Caucasian or light-complexioned), the identities projected onto me often acted as a foil opposite of which residents discerned their national identity.

Despite my self-identification as *American*, *aṁgrez* became the label most commonly applied to me. Just as medieval Europeans referred to any Muslim as *Turk* after the invasion of Europe by Ottoman Turks and Arabs referred to any European as *farangī* following the French, or Frank, invasions of West Asia, many Indians refer to Caucasian Europeans and Americans as *aṁgrez* after the experience of "English" imperialism. In so doing, they collapse most Western-

---

55. The lingua franca of northern India and Pakistan that combines vocabularies derived, in part, from Sanskrit, Persian, and Arabic.

56. Khubchandani, p. 59.

57. Ibid., pp. 90–94.

ers into a single racial category—*gorā*—for cultural comparison, defining themselves in opposition to their description of *aṁgrez*.

Residents often assume that the physical environment of America and India plays an instrumental role in forming more than the physical character of Americans and Indians. One resident of Naugrah's *camṭol* explained that my skin color was becoming like his because of the *ābohavā* (environment). He explained further that if I lived elsewhere in Bihar, such as Ranchi or Dhanbad, my skin color would be even darker because of the iron content of the local water. A resident of Arampur, who also noted my changing complexion, explained, "The *havā* (climate) of this place is black so people are *kālā* (black). In your place, people are *safed* (white)." These observations obviously begin with a stereotyped racial view of Americans and Indians that many residents used to express their pride in what they understood as the unique physical aspects of their nation.

For many Arampur residents, India does more than stand apart from America and other countries because of its unique environment; it stands above them. More than one Arampur resident explained, "No other country has Hindustan's weather. We have *all* the seasons." Moreover, many residents expounded the belief that India's exceptional geography was responsible for the uniqueness of the people of India. The M.A.-educated Panini Singh expresses the opinion of many Indians (especially those inspired by the rhetoric of the RSS, BJP, and VHP) when he describes his identity as *bhārat, bhāratī, bhāratīya*—"India, Indian, Indianization" (his translation). He adds:

> That is not a new thing. It is a very, very, very ancient "tradition." I can read and write that I am "Indian" because I can identify that Indian civilization, like the Sindhu Valley [civilization], is mine. The biggest thing is no other country in the world has such a long history as India's; a history from 600 B.C. to today. From the beginning this has been a peninsula and only one [tradition] has existed. For this reason it is a long, single history. [H]

Balaram Singh added another dimension to this pride in Indian history when he said, "Only in India does Ishvar[58] manifest himself. Jesus was the son of Ishvar. Muhammad was a prophet [*paigambar*]. But only in India does Ishvar come himself—Ram, Durga. The form of God comes through our eternal religion. . . . There is the Himalaya with [Mount] Kailash and Mansarovar. . . . The place is holy. . . . They say that Hindustan is heaven and Bihar is its gate."

This uniqueness provided both a point of pride for residents and an explanation for India's presently poor economic standing. The very fact that India stood so tall made it vulnerable to the envy of other (e.g., Western) nations. Bhalla Caudhri explained,

> India was the bird of gold—there was no country like it. In one country there is this, in another that, but everything is in Hindustan. Your country is cold and

---

58. From the Sanskrit: "Master," "lord," "Supreme Being."

this country is hot. It has four seasons and for this reason it has everything. That is why every country says, "We want to conquer Bharat." Before, the English were only in England. In science, Bharat was ahead of you. . . . Our minds were very advanced. [H]

Among residents, the notion of the plucked golden bird is a common epithet for India.

The role of the British (and, among some, the Muslims) as plunderers of this golden bird becomes central to a nationalist narrative of Indian identity. As propagated by government-sponsored school texts, such a narrative imagines a singular, eternal India. That this narrative informs the worldview that some residents use to interpret contemporary events—both national and local—became apparent one day as I am talking with Ram Nisad, a teacher at an elementary school nearby Arampur. I ask why August 15 is so important in India. He replies, "On August 15, India was delivered from English hands, and so, out of happiness, we celebrate August 15." I ask him how India came to be under English control in the first place. He replies again, "The English . . . came in 1608 in the guise of trading. They took away the freedoms of our country." I then ask how they did this, and he responds, "Just like you come, ask questions, write our history, and will go back to your country to tell them and they will make us slaves." Taken aback, I ask whether he thought that I would do that. He says, "No. But it is the same way" [H].

And so I, a Caucasian Westerner labeled *aṁgrez*, could be mapped by some on the terrain of past foreign interventions and present capitalist arrivals where many Indians see themselves standing tenuously as vulnerable non-Westerners. One resident of a lower-caste, underclass neighborhood pointed to me and said, "*Āp log* (you people) ruled here for a hundred years. In one hundred years *āp log* will return." Throughout my 14 months in the village nexus, I disagreed with some residents when they referred both to me *and* the British rulers of South Asia as *āp log*. Many residents failed to see a difference between the East India Company of yesteryear and the likes of the Enron Company. This American corporation was currently making headlines as a power company that had won a lucrative contract from one Indian state government after spending $300 million to "educate" state politicians.

Concern for renewed foreign economic influence in India has spawned organizations such as the Svādeśī Jāgraṇ Maṁc (National Awareness Association), described by the *Times of India* as "an RSS front."[59] Members of this group scrawled Hindi messages such as the following on a wall in Arampur:

svadeśī ān bān sān hai	Domestic made is pride, quality, and a sign;
videshī jahar samān hai	Foreign made goods are poisonous.
videshī kamp nī yo bhagī yeṇge	Foreign companies will be sent fleeing,
bhārat māṁ kī lāj bacāyeṁ	Save the honor of Mother India!

59. *Times of India.* 19 July 1995, New Delhi edition, p. 4.

jan jan kī hai yahī pukār   This is the cry of the people,
videshī vastu kā vahī kār   the matter, there, of foreign goods.

Such sentiments have increased with the growing national debate about the economic liberalization initiated by former Prime Minister Narasimha Rao.

Besides Western nationalism, the other great negative identity by which many residents define their national selves comes from Pakistan. Among suspicions that I was a CIA operative or some other foreign agent were questions as to whether I worked for Pakistan's intelligence service, the Inter-Services Intelligence (ISI). Because I learned Urdu before Hindi, my pronunciation of these sister languages owes more to the former than the latter. This, coupled with the Cold War American political alliance with Pakistan, suggested to some that I might be an element of Pakistan's insidious "hidden foreign hand," of which national politicians and journalists alike find evidence—both proven and dubious—throughout India.[60] One woman in an impoverished, lower-caste *muhalla* asked rhetorically, yet emphatically, if the village map that she observed me making would be used by invading Pathāns. Yet, resident Muslims have had to suffer far more enduring suspicions about their loyalties. Their common (but not universal) use of Urdu is taken as a token of otherness by many Hindu, Hindi-speaking Indians—a fact that various Hindu chauvinist political organizations use to justify a plank linking Hindi, Hinduism, and Hindu political domination.[61] Ved Singh voiced a like-minded and not rare suspicion that Indian Muslims cheer for the Pakistani cricket team, not the Indian team, during international matches. In this atmosphere, then, my being seen as a Pakistani agent only reflected the far more tragic suspicion among some Hindus that all Indian Muslims are, at heart, Pakistani and not to be trusted as loyal to India.[62]

For this reason, many Muslims take pains to demonstrate their fealty to India. Several Muslim storeowners in Arampur make a point of posting Indian flag stickers on their money boxes, hanging calendar posters of Indian scenery on their walls, and never speaking favorably of Pakistan in public, if they have anything favorable to say. Hindus and Muslims jointly partake in the annual Independence Day (August 15) and Republic Day (January 26) celebrations. These include school holidays and formal events at *thānā*, the block develop-

---

60. George Orwell's *1984* seems to provide a particularly apt foreshadowing of this situation in which successive Indian and Pakistani governments divert attention from pressing domestic issues with the pronouncement of imminent threat from one another. The enemy exists not only across their mutual border but also from traitorous fifth column leaders of suspect national and religious affiliation, strikingly similar to Orwell's ominously named "Goldstein."

61. Vasudha Dalmia details the early expression of this ideal by Hindu publicists in her *The Nationalization of Hindu Traditions: Bhāratendu Hariśchandra and Nineteenth-Century Banaras.* Calcutta: Oxford University Press, 1997. See especially p. 27.

62. Two significant works of scholarship on the tie between language, religion, and nationalism are Paul Brass, *Language, Religion and Politics in North India* (Delhi: Vikas, 1974); and Amrit Rai, *A House Divided: The Origin and Development of Hindi/Hindavi* (Delhi: Oxford University Press, 1984).

ment office, and the high school. Hindu and Muslim pilgrimages that depart from the nexus twice a year combine religious with national historical sites. Thus, the Hindu pilgrimage buses travel for three weeks from Mathura to Mount Abu to the Taj Mahal, and the Muslim pilgrimage tour centers on the *'urs* of the Sufi Muinuddin Chishti in Ajmer yet also includes monuments in Delhi. Hindus and Muslims both participate in the latter. Religious pilgrimage apparently mixes freely with nationalist sight-seeing on these tours.

Yet most Muslims remain sensitive to the suspicions of some of their Hindu neighbors and protest in their own ways. During a conversation about Muslim life at his shop in a bazaar, Sakin Ansari pulls some worn Urdu magazines from a nearby shoe box and opens by memory to a poem by the revered modern Indian Muslim poet, Muhammad Iqbal. It reads,

Maẓhab nahīṅ sikhātā	Religion does not teach
āpas meṅ bair rakhnā	being hostile to others.
Hindī haiṅ ham waṭan	We are Indian,
Hindūstān hamārā	our home is India.

In the next chapter, I explain why I have chosen narratives of the past as the tool by which multiple identities can be explored. It will be necessary to delineate the reliance of identity on space and time as mediated through narrative. Finally, before we can analyze local narratives for multiple identities (chapters 4 and 5), we must first establish a common heuristic space within which historiography, folklore, and mythology can be examined as past narratives without concern for external notions of veracity. That space will be provided through the concept of group memory.

Interconnected worlds: Latif Khan (*above*) prepares one of the 1000 *biṛīs* he makes each day. He rolls chopped tobacco into a tobacco leaf harvested from the neighboring mountains and, at dusk, gives his day's production to a middleman who dispatches it to distant Banaras on one of the daily buses like the "Banarasi Babu" (*below*).

Diversity: The villages of the Arampur nexus vary greatly in size and population. The commotion of Arampur's brick-paved main bazaar (*above*), which acts as a local social and economic center as well as a conduit for pilgrims visiting Shastri Brahm's temple, contrasts with the relative calm of a street in the neighboring Loharani *muhalla* (*below*). *Muhalla*s are defined often by caste.

Village spaces: Area villages tend to economize space by consolidating residential buildings in a densely populated center surrounded by agricultural and pastoral fields. Only a short distance separates this part of Arampur bazaar (*below*) from the village's northern fields and water reservoir (*above*).

Tea stall conversations: Draupati (*above, center*) and Manu (*above, right*) own and operate one of the many tea stalls along Arampur's main road. For years, Sharif Khan (*below, left*) and Vira Singh (*below, right*) shared tea at another shop. As descendants of the brothers Lakshman and Loka Singh, they and their relatives also share a common family identity, despite their divergent village identities and religious identities as Muslims and Hindus.

Places of devotion, socializing, and memory: Although the memory of Raja Vicitra survived longer than his legendary palace, the moat-surrounded fortification mound (*above*) on which the palace sat remains a central reference point to local narratives describing the conflict between him and Shastri Brahm, whose temple now dominates the hilltop. Although far less significant in the daily devotional lives of Arampur area residents, this tomb of a *shahīd* (*below*) is one stop among many in the annual *na'l* procession. Many such devotional places provide social spaces shared by a range of people.

Places of contested memory and shared community: A well for a Hindu raja to bathe his elephants or for local Muslims to wash their hands? A usurped Hindu temple or a Muslim sultan's mausoleum? Despite the communal controversies in which some engage with regard to the local well (*above*) and tomb (*below*), most Arampur area residents relax in each other's company without such concerns while resting at the one and picnicking at the other.

Domestic worlds: Courtyards are a common component of most area homes and amply demonstrate local class and gender differences. Families that work as field laborers (such as the Naugrah family *above*) rely on women to perform not only domestic but also agricultural work. Although often separated by gender when working, these women necessarily have access to public life unavailable to many women of landlord families, who may enjoy a far larger domestic space (such as the Jagahpur home *below*) but have little or no access to the world beyond their door. Female seclusion symbolizes wealth for many families, both Hindu and Muslim.

Integration through education: Children of one of Arampur's recently opened private schools assemble at day's end (*above*). The school founder recruited most of his fellow teachers (*below*) from schoolmates he knew at the government's local high school. Not only do they come from a variety (but by no means a cross-section) of class, caste, and religious backgrounds but also they derive from several villages of the Arampur nexus. Unlikely to have become friends in any other way, their common education provided an environment in which they became familiar with one another. They replicate this experience in their own school, although tuition limits diversity of class.

3

Identity, Narrative, and Group Memory

Just as no one map can adequately demonstrate all the geographic features of a particular terrain, so no one description can hope to depict completely the full spectrum of identities that comprise an individual's sense of himself or herself. The previous chapter provided a broad overview of the geographic, social, economic, religious, and historical context of the Arampur area and the associated range of identities of its residents. This chapter develops the heuristic tool by which we will disclose and analyze various group identities in the final two chapters. First, this chapter considers the village as a focus of study. Second, it evaluates Paul Ricoeur's notion of group self-definition according to shared interests, the past as one of those shared interests, and the essential role of narrative in defining an identity based on those interests. Third, in an effort to create a single field of study that brackets historiographic notions of veracity in favor of local truth claims, the chapter presents the concept of *group memory* as a single, descriptive term for these diverse narratives. Fourth, it demonstrates the utility of this term and the range of narrative styles through an analysis of four versions of a commonly told local story.

The Village as Study Focus

Ronald Inden's critique of village studies offers a useful starting place for my own village-centered project. His *Imagining India* has leveled various criticisms against Western and Indian scholars in an effort to champion a nonessentialist view of rural Indians as self-determined, broadly integrated agents in the construction of their social reality. Inden wants to show that rural Indians do not live in self-sufficient village republics that are the objects, but never the agents, of political and economic change.[1] Although his concerns are justified, Inden overlooks the inherent and necessary reductionism of any ethnographic

1. Ronald Inden, *Imagining India*. Oxford: Blackwell, 1992 (1990), pp. 131–161.

description when he criticizes earlier anthropologists for not depicting all the socioeconomic and historical dimensions of rural Indian life that he deems important.

Returning to Jonathan Z. Smith's observation noted earlier, "'Map is not territory'—but maps are all we possess,"[2] the present project focuses on the village because rural Biharis themselves often make this the locus of self-reference in casual and formal conversations. Because, as we shall see, territory plays an important role in local identification, our use of the map metaphor becomes particularly apt. It is important to recognize both the set of maps that each individual carries in her or his mental map case and the dynamic of selection by which that individual chooses one as temporarily dominant according to social context. Our focus on the Arampur village nexus, therefore, acts merely as a staging point from which to begin a multicontextual analysis of local group identities. The discursive practices of the residents themselves suggest this as our starting point.

In his Hindi novel *The Hunted*, author Mudra Rakshasa uses the character of the city-dwelling journalist Kanchan to reflect his own dilemma as a writer in rural India. Like his fictional newspaperman, Rakshasa struggles to depict for outsiders some aspects of the complexities of a village's social reality despite the impossibility of providing a perfect and complete interpretation.

> During his many excursions to villages, Kanchan had seen the roadsides there and the train tracks, so he believed he knew quite a lot about villages firsthand. What's more, he had acquired no small amount of knowledge about village life from the radio, television, newspapers and books put out by the Department of Rural Development.
>
> But after spending a day-and-a-half in Bhudra [village], Kanchan felt he was seeing a village for the very first time. Villages are not simply mud huts, ox-carts, thatch and ponds. Superficially, villages may seem like two-dimensional, old, quaint photographs, but internally they are as alive and complicated as epic narratives. Each has a history. Not a history like Akbar the Great and Rana Pratap Singh, but an unusual, indefinable history, like a page of the *Rig-Veda* which, because we no longer have Mahindhar's commentary, cannot be understood clearly. They are like obscure Vedic hymns in which one doesn't know if Garhiya is the name of a man or a lake, if *bandhua* is a noun meaning "destiny" or a verb, and if a shoe is a tool to administer a humiliating punishment or something you put on your feet. A village is like the *Adi-Granth*—obscure, impenetrable, and in order to understand it a new *Nirukta* needs to be written. A village is like the first civilization buried in the ground ages ago, for which we need a scientifically organized archaeological dig in order to find out who these people were who performed sacrifices and whose civilization then slipped, and who were those who fought against the sacrificers. Who were Janamejaya, and who were those thrown naked into the fire? After living in the village, Kanchan was amazed to find him-

---

2. Jonathan Z. Smith, *Map Is Not Territory.* Chicago: University of Chicago Press, 1978, p. 309.

self thinking that Kansa and Krishna now were so easily understandable and Harappa was so transparent.[3]

Unlike the journalist Kanchan, Rakshasa is well aware of the dynamics of village life. Like Premchand and many of his Progressivist literary school colleagues, Mudra Rakshasa depicts rural life with a social realism that derives from his experiences growing up in rural South Asia. As a Marxist, the writer appreciates the diverse layers of class and caste that comprise any single village population.

Rakshasa reveals the centrality of the village context and of narrative in the questions that he poses through Kanchan. This journalist character asks, "Who?" "Whose?" "What?" in regard to local life. Yet, perhaps more revealing is what he does not ask. First, Kanchan does not feel the need to ask "Where?" Seemingly apparent to him, the only thing certain about this interpretive jungle is where it stands, where it takes its setting: the village. Second, he does not ask "How?" because he expects that it will be answered within the frame of a narrative, a "history." And so, as the novel unfolds, Kanchan learns about the villagers through a story of class and caste oppression.

Saadat Hasan Manto's short story "Toba Tek Singh" similarly demonstrates the centrality of the village as the setting of social action and interaction and as a focus of identity for many South Asians.[4] Few pieces of fiction have captured the tragedy and confusion of India and Pakistan's Partition in 1947 as powerfully as this short story. It depicts an insane asylum inmate who searches for his village in the vertigo of shifting frontiers and dislocated populations. He desperately questions others about his village's location because he does not know whether it, and thus he, now reside in India or Pakistan. The story inconclusively closes as he collapses in the no-man's-land between the barbed wire of the new borders, declaring that his village exists neither in one country nor the other, yet in both as realized in his person. The audience quickly discerns that not only the village of this refugee has been lost to him but also his identity. It—and therefore he—has fallen off the newly reorganized map.

In some ways, the village itself can become a character in the narratives related by rural residents, as Gyanendra Pandey has argued with his notion of the village as hero.[5] Some Arampur residents personify neighboring villages with singular characterizations of all its residents. So, for example, Lava Pandit of Jagahpur depicted Swami Sarai residents as abrasive, Shivaji Tirth of Swami Sarai called Naugrah a "mini-Pakistan," and Hamzah Ansari of Arampur described the residents of Singhpur as lazy. Panini Singh of Singhpur demonstrated this dynamic best when he narrated a story about a particular village

3. Mudra Rakshasa, *The Hunted*, Robert A. Hueckstedt, trans. New Delhi: Penguin, 1992 (1987), p. 170.

4. Saadat Hasan Manto, "Toba Tek Singh" in *Kingdom's End and Other Stories*, Khalid Hasan, trans. New York: Verso, 1987, pp. 11–18.

5. Gyanendra Pandey, *The Construction of Communalism in Colonial North India*. Delhi: Oxford University Press, 1990, p. 132.

just beyond the outskirts of the nexus. He explained that the comic stupidity ascribed to this village is so profound that stories depicting the outrageous misperceptions of its inhabitants are famous among nexus residents. In one story, he described the following event: "One day, the villagers decided to make a temple. When they were finished, they realized that the temple's door was on the west side. Usually, a temple's door is on the east side. In order to put the door on the east side, a thick rope was wrapped all the way around the temple and all the village's people began to try to turn the temple around. Instead, the temple cracked and collapsed" [H]. Other nexus members confirmed this impression with yet other stories and declared that families avoided marrying their daughters and sons with those of that particular village.

I thought initially that this book would focus on a single village. However, I realized quickly that my focus required an adjustable field of view. Among the residents of any one village, group identities can be found which center on *muhalla*s, castes, and families, while yet other identities correspond to an association with the village nexus, local area, district, state, language area, nation, and, indeed, humanity. Adding to the complexity, some groups identify themselves not with any one particular locale but with a specific set of villages found in a large area. As we shall see in the next chapter, the Khans of Naugrah and Thakurs of Ishwarpur identify each of their extended families with a group of villages—some neighboring and some distant. Then again, some nexus residents allege that Muslims have alien loyalties and, therefore, are not Indian at all, thus denying them an association with the territory in which they reside. Such critics suspect that Muslims' ritual use of Arabic and suspected pan-Islamic identity prove an allegiance to Arab states.

Yet, as the novelist Rakshasa has demonstrated, the focus on the village remains justifiable as long as one recognizes the kaleidoscope of identities, narratives, events, interrelations, and interpretations that swirl through the mental worlds of its residents. During my research, nexus dwellers often referred to themselves via an allusion to their village, whether in conversation with someone from their *muhalla* or from another country. At times, one group in a village might speak as though they alone represented the village, ignoring the existence of other groups. Often, when the Rājpūts of Swami Sarai and the Khans of Naugrah describe their mutual connection and/or enmity (see chapter 4), it seems that the dynamic is between their whole villages, as though no other family or caste lives there. At other times, nexus residents referred to the nexus as "Arampur," conflating the larger locality into the name of a single village. Again, we see that the village can become practically a character in itself at times, a character with which its residents very often identify themselves.

Rakshasa recognized not only that each village is as complicated as an epic narrative, but also that each has "an unusual, indefinable history." Myriad interpretations compose this narrative and, so, no unifying commentary exists by which an outsider can decipher "its meaning." *The Hunted* provides a narrative of the fictional village Bhudra, yet the author problematizes his own work through Kanchan's reflection that demonstrates the tenuousness of any narrative portrait of a village. I make the same disclaimer regarding the narratives considered in this and the next two chapters. I intend neither to portray the history of the Arampur nexus nor to provide a comprehensive account of the identities by which people define themselves and each other. Rather, I seek to show how popularly told narratives simultaneously reflect and construct the multiple group affiliations of those who tell them.

Narrative and Identity

Undoubtedly, individuals express group identities through a very wide range of activities, including ritual, song, and dance. However, narratives regarding the past offer a particularly useful tool of examination because by their very nature they often include important ingredients for identity: references to the present community in time and space. Although he draws on only Western theorists and illustrates his ideas with only Western literature, Paul Ricoeur offers a compelling hermeneutic that can be applied to narratives from other cultural contexts. Ricoeur outlines a notion of group self-definition according to shared interests, describes the past as one of those shared interests, and argues for the essential role of narrative in defining an identity based on those interests.

Ricoeur believes that all people project historical time in an attempt to span the gap between lived time and cosmic time. Phenomenologically, each individual is aware of the passage of time in her or his biological life (i.e., lived time). However, comparison with the immense dimensions of cosmic time threatens to reduce the individual's lived time to insignificance. How can a person's short life compare with the enduring presence of mountains or the inexorable movement of the night sky? Drawing on Heidegger, Ricoeur describes history-as-care as an operation in which a concern for the past attempts to inscribe a meaningful place for the individual in cosmic time. Ricoeur emphasizes that "time becomes human time to the extent that it is organized in the manner of a narrative."[6]

According to Ricoeur, history-as-care spans the gap between lived and cosmic time with the help of three reflective tools: lineages, calendars, and traces. The individual of the present finds a place for himself or herself within cosmic time through association with a lineage of successive generations. These generations and the events ascribed to them are evidenced through traces such as monuments and artifacts. The individual of the present arranges each generation relative to others according to some calendar or calendars. Drawing on the work of Alfred Schutz, Ricoeur describes how the individual of the present ("I") experiences a sense of belonging to a group ("we") through a personal connection to public time via a lineage. Without a personal connection, pre-

---

6. Paul Ricoeur, *Time and Narrative*, vol. 1, Kathleen Blamey and David Pellauer, trans. Chicago: University of Chicago Press, 1984 (1983), p. 3.

vious generations would remain only a distant "them" to the "I." The degree to which the individual becomes involved in a shared identity (shared among "us") is the degree to which she or he has spanned the gap in time. Thus, public or historical time allows the individual to transcend private or lived time and find a meaningful place in cosmic time.[7] Again, this historical time can be realized only if organized in narrative form.

Group identity, therefore, becomes central to Ricoeur's understanding of the human effort to reconcile the personal, finite lived time of the individual with the impersonal vastness of cosmic time. Group identity acts as the arch upon which lineage bridges cosmic time. The "narrative identity," by which Ricoeur means the continuity of identity associated with a narrative subject always in the process of transformation, can be that of an individual or a group. Through the narrative that it creates for itself, the group, like the individual, defines not only its place in time but also its very identity. Ricoeur warns that "narrative identity is not a stable and seamless identity. Just as it is possible to compose several plots on the subject of the same incidents (which, thus, should not really be called the same events), so it is always possible to weave different, even opposed, plots about our lives." Of course, this must be the same for the group as well, as we shall later see among the diverse retellings of the same basic narrative.[8]

As useful as Ricoeur is, he fails to recognize one other reflective tool of history that connects lived time with cosmic time: place. Whereas Ricoeur describes the roles of calendars that measure the temporal distance between "us-now" and "them-then," lineages that trace a line across this distance, and relics that give evidence of "them-then" to "us-now," he misses the importance of place as meaningful space shared by both "them-here" and "us-here." Place resists the vicissitudes of cosmic time—forests may be cleared and buildings demolished, but a place may remain associated with events and/or persons indefinitely. The physicality of place adds another dimension to personal and group identity when experienced in conjunction with narrative.[9]

The Muslim commemoration of Muḥarram offers a useful example of the roles of all four reflective tools of history. Muslims who celebrate the martyrdom of Husain at the Battle of Karbala 1,300 years ago process during the tenth day of the month of Muḥarram to a permanent shrine known as Karbala. In the Arampur area, this day follows an earlier celebration of the horseshoe (*naʿl*) of Husain's charger. On the day itself, the procession includes a rickshaw-borne tape recorder blaring a narrative of Husain's heroism and sacrifice. In this short example, we readily discern Ricoeur's three tools of history in action. First, the

7. Paul Ricoeur, *Time and Narrative*, vol. 3, Kathleen Blamey and David Pellauer, trans. Chicago: University of Chicago Press, 1988 (1985), pp. 100–115.

8. Ibid., pp. 246–248.

9. For a novel examination of this theme in the context of the loss of places and the resulting personal impact, see Peter Read, *Returning to Nothing: The Meaning of Lost Places*. Melbourne: Cambridge University Press, 1996.

Islamic *calendar* (itself fixed relative to an event, the Prophet Muhammad's *hijra* or "emigration" to Medina) marks a specific day for the annual commemoration according to the day and month of the original event. Second, Muslims (particularly Shii Muslims, who consider Husain, his brother, and father as revered leaders of their group) may feel a sense of *lineage* to the early Muslim community. The annual repetition in personal lived time of the commemorative narratives and rituals describing the Karbala battle use this formative and definitive event to promote a connection with the past. Third, the *na'l* provides a *trace* or relic of the battle itself, while the Karbala shrine re-creates ritually the place in Iraq where Husain was buried. As the processions converge on this place, participants share a community physically through these traces in a way that complements the intellectual sharing through oral and written expressions of the narrative.

The correlation between space and identity has been drawn by too many authors to review fully here. As mentioned in the previous chapter, Satadal Dasgupta broadly examines rural caste, kinship, and community associations in West Bengal through analysis of various levels of community integration. However, Dasgupta's model and descriptions are static, demonstrating only the seemingly constant forces of self-identification, acceptance, and integration. We need to examine how groups identify and exclude others—in effect, disintegrating community—as contexts change and how this can shift as quickly as the social circumstances to which they respond. Later, we consider also the link that Maurice Halbwachs makes between space and memory.

As social constructions, identities evolve through the dynamics of exclusivity, controversy, and disintegration. Individuals within any one group may disagree regarding who should and should not belong. Local residents demonstrate these dynamics of identity construction through their narratives of the past, by which they may alternately question, support, and undermine the claims of others while projecting their own. This book attempts to depart from others in its depiction of the intersubjective construction of group identity among individuals through their discourse. The diversity among variations of one particularly popular local narrative demonstrates the variety of narrative styles with which they depict the past.

Group Memory and the Raja, *Brahm*, and Sultan

Before we can properly analyze these narratives, we need to find a common field upon which they can stand equally and be compared fairly. The narratives share the common feature that those who communicate them believe that the stories depict *actual* events of *their* past: "actual" inasmuch as they do believe the events to have happened and "their" because the narrators consider themselves connected somehow to the events, through a shared identification with the actors and/or the place. This approach, then, privileges the narrator's understanding of these events and brackets ours. Thus—no matter whether it involves Brahman ghosts, deities, or a unified nation—we suspend the analyst's judgment as to the veracity of the story and acknowledge (but not necessarily embrace) the narrator's perspective. This matter of bracketing truth claims makes our search for an appropriate term for all the narratives most difficult. *History* and *myth*, inevitably the first two terms that English speakers reach for, still imply for most a judgment of truth by outsiders upon the narratives of insiders. Although several recent authors such as Paul Veyne and Wendy Doniger have challenged the common association of *history* as event-that-happened and *myth* as event-that-they-believe-happened-but-we-know-did-not, the common understandings of these terms are too tainted with an expectation of judgment to serve our purpose.[10]

A separate designation becomes necessary to achieve two ends. First, narratives of the past in South Asia have too often been dismissed as "myth" simply because they did not conform to historiographic standards. The result has been a Western conclusion that South Asians have no interest in the past or, at best, a deficient one. Trinidad-born V. S. Naipaul, a keen observer and vociferous critic of India, has written,

> Indian interpretations of their history are almost a painful as the history itself; and it is especially painful to see the earlier squalor being repeated today. . . . A people with a sense of history might have ordered matters differently this is precisely the saddening element in Indian history: this absence of growth and development. It is a history whose only history is that life goes on. There is only a series of beginnings, no final creation.[11]

Yet, as Ricoeur has argued, all people have an interest in the past. But whereas Ricoeur labels this concern *history*, I would argue that the overly broad use of this concept threatens to both obscure with Western assumptions culturally alternative depictions of the past and undermine the unique techniques by which Western cultures make their own truth claims regarding the past. By bracketing the notion of veracity, we can concentrate on the subtleties of *myth* as demonstrated by Paul Veyne and Wendy Doniger; that is to say, this bracketing allows us to consider the role that the narrative plays in its society, sensitive to types of truth claims separate from our notions of historical truth while avoiding the battle of what-*really*-happened-to-whom-when-and-where.

The notion of group memory offers this ability to bracket issues of veracity, sidestepping the multiple and contentious understandings of *history* and *myth* while allowing analysis of the social role of narratives regarding the past. An examination of one example of the commonly told narrative of the local raja, a vengeful *brahm*, and the Delhi sultan will help initiate my outline of a theory of group memory.

---

10. See Paul Veyne, *Did the Greeks Believe in Their Myths? An Essay on the Constitutive Imagination*, Paula Wissing, trans. (Chicago: University of Chicago Press, 1988 [1983]; and Wendy Doniger O'Flaherty, *Other People's Myths: The Cave of Echoes* (Chicago: University of Chicago Press, 1988).

11. V. S. Naipaul, *An Area of Darkness*. New York: Macmillan, 1965 (1964), p. 213.

The Recollections of Lakshmi Devi and Mujun Khan

As I pass through Arampur Bazaar one day, Krishna Sah calls out to me from behind the sooty smoke of his tea shop's glowing braziers. He thrusts a glass of hot, milky tea into my hand and motions for me to sit on one of the wobbly benches behind him. I greet his mother, Lakshmi Devi, who sits beside her son among sticky pyramids of variously colored sweets. I ask them, "How long has your family lived here?" Lakshmi Devi answers in Hindi, "Three generations." "Where did you live before?" I ask. "I was born here and I was married here, so I do not know anything more than here." "Did your family live outside Bihar?" "I'm not from Hindustan or Pakistan—I'm from here," she says with sudden defiance. Referring to her family, she adds, *"Ham log Biharī hai"* (We people are Bihari).

A bit later, I point to the temple of Shastri Brahm and ask, "Will you tell me why the temple up there is so famous? Who was the Shastri Brahm?" *"Rājā the"* (He was a raja), she begins, using the most common, two-word introduction residents employ to begin their versions of this narrative.[12] Lakshmi Devi continues, "Vicitra was raja here. His capital was here. Shastri Brahm was his pandit who became a *preta*.[13] The raja had already married and had had a daughter. There was no son, so there was no family line. The pandit said, 'Take another wife—so you can have a boy and your family can continue.' The rani became angry at the pandit. She took to bed and would not drink any water. So the raja asked, 'Why aren't you taking anything?' The rani said, 'The palace of Shastri Brahm is so tall. Destroy it; he doesn't need to make it so large. Until you do, I won't drink any water.' She said this to the raja and also gave him alcohol. He destroyed the entire palace. Shastri Brahm, after the destruction of the palace . . . fasted to death. . . . But before this, the daughter of the raja gave him water and sherbet. So for this service, he told her to flee to the mountains. There were to be no descendants of the raja and the girl understood this. When the raja became scared of the *brahm*,[14] he became depressed and died. After that Shastri Brahm made the pandit folk successful, so they created an image of him. People worship him to this day."

After Lakshmi Devi finishes her telling, I ask what happened to the raja after the death of Shastri Brahm. She responds, "No one remained. Everyone died." "The daughter too?" I ask. "Yes. Everyone died," Lakshmi Devi answers, "The daughter died, but her family continues on." "Where?" I ask. "There—" uncertain, she hesitates. A bystander responds, "Ishwarpur." Lakshmi Devi echoes this answer as she points toward that distant village. "How do you know this?" I ask. "There is a book here," she says, "Everyone says so." "Did you read the book or hear about this?" "I heard about it." "From whom?" "From people," she concludes.

---

12. The Hindi verb "to be" in the third-person plural past tense—*the*—denotes respect.
13. The ghost of someone dead.
14. The ghost of a Brahman who died unjustly.

Later, having finished both tea and conversation, I return to my walk through the Bazaar, when Mujun Khan hurries up behind and stops me. He had been present when Lakshmi Devi had told about the raja and the *brahm.* "She has told you mistakes," he announces in the middle of the busy street in Hindi. "Raja Vicitra died because a war happened. Whose mausoleum is that?" he asks as he points to the large tomb hidden from view from the shop-fronted street. "Bakhtiyar Khilji," he says in answer to his own question. "What happened?" I ask. "He was conquered," Mujun Khan replies, referring to the raja. "He was not killed by Shastri Brahm?" "No. Shastri Brahm starved himself to death. History is one thing and what the pandit folk say is another—a thing to make money. They make a million rupees a year." "Why did Bakhtiyar Khilji come here?" I ask. He responds, "Others can say—older people." "How do you know about this?" He answers, "*Sunā-sunāī*" (Hearsay).

The narration of Lakshmi Devi and the counternarration of Mujun Khan separately, and in their connection with one another, both typify a common way in which residents orally express narratives of the past and demonstrate the challenge for Westerners of labeling these narratives. Both of these Arampur residents communicated their narratives orally in public settings: the tea shop and the Bazaar street. They both referred to previous oral accounts when asked, "How do you know about this?" When Mujun Khan said, "*sunā-sunāī*," he used a term commonly employed in variant forms by both Hindi and Urdu speakers to explain the oral transmission of narratives and other matters.[15] The English translation *hearsay* is a term that provides a perfect insight into the dynamic of transmission in this system: hearing and, then, saying. No formal styles of transmission rule this system beyond those governing everyday discourse. Significantly, however, neither Mujun Khan's phrase nor the more common phrase *sunī-sunāī* have the sense of doubtful veracity for these narrators (nor for most nexus residents) that *hearsay* has for English-speaking audiences (suggesting *gossip, scurrilous, untrustworthy*). Perhaps this reflects the primacy of oral narrative for many rural north Indians and the dominance of textual narrative for most urban and suburban Westerners. The latter commonly suspect "word of mouth," preferring "word of print."[16] Many Arampur residents used *sunī-sunāī* in a manner synonymous with *itihās* and *history*, a correlation with which, I think, most English speakers would be uncomfortable.

So should I regard the narratives of Lakshmi Devi and Mujun Khan as hearsay, despite that term's association with words that insinuate dubious truth claims such as *gossip* and *rumor*? Or should I follow Ricoeur's lead in designating them as *history*? If I do, can I accept a ghost as a historical agent? Would not I be calling these narratives *history* but always consider them as less histori-

---

15. Other variations of this phrase include *sunī-sunāī* and *kahī-sunāī.* The literal meaning of these is "hearing and causing-to-hear."

16. For an insightful exploration into the social life of oral and written "histories" in rural America, see Stephen William Foster, *The Past Is Another Country: Representation, Historical Consciousness, and Resistance in the Blue Ridge.* Berkeley: University of California Press, 1988.

cally true than others? As we shall see later, historiography plays a pivotal role in Western constructions of identity and should not be undermined. Bruce Lincoln argues provocatively that what distinguishes history from fable and legend is that a group accepts history as a narrative of past events because of its credibility and truth claims. However, he suggests that a myth differs from history because a group not only accepts the credibility and truth claims of myth but also grants it an authority to act as a paradigmatic vision for the construction of society.[17]

As an example of this dynamic, Lincoln depicts the 1979 Iranian revolution as a struggle between two histories used by different leaders to rally support. The contemporary ruler, Reza Shah Pahlavi, depicted Iran in terms of the history of the Achaemenian Empire, using the ancient kingdom as a template for modern political life with his family cast as the dynastic head. To this end, the Shah infused Achaemenian symbols and themes in many of the rituals by which he celebrated the nation and his family's rule. The Iranian *'ulamā* (body of Muslim scholars), who resisted the Shah's often oppressive regime, organized opposition to him with considerable reference to the Battle of Karbala in which the Prophet's grandson, Husain, died resisting an illegitimate government led by Yazid. The opposition movement gained increasing momentum as the *'ulamā* successfully interpreted current events by using allusions to the events of Karbala.[18] In this way, attempting to encourage supporters after the massacre of fellow protesters, Ayatollah Khomeini explained,

> It is as if the blood of our martyrs were the continuation of the blood of the martyrs of Karbala, and as if the commemoration of our brothers were the echo of the commemoration of those brave ones who fell at Karbala. Just as their pure blood brought to an end the tyrannical rule of Yazid, the blood of our martyrs has shattered the tyrannical monarchy of the Pahlavis.[19]

As part of the successful political struggle which toppled the Shah, the *'ulamā's* narrative proved more popular and powerful than the Shah's and became a socially constructive myth.

However, this model cannot discern the different types of truth with which people understand myths. The narrative of Adam and Eve can remain a paradigmatic vision of the world even for those who do not consider it a credible account of the origin of humanity. A perusal of current American advertising finds any number of references to and depictions of the first couple. Uninterested in truth claims regarding the existence of the two, the ads promote their products or services by tapping into the themes of innocence, sexuality, transgression, and punishment that most Americans associate with a story many of them are likely to call a myth. The term *myth* usefully denotes a broad range

17. Bruce Lincoln, *Discourse and the Construction of Society: Comparative Studies of Myth, Ritual, and Classification.* New York: Oxford University Press, 1989, pp. 23–26.

18. Ibid., pp. 32–37.

19. Imam Khomeini, *Islam and Revolution*, Hamid Algar, trans. Berkeley: Mizab, 1981, p. 249.

of types of truth and should not be overly constrained to fit within some semblance of historical truth.

Not only do we need a term that accommodates the difference between Western and other understandings of the past without judging the veracity of their claims but also we need a term that can encompass the varying and, at times, discordant narratives of the past found even among neighbors. We seek a heuristic tool that clears a neutral space in which similar and divergent accounts—such as those of Lakshmi Devi and Mujun Khan—can be analyzed for the group identities that they reflect. The concept of *group memory* provides this tool.

Western Theories of Group Memory

Developed by Maurice Halbwachs and expounded by Paul Connerton, *group memory* reveals the social orientation of concerns for the past, even on the part of individuals. Although both of these sociologists explicitly separated historiography from memory, I contend that the former is but another type of the latter. In this way, I examine the theories of both Halbwachs and Connerton, then describe how my own understanding of group memory suggests the inclusion of historiography within this category of social knowledge. Current scholarship in the human sciences reflects an increasing tendency to support this perspective. Some residents of the Arampur area also view narratives of past events as memories that are social by nature. Group memory thus fits into indigenous categories.

The works of Maurice Halbwachs (1877–1945) reflect his early departure from Henri Bergson's psychology in favor of Émile Durkheim's sociology. Although critical of a purely psychological treatment of the individual, Halbwachs did not eschew Bergson entirely but incorporated some of that psychologist's thought into his works. This is particularly evident in his books *Les cadres sociaux de la mémorie* (*The Social Frameworks of Memory*, 1925), *La topographie légendaire des évangiles en terre sainte* (*The Legendary Topography of the Gospels in the Holy Land*, 1941), and *La mémoire collective* (*The Collective Memory*, 1950). These works argue, in part, that individual memory and community belief must associate with some group memory of events, what he called *collective memory* and *group memory*.[20] His later interaction with Annales School historical theorists Marc Bloch and Lucien Febvre, with whom he shared appointments at the University of Strasbourg in the interwar period, hardened his reflections on historiography apropos of society and collective memory. Halbwachs's work, therefore, provides a useful starting place for our examination of the overlap between memory and history among individuals and groups.

---

20. Although Halbwachs (in translation) more commonly uses the term *collective memory*, I prefer the term *group memory*, which he uses interchangeably, because it distances us from the Jungian notion of *collective consciousness*, which bears little resemblance to Halbwachs's ideas.

True to his early psychological views, Halbwachs takes the experiences of the individual as the starting point for his study of group memory. However, his attention moves between two poles as he examines the individual only within society and society solely as expressed by the individual. Because humans are not simply individualistic, he explains, memory is not either. In fact, he argues, all individual thoughts and feelings have their origins in particular social milieus.[21] Humans cannot be understood merely as "isolated beings" and must be considered within the social contexts in which they commonly recall and recount their memories. Memories require a social framework to which they can attach themselves and from which they may be retrieved.[22] This framework exists in the individual as a matrix of influences deriving from the various groups to which the individual belongs. Therefore, as the individual moves from one group to another, the memories he or she recalls change as well. The groups, meanwhile, may change over time and alter the dynamic between group, individual, and memory.[23] Halbwachs underscores the ideas that individual memory exists only within a social sphere and that the group memory can be expressed only by individuals. The memories that individuals express reflect the groups to which they belong and their relations to that group.[24]

Although the group provides the milieu in which memories form, Halbwachs argues, the individual uniquely arranges and expresses these memories, according to her or his particular position among many groups. The similarities and differences among different group members in their individual recollections of the same event reflect the individual member's relation to that and other groups.[25] Halbwachs writes that "our recollections, each taken in itself, belong to everybody; but the coherence or arrangement of our recollections belong to ourselves—we alone are capable of knowing and calling them to mind."[26] The member often fails to recognize the influence of the group memory because this individual creativity provides the illusion that his or her ideas and recollections derive uniquely from the member.[27] Despite this illusion, the individual would not remember without the involvement of others. We tend to tell others about the events that we deem important. Each telling reinforces the recollections from which they derive. Later, the same audience may remind us of these events in another context. Without some cohesion in the experience and remembering of the past, our group would have little sense of unity. Therefore, Halbwachs, like Ricoeur, conceives a group as defined by its common interest in the past. However, Halbwachs takes this argu-

21. Maurice Halbwachs, *The Collective Memory*. Francis J. Ditter Jr. and Vida Yazdi Ditter, trans. New York: Harper Colophon, 1980, p. 33.

22. Maurice Halbwachs, *On Collective Memory*. Lewis A. Coser, trans. Chicago: University of Chicago Press, 1992, pp. 38–43.

23. Ibid., p. 172.

24. Ibid., p. 40.

25. Ibid., p. 52.

26. Ibid., p. 171.

27. Ibid., p. 48.

ment in another direction when he argues that the individual cannot remember without the help of others, and society cannot stand without some unity of outlook.[28]

Halbwachs clearly describes group memory as more than the aggregation of individual memories from shared experiences. Because of the discursive nature of group recollection, memories of events can be shared by group members who never directly experienced those events. He differentiates group memory from autobiographical memory—those recollections that derive only from personal experience of events.[29] An individual may remember many events experienced seemingly outside the influence of any group memory. Most of us have memories so personal that we share them with few others, if anyone. Yet, these "autobiographical memories" do not stand as independently as we might imagine. Halbwachs argues that autobiographical memory never remains entirely without influence from group memories, as we associate the recollections of others with our personal memories. We construct a framework of memory through social interaction and personal experience that acts as a matrix for a variety of memories.[30]

Whether they are autobiographical or group memories, Halbwachs stresses that we do not *preserve* memories but rather *reconstruct* them according to the concerns of the present.[31] He repeatedly describes the dynamic and changing nature of both groups and individuals. Memories alter in response to the changes among both the groups that form them and the individuals who recall them. As individual experiences compel a person toward change, that person's memories adapt to these new experiences and maintain coherence with previous memories.

Halbwachs takes an extreme position. His language edges toward the claim that *all* memories derive from social interaction and that *all* group memory has social utility. I would argue that group memory often has a social purpose but that the more fundamental impulse to remember arises from what Ricoeur describes as a basic human need to place ourselves in time. Ricoeur stresses the narrative nature of this projection into the past. Halbwachs unwittingly contributes to this issue when he describes how narratives are formed in a social context and remembered by individuals who associate with various groups.

Halbwachs more obviously reinforces Ricoeur's notions of the interaction between time and reflection on the past while he includes an area overlooked by Ricoeur—space. We might recall that Ricoeur identifies three devices by which individuals project themselves into the past: lineage, calendar, and trace. The first two obviously mediate time. Lineage allows humans to imagine a generational chain through time, while calendar provides a temporal map established according to quantifiably discrete yet measurable time periods. A trace,

---

28. Ibid., p. 182. "Unity of outlook" need not imply unanimity of opinion.
29. Ibid., p. 51.
30. Ibid., p. 70.
31. Ibid., p. 40.

identified as surviving material from an event, may act to symbolize that event. Although traces often mark space, Ricoeur does not make this explicit. Halbwachs, however, demonstrates how places—such as relic-strewn Jerusalem, which he examines in *The Legendary Topography of the Gospels in the Holy Land*—become associated with events so that the mention of or visitation to them evokes memories propagated by groups.[32]

In summation, Maurice Halbwachs's idea of collective memory attempts to account for the psychological expressions of a social phenomenon: the ability of group members to share recollections of events, even of those that no living member witnessed personally. He argues that the inherently social character of humans reveals itself in memory, even the seemingly most personal recollection. Individual memory negotiates an internal social framework composed of the intersections of the group influences in a person's life. Reflecting the dynamic nature of the individual and the groups with which the individual associates, this social framework and the memories attached to it change according to the needs of the present. He cautions, however, that within a group some may retard this adaptation by maintaining memories no longer considered relevant by others. In either case, recollection never retrieves immutable memories but always recasts them to suit the needs of the present community. Using the example of the meaning of the "Holy Land" for many Western Christians, Halbwachs demonstrates how groups maintain and alter memories by using text, ritual, and space. Space, then, becomes one more strategy of narrative reference and social integration that we can add to Ricoeur's list.[33]

What Halbwachs most contributes to our study of the Arampur area derives from his insistence that the individual acts as the final arbitrator of group memory and that this arbitration occurs in a psychological realm composed of competing group identities (and the memories associated with them). Yet, however much he prompts us beyond Ricoeur's focus on time and narrative by asserting the importance of space, Halbwachs describes a merely cerebral group memory that is at play in the individual and the group. In contrast, the residents of Arampur create lived spaces—areas with which people interact physically—that, in turn, help form their sense of identity. Their interaction never remains only mental. However, Paul Connerton furthers Halbwachs's thesis and provides a heuristic by which the physical interaction with space, in time, and with groups defines group identities alongside mental constructs.

The work of Halbwachs furnishes a starting point for Paul Connerton's argument in *How Societies Remember*. Connerton applauds his predecessor for his theory regarding the social origins of all memory and the orbit of group

---

32. Maurice Halbwachs, *La topographie légendaire des évangiles en terre sainte*. Paris: Presses Universitaires de France, 1971 (1941).

33. For a fascinating example of space used in a reenactment of a past event by Fidel Castro, Ché Guevara, and Camilo Cienfuegos in an effort to harness popular group memory to their revolutionary agenda, see Eric Selbin, "Revolution in the Real World: Bringing Agency Back In" in *Theorizing Revolutions*, John Foran, ed. New York: Routledge, 1997, pp. 123–136.

memories around shared interest and space. Yet, he finds that Halbwachs's argument insufficiently explains the transmission of memories from one generation to another. To address this deficiency, Connerton focuses specifically on commemorative ceremonies and their reliance on bodily practices. He seeks to demonstrate the nondiscursive nature of these practices as embodied in rituals and links this nature with their resistance to change.

> If there is such a thing as social memory, I shall argue, we are likely to find it in commemorative ceremonies; but commemorative ceremonies prove to be commemorative only in so far as they are performative; performativity cannot be thought without a concept of habit; and habit cannot be thought without a notion of bodily automatisms. In this way I shall seek to show that there is an inertia in social structures that is not adequately explained by any of the current orthodoxies of what a social structure is.[34]

Connerton's major departure from Halbwachs stems from his argument for the bodily incorporation of some social memory that undergirds a distinction between innovation and inertia among group memories.

Among Connerton's theoretical sparring partners is a group of scholars who argue against the common notion of tradition as something originating from the past and handed down to the present. Rather, they assert, current social orders invent traditions to suit present conditions.[35] While acknowledging the role of present concerns in the remembering of the past, Connerton endeavors to demonstrate that the group memory of commemorative ceremonies cannot be manipulated entirely through discursive practices because much of it has no discursive element. In other words, much of ritual derives from bodily practices so completely incorporated into everyday life that they are habitually performed without conscious reflection. New generations learn these habits through nondiscursive transmission and incorporate them in their own bodily behavior without deliberation. In this way, some group memories contribute to a social inertia that resists change. By not accounting for this inertia, Connerton argues, some scholars have overstated their claim for the invention of tradition.[36]

As one of the illustrations of his argument, Connerton refers to the liturgy of the Mass in the Roman Catholic Church. As a commemorative ceremony, the Mass evokes the memory of Jesus' Last Supper through habitual action, not prepositional statement. Gestures particular to the rite, such as the communal eating of bread, reproduce gestures associated with Jesus in the Bible. The space in which the Mass is performed reflects the two bodily practices that

34. Paul Connerton, *How Societies Remember*. New York: Cambridge University Press (1991), pp. 4–5.

35. Prevalent examples of this view include E. Hobsbawn and T. Rangers, eds. *The Invention of Tradition* (New York: Cambridge University Press, 1983); David Lowenthal, *The Past Is a Foreign Country* (New York: Cambridge University Press, 1990); and Benedict Anderson, *Imagined Communities* (New York: Verso, 1991).

36. Connerton, pp. 101–103.

Connerton discerns: inscribing and incorporating practices. Bodily practices of inscribing physically store meanings after an act of transmission. By contrast, incorporating practices transmit meaning through sustained activity. For example, the Mass creates space and time for both types of bodily practice. The first half of the ceremony, the Liturgy of the Word, centers on the pulpit and the reading aloud of selections from sacred inscriptions—the Bible. In contrast, the second half, the Liturgy of the Eucharist, centers on the altar and the preparation of the Eucharist through a series of incorporated gestures. These gestures both represent and re-present a group memory of the events in Jerusalem during the first Easter as evoked through bodily movement. As the author says, "The liturgy is, as it were, the permanent making present of that temporal situation."[37]

Connerton stresses, however, that too many scholars have mistakenly attempted to read rituals as they would texts. They have tried to use the techniques for understanding the content of inscriptions to discover the meaning of incorporated actions. Connerton argues that the mistake lies in the effort to discern the content of the ritual when the meaning resides in the form itself. Bodily habits do not act as signs that deliberately imply meaning for other minds to know. Rather, it is the body that knows.

Connerton gives the example of a typist who habitually knows or remembers the place of each letter on the keyboard, who does not think, "This is *L*." Rather, through long-term practice, habit allows the typist's hands to know how to extend or retract to press precisely the proper key. Nor do typists consciously bring to mind the memory of the first time they learned that this particular key, when pressed, typed the letter *L*. Connerton explains, "We remember this through the knowledge bred of familiarity in our lived space." He adds, "Habit is a knowledge and a remembering in the hands and in the body; and in the cultivation of habit it is our body which 'understands.'"[38] The difference, of course, between the habit of typing and the habit of the Mass rests in the shared nature of the latter. Whereas one could claim that the typist's hands remember and reenact (albeit unconsciously) the typist's first lesson as a personal memory, the participants in the Mass remember and reenact (often, too, without reflection) the Last Supper as a group memory. Westerners may struggle to accept this because of the cultural importance of action guided by reflective thought. Ritual often seems meaningless if participants cannot verbally explain why they do what they do. In a post-Enlightenment and post-Reformation world, customs without obvious intellectual content are commonly disparaged as "empty ritual."

Perhaps the greatest significance of the incorporated and habitual nature of some group memories for Connerton derives from the inertia they create in social institutions. He wants to argue against those who overstate the case for tradition as a product of present social forces. He does this in two ways. First,

---

37. Ibid., p. 70.
38. Ibid., p. 95.

echoing Halbwachs, Connerton asserts that no beginning springs entirely from innovation. Even revolutionary social orders perennially delve into the old and familiar to create the new. Using examples from the French Revolution and the Third Reich, Connerton demonstrates how those who would establish a new social order overwrite previous practices with new meanings. So, for example, Hitler created ceremonial holidays to commemorate events in the formation of National Socialism and overlaid them atop the feasts of the Christian calendar "in much the same way as the latter had been related to the seasonal celebrations of the pagan era."[39] Connerton wants to draw our attention beyond the simple co-opting of institutions and calendars. He wishes to argue that the habitual behavior associated with these social constructs has been usurped as well, perhaps even unconsciously.

Second, Connerton contends that this behavior, as incorporated performance, resists change and maintains traditions *because* of its unreflective nature. Whereas the Bible and Roman law have undergone changes in interpretation over time,[40] the fixity and nonreflectivity of performance have preserved the Mass in almost the same form as when it was created nearly two millennia ago. He demonstrates this to be true for other religious ritual as well. Returning to the era of the Third Reich, we notice that the Harvest Festival—previously pagan, then Christian—becomes "a National Socialist Festival of the German peasantry."[41] We can extrapolate from Connerton's other arguments that the Harvest Festival continues as a tradition associated with specific physical circumstances (i.e., seasonal variations, agricultural conditions, performative behavior), although the meanings ascribed to it by leaders of the religious and/or political order have varied over a millennium.

Connerton, then, offers an important, additional dimension to Halbwachs's notion of group memory. Whereas Halbwachs demonstrates the survival of verbally shared and negotiated narratives across generations of a group, Connerton describes a group memory located in performance that is often associated with narratives but seldom dependent upon them. Rather, narratives, if only orally communicated, exhibit a susceptibility to change that habitual behavior does not, due to the vulnerability of oral narrative to reflective thought. The less reflectively inclined nature of performance aids in its survival at the same time that it hides it from the reflection of both the performer and the scholar.

What Connerton particularly offers our study is the insight into the physical dimensions of group memory. Whereas Halbwachs complements Ricoeur by adding the importance of space alongside that of time, Connerton shows the ways in which groups physically interact with that space and make it lived space. Although I focus only somewhat on memory evoked through bodily habit (as glimpsed in the discussion of Muḥarram earlier in this chapter), we will see the importance of the interaction between space, time, narrative, and group memory.

39. Ibid., p. 41.
40. Ibid., pp. 98–100.
41. Ibid., pp. 42–57.

Historiography[42] *as an Expression of Memory*

Both Halbwachs and Connerton explicitly argue against any consideration of historiography as a group memory. Yet, we must challenge both authors to construe their own concepts more broadly.

"But past events read about in books and taught in schools are selected, combined, and evaluated in accord with necessities and rules not imposed on the groups that had through time guarded them as a living trust."[43] This short passage from Halbwachs illustrates his (and many of our) underlying assumptions regarding historiography as a discipline. He associates historiography with textuality ("books") and formal education ("schools"). He sees it as a system defined by formal boundaries ("necessities and rules"). By juxtaposing historiography with a description of group memory as "a living trust," he implies that the former survives independently of groups that actively maintain their memories. Indeed, far from being a social endeavor, "The study of history in this sense is reserved only for a few specialists," and these few are differentiated by their uncommon erudition.[44]

In three ways, Halbwachs has described historiography in too constricted a manner. First, by focusing on the minutiae of the academic discipline, he has failed his own method by not situating this activity of historiography within its larger social context. After all, historiography is the realm not simply of historians but of those who read its products as well. Modern books of history require publishers, who, in turn, require readers to realize the profit that allows them to survive as businesses. Therefore, the activity of historians must respond, in part, to the intentions of some members of society to consider the past. The recent debate concerning the multicultural textbook selected by California for its public school children reflects how the narratives chosen to depict the identity of the group can be contested because members of the group challenge the nature of that identity. For example, some state residents may claim, "Californians are primarily European-Americans, so California history should be about European-Americans," while others would counter, "Californians descend from Europe, Latin America, Asia, Africa, and Native America and our history must reflect this."[45]

Second, by focusing exclusively on historiography as a scholastic discipline, Halbwachs fails to recognize it as but one epistemology of the past among many. The historiographic systems of authorization, verification, and transmission need not be opposed to group memory. Rather, they can be considered as one set of systems (albeit a more consciously formalized set) among others, each

---

42. By "historiography," I refer to the writing of a narrative of the actual past events ("history") as practiced and regulated by the intellectual discipline ("History") found in any of many cultures.

43. Halbwachs, *The Collective Memory,* p. 78.

44. Ibid., pp. 79–80.

45. See Robert Reinhold, "Class Struggle: California's Textbook Debate" in *New York Times Magazine* (September 29, 1991), pp. 26–29, 46–47, 52.

serving a different type of group memory. The ways in which historiography rests on a spectrum of group memories are demonstrated in the following section.

Third, in his effort to distinguish historiography from group memory, Halbwachs characterizes historiography as a process by which memories are separated from the groups that maintain them and, then, are placed within frameworks external to the group. Periodization is one such framework, which replaces a streamlike temporal flow of the group memory with a system of discrete periods of unique character. "History divides the sequence of centuries into periods, just as the content of a tragedy is divided into several acts."[46] We can imagine that another external framework that Halbwachs might find in historiography would be the paradigms of historical action and actors considered earlier. Can a merciful god be a historical agent? A vengeful ghost?[47]

A response to this point leads us to the broadest application of Halbwachs's idea of group memory, one that he does not make explicitly yet which logically extends from his argument. Three points comprise this response. First, a group need not be defined by absolute unity of view; that is to say, groups orient themselves around common concerns, among which are similar interests in the past. Contained within these concerns may be multiple perspectives on particular events. In brief, the *debate* regarding an event commonly considered significant may be more important to the definition of the group than *agreement* concerning the narrative of that event. Therefore, the perspective of one part of a group may seem foreign or external to another part, yet they may still agree (through disagreement) that they are all members of the group. Orthodox Jews who understand the Torah as literally true might accept the Genesis

---

46. Halbwachs, *The Collective Memory*, pp. 80–84.

47. Besides these three sets of oppositions, Halbwachs poses a series of additional differences between group memory and historiography in *The Collective Memory*. Unfortunately, these contradictory objections seem a less reflective component of his argument. The sociologist argues that historiography concerns itself with long durations while the duration of a group memory lasts as long as a human life (p. 86), despite the fact that he argues only pages earlier, "The memory of a society extends as far as the memory of the groups composing it" (p. 82). Then again, Halbwachs states that historiography simplifies while memory has uncertain boundaries (p. 80). Yet, he argues elsewhere for historiography as a "record of changes" in contrast to group memory, in which nothing really changes because it focuses on the resemblances within a group (pp. 85–86). We have also already seen that he believes memories to tend toward cohesion and conformity, forgetting the unusual so as to simplify the complex. Finally, Halbwachs describes group memory to be comprised of several memories, whereas historiography strives to unify and universalize all accounts of a particular event (p. 83).

I would suggest that these contradictions actually demonstrate historiography to be a form of group memory. In fact, group memories can survive very long durations or not. Historiography can tend toward the simplistic or the complex. And any library catalogue search regarding a particularly noted event of history—say, the Holocaust—will harvest a crop of many divergent and nonuniversal, if not downright inimical, accounts of that event. Broadly speaking, the same dynamics that Halbwachs describes as at work in group memory also exist within historiography, although as more formalized expressions.

narrative as an accurate portrayal of actual events. Reform Jews, influenced by techniques of historical criticism, may consider it as an insightful allegory derived from antecedent Mesopotamian sources. Despite the severity of the disagreement, some Orthodox and Reform Jews recognize one another as Jews—belonging to different communities, for sure, yet bound together into a larger group through their common regard for Torah that makes the debate about its proper interpretation so significant.

Second, historiography does not stand as an isolated intellectual endeavor located outside a group, as Halbwachs suggests, but acts as one more system and expression of group memory. The ideal of the supposedly external perspective of historians (a.k.a. objectivity) represents yet one system among many used in the recollection of past events by a group. Because groups create their identities, in part, through recollections of the past, the more important of these recollections become regulated; that is to say, groups authorize, verify, and transmit recollections according to certain rules and habits. Historiography differs from most expressions of group memories only in the degree to which these rules have become explicitly formalized and the focus of intense methodological discussion. Through the examples given in the second half of this chapter, we will see how historiography resides along a spectrum of types of group memory.

Connerton's objections to the inclusion of historiography within group memory stem from his failure to recognize these systems of regulation as also operative in nonhistoriographical narrative traditions. He argues that historians rely on traces that they interpret without accepting the explicit claims these traces may make. The historian, he writes, must question every claim made by those about whom he writes. Historical methodology stands apart from the everyday.[48] Connerton sums up his central objection succinctly: "A historically tutored memory is opposed to an unreflective traditional memory."[49] So far as he applies this objection to habitual action as group memory, Connerton is correct. Yet, as we shall see in the examples of the next chapter, orally transmitted group memories are far from unreflective. They commonly may undergo a constant engagement of intersubjective reconstruction through public questioning and debate. Informal rules of authorization, verification, and transmission often regulate this reflective dynamic. Habitual action, too, is regulated, as evidenced in the directions and corrections that adults give children regarding the "proper" way to behave. Therefore, Connerton's reflective-nonreflective dichotomy makes the same mistake as Halbwachs's social phenomenon–academic discipline opposition; both fail to understand that the difference between group memory and historiography is not one of kind but one that does not exist at all. Historiography *is* an element of group memory—a very particular type of element, to be sure, characterized by the

48. For a perspective opposed to this point, see Carl Becker, *Everyman His Own Historian: Essays on History and Politics*. Chicago: Quadrangle, 1935.
49. Connerton, pp. 13–16.

formalized rules that govern it and the small percentage of people these rules allow to forge the narratives considered authentic.[50]

Third, we come to the final point regarding Halbwachs's objection to historiography's externality, one he does not raise, but we must consider. How can historiography express a group memory for the historian who portrays an event involving groups with which he does not associate? For instance, how can the study of medieval German history by a Chinese historian be construed as an exercise of his group memory? The answer lies in the imagination, relatively recent in the Western world, of a global human identity.

The notion of global humanity that most of us take for granted today rarely existed among Westerners before the seventeenth century.[51] Herodotus and Pliny, the great ethnographer and encyclopedist of the ancient Mediterranean, created a world map that extended from a center of Greek humanity toward lands of monstrous humans and, ultimately, to the simply monstrous. These Greek writers, as well as the Bible, maintained such a hold over the European imagination of Asia (and other continents) that the new, and often contradictory, accounts of other cultures produced by European travelers could not displace them, even as late as the midseventeenth century.[52] This situation held true with the European imagination of the past as well. However, from the late seventeenth century on, extensive reports by world travelers, as well as the scholastic challenge to the revered ancient Greek and Hebrew sources, led to an intellectual development that allowed Edmund Burke in 1777, in describing William Robertson's *History of America*, to say that "the Great Map of Mankind is unrolld at once."[53]

Not coincidentally, this period also initiated the development of historiography in Europe. Historians began to systematically research and narrate the pasts of non-European cultures. "History" became included among lists of topics that homebound contemporaries prompted travelers to record during their observations of foreign cultures.[54] In this way, the memories of extra-Continental groups were appropriated, processed, and reconstituted to fit

50. Some historians make similar arguments as Halbwachs and Connerton in defense of the distinctness of their discipline. See Natalie Zemon Davis and Randolph Starn's "Introduction" to the special issue on "Memory and Counter-Memory" in *Representations* 26 (Spring 1989), pp. 1–6.

51. The tenuousness of this idea of humanity can be discerned even today in the comment of a Kendra man that I was unusual for a Westerner because I did not have "the eyes of a cat," the fretting of a New Jersey mother who lived next to a newly opened temple when she heard that Hindus commit "child sacrifice," and the tales of cultural bizarreness and barbarities that fill the "global news" columns of many American and Indian newspapers. For a consideration of strategies of dehumanization, see Sam Keen, *Faces of the Enemy: Reflections on the Hostile Imagination*. San Francisco: Harper, 1991.

52. P. J. Marshall and Glyndwr Williams, *The Great Map of Mankind: British Perceptions of the World in the Age of Enlightenment*. Toronto: J. M. Dent, 1982, p. 7.

53. Ibid., pp. 1–11.

54. Ibid., pp. 45–46.

European frameworks of group memory under the guise of "history."[55] The seeming arrogance by which many Europeans judged native accounts under the general rubric of "myth," "legend," and "history" demonstrates, among other motives, the desire to create a universal history—that is, a memory for global humanity—that would accord with the prejudices of European systems of remembering. My argument for group memory attempts to allow a comparative study of narratives of the past that respects each culture's paradigms for discerning the truth claims made on that past without undermining my own culture's paradigms through some extreme form of cultural relativity.

The notion of group memory finds an increasingly familiar place in both American mass media and academic writings. Many Western scholars of the humanities and the social sciences use the concept.[56] In popular culture, mass media presentations commonly imply that groups remember certain events long after those who witnessed them have died. For instance, a front-page item in the *New York Times* echoes Halbwachs's reflections on the Via Dolorosa and the Stations of the Cross, as well as Connerton's notions of ceremonial commemoration. Beneath a picture of a man carrying a cross facing women with covered heads and accompanied by a priest under an umbrella runs the bold-printed line, "Christ's Suffering Is Remembered." Below this, a description adds, "Observing Good Friday, Members of St. Columbia Roman Catholic Church in Manhattan re-enacted the Stations of the Cross. Here they portray the eighth Station, when Jesus meets the women of Jerusalem." In the next column, an article describes the efforts of Oklahoma City residents to create a national memorial in memory of the bombing of the Federal Building in their downtown on April 19, 1995. The article implies that, beyond the myriad memorial services happening on the anniversary of the event, there is a need for a permanent monument to remind present and future Americans of what many consider a national event.[57]

---

55. Part of the uniqueness of the work of Leopold Ranke (1796–1886) rests in his understanding of a "universal history" within which he concentrated on Western civilization yet admitted that "the final goal always remains . . . a history of mankind." Trygive R. Tholfsen, *Historical Thinking: An Introduction*. New York: Harper and Row, 1967, p. 171. For more on the development of the Western notion of history, see R. G. Collingwood, *The Idea of History*. New York: Oxford University Press, 1956.

56. Among anthropologists, Debbora Battaglia, *On the Bones of the Serpent: Person, Memory, and Mortality in Saharl Island Society* (Chicago: The University of Chicago Press, 1990); James Brow, "Nationalist Rhetoric and the Local Practice: The Fate of the Village Community of Kukulewa" in *Sri Lanka: History and the Roots of Conflict*, Jonathan Spenser, ed. (New York: Routledge, 1990); and Nancy Munn, *The Fame of Gawa* (New York: Cambridge University Press, 1989). Among historians, Jacques Le Goff, *History and Memory*, Steven Rendall and Elizabeth Claman, trans. (New York: Columbia University Press, 1992); Michael Roth, "Remembering Forgetting: *Maladies de la Mémoire* in Nineteenth-Century France." *Representations* 26 (Spring 1989), pp. 49–68; George Lipsitz, *Time Passages: Collective Memory and American Popular Culture* (Minneapolis: University of Minneapolis Press, 1990); and the journal *History and Memory: Studies in Representation of the Past*.

57. The *New York Times*, 6 April 1996, p. 1.

The notion of group memory, then, provides a category of knowledge familiar to many Westerners, who may favor historiography as the medium for narrating the past but who, nevertheless, can understand historiography as one (albeit the preferred one) among numerous narrative strategies that express their communities' memories and identities.

Local Terminology

The Western notion of group memory finds parallels in north India. Among scholars, Sudhir Kakar writes of "collective memories" and "cultural memory,"[58] Gyanendra Pandey refers to "historical memory,"[59] and Akeel Bilgrami discusses "the scars and memories of Western colonial rule."[60] In the Arampur area, residents occasionally use terminology suggestive of group memory to express an understanding that groups, notably families, transmit memories across generations. This section examines these linguistic practices and, then, using the example of a set of narratives roughly similar in their plots and characters, demonstrates how different groups use various systems to authorize, verify, and transmit memories. We shall see how historiography represents but one type of group memory that formalizes what other groups maintain less formally.

As we sat talking about the upcoming Baqar 'īd celebrations, I asked Rati Khan why this Muslim holiday is so special. "*Zikr karne mem ta'rīf karte haiṅ*" (We praise him by remembering him), he replied in Urdu, referring to Ibrahim, who is celebrated by Muslims for having offered his son Ismail in sacrifice to God. When he said "*zikr*," Rati Khan used but one of the many terms indigenous to the Arampur area for *memory*. These also include *yād*, *smṛti*, and *memory*. Residents most commonly use these terms in reference to individual memory yet, at times, refer to an implicit group memory.

My conversation with Rati Khan illustrates well the ideas of Ricoeur and Halbwachs regarding intersubjectivity and the reconstruction of memory within a group. When I ask Rati Khan how he knew about Ibrahim, he answers, also in Urdu, "*In kī bāt hamāre bīce calte haiṅ. Bāt cīt karte haiṅ. Un kī ta'rīf calte haiṅ*" (We talk about him among ourselves: we talk and his praise continues.) "We" connotes Muslims, particularly the Muslims with whom he commonly associates—those of the villages surrounding Arampur. Muslims remember Ibrahim as they talk about him, retelling the narratives that they have heard regarding him. Many say that by obeying the command of Allah and preparing to sacrifice his son, Ibrahim demonstrated himself to be a good Muslim—one who submits to Allah. Therefore, Muslims praise him by recollecting the event as described to them by their elders and other sources. In so doing,

58. Kakar, pp. 12, 17.

59. Pandey, *The Construction of Communalism*, p. 115.

60. Akeel Bilgrami, "What Is a Muslim? Fundamental Commitment and Cultural Identity" in Gyanendra Pandey, *Hindus and Others: The Question of Identity in India Today*. New York: Viking, 1993, p. 282.

these Muslims help sustain what van der Veer adroitly calls a "constituency of participants."[61]

Connerton's assertion that habitual action and commemorative ceremonies often constitute group memory finds parallels in the descriptions of some Muslims of this holiday. Among the terms for *memory*, *yād* certainly is used the most. "*Is din kī yād mem qurbānī khāte haiṅ*" (We eat the sacrifice in memory of this day), Sayyid Afifuddin said in his explanation of Baqar 'īd. "This day" refers to the attempted sacrifice by Ibrahim of his son Ismail, an event that he had just narrated for my benefit. What Connerton described using the example of the Christian Mass finds a parallel in what Afifuddin narrated in regard to Baqar 'īd. The family of Afifuddin, like those of most Muslims in the area, sacrifices a goat or another animal in bodily recollection of the slaughter of the ram provided by Allah to Ibrahim in place of his son on "this day." When Afifuddin said, "*Ibrahim kī yād mem qurbānī khāte haiṅ*" (In memory of Ibrahim we eat the sacrifice), he suggested that local Muslims remember not only the name *Ibrahim* but also the narrative associated with him and the religious ideal that the narrative demonstrates. Both ritual action and verbal narrative generate and are generated by this recollection. Yet many, if not most, Muslims and Hindus, when asked why they commit a particular commemorative act, simply shrug and say, "Because we have always done it this way." This demonstrates Connerton's point concerning the unreflective nature of ritual and the resulting inertia of tradition.

Residents who associate memories with a particular material marker deliberately constructed to evoke recollection may refer to it as a *yādgār*, *smārak*, or *memorial*. Upagrah Singh did so as we sat with the other teachers of his private elementary school in the village of Swami Sarai. After responding to my question about an ascetic's tomb nearby, he asks me if I know about the neighboring, far more massive tomb of Bakhtiyar Khilji. After identifying it and describing the former military commander, he adds in Hindi, "*Vahīṅ unke yādgār hai*" (There is his memorial).

"Why do you call it a *yādgār*?" I ask.

He replies, "So that after death the *yād* (memory) should remain that he is there."

I ask, "Why should it remain?"

Upagrah says, "Just as you asked 'what is that?' so people will explain *memory kī rūp mem* (in the form of memory)."

Finally I ask, "How is it a memory if it is so old?"

He answers, "You did not know your grandfather but your mother and father told about him, showed you his photo. In this way *itihās jānte haiṅ* (we know history)."

Through his use of the term *yādgār*, Upagrah Singh demonstrated the way in which some local residents associate memory, relic, history, and narratives passed down from one generation to another. The memory of Bakhtiyar Khilji

---

61. Van der Veer, p. 82.

survives when someone sees his memorial (a relic of his rule), asks about it, and has a story about him explained by others through a narrative. Yet, there does not exist any clear-cut and universal distinction between memory and history in the Arampur area. Not everyone shares the conflation Upagrah Singh makes between *yād* and *itihās* or the other local terms for the latter: *tārīkh*, *history*,[62] and, occasionally, *dāstān*. After describing to me events that he claimed occurred 500 years ago, Harun Ansari explained that he knew about them through the "chain-by-chain"[63] communication from father to son over generations that he will continue with his own progeny. He added, *"Ko'ī itihās hamāre pās nahīṅ"* (We don't have any history). For him and many others, history can be found only in books. Some distinguish between "oral history" and "written history." Finally, others, like Upagrah Singh, find a continuity between memory and history.

In conclusion, indigenous terminology includes words for the loss of memory, such as the verbs *bhūlna* and *to forget*. I asked Rukn Khan how he knew about the events of last century that he had just narrated to me. In Urdu, he replied, *"Sunī-sunā'ī kī bāt—oral history"* (It is a matter of hearsay—oral history). Then he added, *"Log history bhūl gaya"* (People have forgotten history). We examine the role of hearsay later. Suffice this to show for now that some Arampur residents equate certain oral narrations with history and believe that these narrations can be forgotten as well as remembered, as Rukn Khan implies.

Local Systems

Group memory, therefore, finds a natural resonance with ideas of knowing the past in English, Hindi, and Urdu. Justification for using the term, finally, requires a demonstration that it does provide a common ground on which various oral and written narratives can be comparatively analyzed. We can accomplish this by showing how groups reflect their concern for their past through the systematized regulation of the narratives that express that concern. In an attempt to portray some of the various means by which groups systematize their memories with strategies of authorization, verification, and transmission as remembered by individuals, we shall examine four versions of one of the most commonly repeated narratives in the Arampur area. In the first eight months of my stay in their locale, no fewer than twenty-six residents recollected a version of this narrative about the area's past for me. Many more referred to it in their conversations describing the nexus. It became a routine way by which residents introduced themselves and their area to me. A common conversation upon meeting someone for the first time often went like this:

> *Resident:* "Who are you?"
> *Me:* "My name is Peter."

---

62. Adjectival forms in use include *aitihāsik* and *historical*.
63. He used this English phrase in the midst of our conversation in Urdu.

Resident: "Where are you from?"
Me: "America."
Resident: "What are you doing here?"
Me: "I am studying the rural life of Bihar."
Resident: "Where do you stay here?"
Me: "I live with the family of Mahan Singh."
Resident: "Have you seen the fort over there [pointing to Arampur fort]? It is the fort of Raja Vicitra."

And from this juncture the resident often provided a narrative depicting the local raja, his slighted Brahman, and the Delhi sultan.

The four versions that I have chosen for comparison include the oral telling by a low-caste woman, the publication of a Brahman man, the oral telling by another Brahman man who plans his own publication, and a multivolume history of Bihar published by the state government. I chose these particular recollections to demonstrate the varieties in styles of transmission, verification, and authorization for narrated remembrances. Through an examination of how narrators qualify their narrative with regard to these, we gain an insight into the systematized ways in which narratives are considered by those who recollect, hear, and recast them.

The distinction between transmission,[64] verification,[65] and authorization[66] should be understood only in a heuristic sense. These are neither mutually exclusive nor the only qualifications for narratives regarding the past. They serve us only as a useful way to demonstrate and examine the dynamics of the diverse systems of group memory among different people. As an example, we might imagine three people's conversation about the story of Noah's flood. The first considers the Bible as the utmost authority on this story and all of the ancient past because it arrived through the ultimate form of transmission—direct revelation from God—and has been rigorously preserved and transmitted to succeeding generations through meticulous copying and vigorous study. As such, it is considered verified by God and religious tradition. The second may reject the Bible as transmitted from God through revelation while accepting its communication via tradition and thus understand the story as an allegorical myth. Even though the second person does not believe that God verifies the truth of the story, he or she trusts the millennia-old religious institutions to verify the accuracy of the transmission, acknowledges its authority to structure the life of the religious community, but denies its authority to describe the past accurately. Finally, a third considers the Noah narrative as a folktale common to those communicated by other ancient Mesopotamian religions, with changes, through hoary texts. The third believes that the narrative's accuracy can be verified only through geological proof of a massive flood or a

---

64. The manner and means by which a narrative is communicated by one person to another.
65. The ways of assessing the truthfulness of a narrative that claims to describe events of the past.
66. The socially sanctioned power to evaluate and declare a narrative's truth claims.

carbon-dated relic of the ark. All three of these people know the narrative, but in vastly different ways. Their different strategies—influenced by the groups to which they belong—of evaluating a narrative's transmission, verification, and authorization form part of their overall hermeneutic.

Through an examination of the role of these categories in various recollections regarding the past of Arampur, we shall debate the claims of both Halbwachs and Connerton that only historiography reflectively critiques its own accounts. Although perhaps less formalized and less self-conscious than historiography, other modes of discourse regarding the past address similar concerns regarding proper transmission, authorization, and verification of group memories. As we shall read, then, historiography can be included as one set of systems found on a wide spectrum of many group memory systems. In so doing, we create the necessary heuristic space by which we can compare various local narratives of the past that have a wide variety of discursive techniques while bracketing the veracity of their truth claims.

Four Versions of the Raja-*Brahm*-Sultan Narrative

The Recollections of Lakshmi Devi and Mujun Khan (Continued)

In my experience among the residents of Arampur, nearly anyone at almost anytime and practically anywhere could recollect the matter of the local raja, his Brahman priest, and the Delhi sultan, often alluding to *sunā-sunāī* as a reputable source. The simultaneously consensual and conflicting versions of Lakshmi Devi and Mujun Khan have been described previously. Here, we must analyze them as one of many local group memories, each of which relies on techniques of communication, verification, and authorization in its claim for the veracity of its account of the past.

Despite her reliance of *sunā-sunāī*, we must not overlook the fact that Lakshmi Devi gave two answers to my question, "How do you know about this?" She first answered, "There is a book here." When pressed, she explained that she had not read the book but had heard about Shastri Brahm from others. Why did she mention the book then? Perhaps she wanted to feign a literacy that she does not exercise. Perhaps she thought that a book, rather than conversation, was the type of source about which a foreign researcher preferred to hear. In either case, the answer of Lakshmi Devi suggests a source of authority that she recognizes. It became not uncommon that residents, having recalled some local or national event, referred to a book as being not the source of their narrative but as confirmation of its veracity. In this way, we can see that authority and verification often overlap. If someone considered authoritative in the recollection of the past acknowledges a narrative, then that, too, is verification of its truthfulness. Residents, therefore, recognize certain examples of what Connerton calls "inscribing practices" to substantiate their memories.

Yet, verification cannot be entirely subsumed within authority. Objects and phenomena can verify a narrative's truthfulness quite apart from the presence of an authority.[67] Note how Mujun Khan followed his contradiction of the preceding account of the raja's death. "Whose mausoleum is that?" he asked rhetorically, as he pointed toward the unseen tomb, expecting me to recognize it as verification of his account. Each figure in the raja-*brahm*-sultan narrative has a relic in or near Arampur commonly associated with him or her, and that verifies certain events for most residents. In particular regard to this limited telling, the raja is associated with the ruined fort, the *brahm* with his active temple, and the sultan with his massive mausoleum. Residents usually refer to these traces as they recollect the events associated with these characters—events for which these relics act as traces.

Informants make this association both bodily and verbally, as when Mujun Khan pointed in the direction of the mausoleum when he referred to the sultan. This habitual behavior among many, if not most, residents constitutes what Connerton describes as one type of technique of bodily practice—what he calls "referential gesture."[68] These acts of pointing effectively map the Arampur area, an area with which most identify as residents. Even when informants pointed to objects out of their sight, they most often pointed in the precise direction. This demonstrates the manner in which traces of past events that are commonly incorporated into narratives play a role in mapping a locale that residents know intimately and with which they identify. It also shows how the tellings of narratives, as well as associated posturing, help residents inscribe the terrain with the narrative. Ultimately, because they and their families and other groups have a place on this terrain, the tellers and listeners of group memories emplot themselves within the map and narrative of the past.

Returning to the issue of authority, we see that both informants refer to "others" from whom they have heard about the events surrounding the raja and the *brahm*. As mentioned before, "the book" that she refers to seems to operate as an authority for Lakshmi Devi. This is true even if it is only to the degree that she believes that it is an authority that I, as a Western scholar, will recognize. Several informants referred to books as the source of their recollections, although most had said that they had never seen them, suggesting the implicit authority in the eyes of many residents that a publication merits simply by supposedly existing.[69]

Mujun Khan specified his allusion to authority with his reference to "older people." The most common authority in everyday oral recollections of nexus men are elder men. Very often, having pursued questions regarding a recollec-

---

67. Of course in the long run, authoritative figures play a role in determining within a group what objects and phenomena act as proper verification.

68. Connerton, p. 81.

69. Narayana Rao, scholar of South Asian literature, argues that many oral traditions in South Asia have long made use of references to written texts as proof of their veracity, even when no such text exists. Narayana Rao, personal conversation, October 22, 1996.

tion, I would be directed to a particular older man, who, I was assured, would answer my questions. Younger men almost always deferred to the authority of the older men in their family or caste. Some younger men simply stopped talking once an older member of the family arrived. Immediately preceding my talk with Sayyid Afifuddin regarding Baqar 'īd, his son had been recalling the circumstances of the sacrifice of Ibrahim. At the moment Sayyid Afifuddin arrived, his son ended his conversation as quickly as his father began his own. Certain elders are considered the highest authorities of recollection, not only for the village in which they belong but also for the entire village nexus. Baba Singh, certainly the most recognized authority on the past, received respect from male residents of the area without distinction of religion, caste, or class. However, men are not accorded respect as authorities due to their age alone. Plenty of younger men question, contest, and even ridicule the recollections of some older men. Education, intelligence, character, and social status all contribute to the evaluation of authority.

As a final note on authority, we recognize that while he contested the veracity of the narrative of Lakshmi Devi, Mujun Khan disqualified the authorities from which, he implied, her narrative derived. By juxtaposing history (*itihās*) to what "the pandit folk say," he sought to contrast the authority of supposedly authentic recollections with those which, he charged, temple priests constructed for their own fiscal benefit. We see, then, that residents do not rely on the "unreflective traditional memory" that Connerton would contrast with the self-scrutiny of historical methodology. The recollections of both Lakshmi Devi and Mujun Khan demonstrate informal systems within which residents reconstruct heard narratives and re-present them to an audience. Within this system, choices are made regarding the sources of authority and manner of verification that others may contest, as Mujun Khan has done.

Brahm Prakās *by L. Tripathi*

Panini Singh, the friend from Banaras who introduced me to the Arampur area, where he grew up, sat with me and a number of his home nexus friends on strung cots overlooking the Bazaar during my first visit to the area. Those present alternately ask me about myself and my home and told me about themselves and their homes. Talk turns to the ruined fort of the raja and the temple of the *brahm*. Panini Singh suddenly leaps up and runs down the street, out of sight. In a few minutes' time, he returns with a faded blue pamphlet that he offers to me, saying that it will tell me the whole story. Printed on the cover is the Hindi title *Brahm Prakās*. Many times during the next 14 months, residents would refer to this text as we talked about the area. It represents another system of group memory, distinguishing itself from the narratives of Lakshmi Devi and Mujun Khan according to mode of transmission, authority, and verification.[70]

---

70. Lakshmi Devi may have been referring to this book or no actual one at all.

The thirty-two-page Hindi publication can be bought in two places. Panini Singh had dashed off to the first: Pandey Book Palace. Throughout the year (depending on stock), this store displays it among its many Hindu religious texts, comic books, and school texts in Arampur Bazaar. Second, during important Hindu religious celebrations and events relating to Shastri Brahm, one or two temporary bookstalls sell the pamphlet as they bid for floorspace on the crowded path leading to the temple of the *brahm* in the Arampur fort among merchants of devotional offerings, multicolored bangles, plastic toys, gooey sweets, and a host of other articles. In these stalls, the text lies among thin, stapled copies of *vratkathās* (books on fasting) and thick, bound copies of the *Rāmacaritamānas*,[71] as well as framed photographs of the *brahm mūrti*.

Atop the first page of the pamphlet, the text's title stands prominently. Below it is a two-tone photograph of the *mūrti* of the *brahm* within its temple. Immediately below this and to the right sits the author's name, L. Tripathi. The back cover has a picture, much smaller than that on the front cover, that depicts the author above his name, which, in turn, stands above the words, "Teacher of grammar and literature, double M.A., gold medal recipient." In the right-hand corner below this reads the price, "6.00 rupees." The title page of the booklet repeats the title, author's name, and qualifications as printed on the back cover. To this is added the name of the author's village, the name of the publisher (followed by the title, "teacher"), and the name of the "vendor"— Pandey Book Palace. A dedication follows in which L. Tripathi explains that others have insisted that he "shed some light in connection with the life of Shastri Brahm." L. Tripathi then concludes his dedication with a four-line devotional poem ascribed to himself.

The text that follows is of a highly Sanskritized Hindi that some Hindi-speaking residents said they could not understand. Certain local residents use this type of Hindi to confer a note of formality to the material and/or erudition, if not authority, to their speech and writing. The text begins with a brief geographic description of the general Arampur area. The author locates the not-too-distant Mundeshvari temple relative to local mountains, rivers, and (finally) villages. Associated with this, he narrates the depredations of the brothers Cand and Mund, the *rākṣasa*[72] governors of the area and their destruction by an avatar of the goddess Candi. Like those who orally narrate this commonly told story, L. Tripathi associates particular villages and temples with these events: the ancient name of Arampur—Mundpur—derives from the demon Mund, the name of a neighboring village derives from that of the wife of Cand, and so forth. On the page following these two, the author describes the political fortunes of the Arampur area from Gupta rule in 380 C.E. to the ascent of Raja Vicitra in 1388 C.E. The remaining twenty-five pages of the pamphlet recount the rule of the raja, his marriage to his rani, the injustice that she prompted

---

71. Tulsidas's sixteenth-century version of the life and adventures of the avatar Ram written in a Hindi dialect.

72. An ogrelike demon.

him to commit against his priest and minister Shastri Pandey, the latter's post-mortem revenge, and, in conclusion, the invasion by the Delhi sultan.

L. Tripathi uses a variety of sources to claim authority for his narration. The educational and professional qualifications that he lists for himself on both the back cover and the title page are meant to suggest that the author's learned nature makes him a competent source for the printed information. It is possible that some readers will grant Tripathi some authority on the basis of his recognizably Brahman name. By stating that others compelled him to write the present book, the author implies that they consider him authoritative and that his motive is not self-serving. His devotional dedication of the booklet to Shastri Brahm reinforces the latter implication. His Sanskritized Hindi also hints at authority.

Like Mujun Khan, L. Tripathi implies the use of *itihās* as a means of both authority and verification for his narrative. He gives the sense that he has examined *itihās* and *aitihāsik* sources for his work. In his dedication, the author writes that he will shed light on Shastri Brahm "*pramānik aitihāsik tathyoṅ ke sambandh meṁ*" (in connection with authoritative, historical facts).[73] Later, he admits that he has no "authentic, historical evidence" to prove his contention that the name *Arampur* (place of rest) derives from the peacefulness that once typified this place. He adds, however, that it was known to have been given in the era of the rule of Ashoka.[74] In the same way, the author challenges the "rumor" that the raja compensated for a lack of Brahmans by having members of other castes wear the sacred thread associated with the former when he argues, "Indian history cannot confirm the creation of new Brahmans."[75]

In part, L. Tripathi verifies his work through written Sanskrit texts and, therefore, suggests the precedence of written texts over oral ones. Despite the wealth of narratives among local residents and the Brahman families that service the Shastri Brahm temple, L. Tripathi refers to no oral source in his booklet. For instance, he cites the *Mākaṇḍey Purāṇa*[76] and *Devī Bhāgavat*[77] regarding the battle between Cand and Mund and the Candi avatar while ignoring the many oral tellings for this event.[78] As a resident of a local village, he cannot have been ignorant of these narratives but simply dismissive. Because he creates his own written narrative of these happenings, it is obvious that the author considers such a text as not just most authoritative and properly verified, but as a more proper mode of transmission as well.

73. L. Tripathi, *Brahmprakāś*, Bhabhua: Ruchika, 1995, p. 3.

74. Ibid., p. 6.

75. Ibid., p. 8.

76. A Sanskrit text (entitled in that language *Mārkandeya Purāṇa*) comprised of behavioral proscriptions, didactic stories, and narratives connected with the *Mahābhārat*. Written before the sixth century C.E.

77. A Sanskrit *purāṇa* (entitled in that language *Devī Bhāgavata*) written no earlier than the mid-tenth century C.E.

78. Tripathi, p. 5.

The Envisioned History of Surya Pandey

During the first week of my arrival in Arampur, I spoke with Satya Pandey about the locale. He suggested I talk with his 32-year-old brother Surya, whom he described as someone "educated" who could tell me about the area. Surya happened to be visiting Arampur then, having taken leave from his post as an assistant librarian in one of India's largest libraries. And so we meet. Under the warm winter sun, we sit in front of his family home, with its large, hand-painted sign advertising his eldest brother's services as a priest at the temple of Shastri Brahm. This Brahman family, among many others in Arampur, caters to the ritual needs of pilgrims who seek help with conception, exorcism, and other favors from the dead, yet efficacious, Brahman.

No sooner do we settle into our seats and pass through the usual introductory questions than Surya Pandey begins to describe the *itihās* of the area and a story of Shastri Brahm. He begins with the rise of the Guptas, a "golden period" for Arampur in which, as he describes, the village evolved because of its proximity to a university. A period of decline followed until Rājpūts, dislodged by Muslim attacks in the Delhi area, established local kingdoms, including one at Arampur. Raja Vicitra came to inherit this kingdom. His wife, angry at the suggestion of her husband's priest and minister that the heirless raja should remarry, instigated the raja's decision to damage the priest's house and seize his property. The priest, Shastri Pandey, starved himself to death in protest, went to Delhi as a *brahm*, and convinced the sultan, Mubarak Shah, to invade the raja's realm. The raja died, and the sultan gave a non-Rājpūt *jāgīrdār* control of the area. Residents of the locality, especially the fort, continued to sense the presence of the *brahm*, who aids those who make offerings to him and punishes those who trespass against him. So when Bakhtiyar Khan reconquered the area from a descendent of Raja Vicitra and then looted the fort's treasures to build tombs for his father in Sassaram and for himself in Arampur, the *brahm* slaughtered his entire family. Surya Pandey then concludes with descriptions of the annual ritual calendar for the temple of Shastri Brahm and the abilities of the *brahm* in exorcism.

The narrator explains, upon my asking, that he had first heard this narrative from his father—who was an important priest at the Shastri Brahm temple—and other locals. But, he continues, he had not been satisfied with it, and so, while working in his current position as assistant librarian, he had read district gazetteers and other documents about the area. Surya Pandey now intends to write his own "history" (his word) of Shastri Brahm and plans to approach the Indian Council of Historical Research for funding. The other sources that he refers to includes Chinese pilgrim Fa Hsien and British travelers William Crooke, Buchanan Hamilton,[79] and T. Blochmann. Surya Pandey also mentions a "very old" Sanskrit text, *Brahm Mumtāvalī*, which he has not seen but understands to be hidden somewhere in Bihar or Uttar Pradesh. When asked

79. Also known as Francis Buchanan.

about the *Brahm Prakās* by L. Tripathi, Surya Pandey immediately disparages it as "totally false" and based on "local experience." The author, he said, has no relation to the Shastri Brahm temple, had not studied the complete history of Bihar, only had an M.A. in Sanskrit, and falsely reported names and stories.

In terms of group memory, then, Surya Pandey drew from one set of memories and sought to refine them through another set. He drew originally on the memories of his family and caste group—those who service the temple and profit from devotees. But, after receiving a multidegree education at Banaras Hindu University, he became dissatisfied with these narratives. Referring to them as "legendary" and "folktales," he suspected that the recollections are in some way flawed and, so, went to sources that he considers to be more authoritative: the written recollections of observers from previous centuries—Chinese, British, and local. Yet, he did not unreflectively grant authority to any author of written texts. Besides his critique of Tripathi's pamphlet, Surya Pandey accused medieval Muslim historians in their books of ignoring the fact that Bakhtiyar Khan prohibited devotees from entering the temple. He implied that these authors, because of their religious prejudices, do not reliably recall the entire narrative.

Surya Pandey deliberately chose one medium of transmission over another. He explained how his father knew the story because it has been "continuing since 1430" from one generation to the next. Although this oral narrative may remain the foundation of his own version, he supplemented it with information from recorded accounts. The plan of Surya Pandey to write and publish a "history" indicates also a preferred mode of transmission that he said he relied on to preserve the recollected narrative that he pieced together from so many disparate sources.

In regard to verification, Surya Pandey depended on oral, textual, and material evidence. Although he doubted elements of the oral recollections from his family and caste, he implied that these narratives' survival since 1430 lends them some sort of credibility. This derives from both the duration of their survival and the span of their popularity, as evidenced when he said approvingly that the story of Shastri Brahm is not only very old but also popular among both literates and illiterates throughout north India.

In his attempt to recast his own narrative memory from "folktale" to "history," Surya Pandey drew on textual sources recording the recollections of much earlier researchers. During his narrative to me, he often qualified his own discourse by noting the ways in which writers verified what he said. For instance, following his description of local conditions in the post-Gupta period, Surya Pandey added that Fa Hsien's account mentions Mundeshvari temple. He then went on to say that in 1811 Hamilton Francis found a broken inscription that described one of the post-Gupta rajas and other local figures. The inscription, he added, is now in the Calcutta National Museum. In this way, we can see that the authority that Surya Pandey invested in a British traveler whose descriptions verify elements of local oral narrative includes an authority to identify and interpret traces associated with places, people, and objects in the narrative. When Surya referred to the Calcutta National Museum as the repository of an ancient inscription found in the area that proved an aspect of his narrative, he conferred authority to the museum as a collection of institutionally recognized traces. The mere presence in the museum of an artifact of an ancient period, Surya Pandey suggested, helps verify a local narrative depicting that period.

The Historiography of Hasan Nishat Ansari

The fourth example of a systematized memory of Shastri Brahm can be found in the *Comprehensive History of Bihar*. Opposite the title page for each of the six volumes of this tome is the English translation of a quote from the *Rājataraṅgiṇī*:[80] "He alone is a worthy and commendable historian, whose narrative of events in the past, like that of a judge, is free from passion, prejudice and partiality." By quoting this twelfth-century chronicle, the editors seem to be setting the standard for historians and the historiography they write, a standard which, they imply, has remained the same for at least eight centuries. Borrowing a term from the pre-postmodern age of historiography, we might call this quality "objectivity" as opposed to "subjectivity." Although postmodern and subaltern historians challenge this notion, historians in India and the West by and large still recast memories within a realm of formalized rules of transmission, verification, and authorization.

This becomes clear in the version of the narrative regarding the raja, his priest, and the sultan found among the 4,380 pages of the Bihar state–sponsored, English-language history. Or, rather, this becomes clear in the light of the fact that there is no such version. Despite the varieties of styles of historiography today, few, if any, professional historians can accept a ghost as a historical agent. Any source, whether textual or oral, that claims that Shastri Brahm played an instrumental role in the Delhi sultan's defeat of Raja Vicitra would not likely be accepted as authoritative or as verification. Historians may take note of local oral narratives, but these stories remain under heavy skepticism until more authoritative sources substantiate their claims. Oral narratives seldom gain the stamp of authority that allows them to stand alone.

An examination of one example of Indian historiography demonstrates how historians weigh local oral narratives in light of the formalized rules of historiography. In the case of the raja-*brahm*-sultan story, "Shastri Brahm" is not mentioned anywhere in the *Comprehensive History of Bihar*, and a ruler with the raja's name is found associated only with a realm nearly 240 kilometers distant from Arampur. Only Bakhtiyar Khalji[81] appears as a historical actor in the multivolume text, and so we will examine the historiographical essay re-

80. The twelfth-century Sanskrit account of the kings of Kashmir written by Kalhana.
81. Because of the common omission of short vowel signs in Persian and Urdu orthography, this name can be read in those scripts as either *Khilji* or *Khalji*. *Khalji* used here reflects Ansari's rendering. *Khilji* used elsewhere portrays common pronunciation in the Arampur area.

garding him, "Early Muslim Contact with Bihar and Invasion of Bakhtiyār Khaljī," written by Hasan Nishat Ansari.

Reflective of the broad concerns of all six volumes, Ansari narrates a military and political history of Bihar from the eleventh century to the thirteenth. Chronology structures the narrative development: first Pala and Sena rulers control Bihar politically, then Turkish raids begin as these rules weaken, then Bakhtiyar Khalji invades and conquers Bihar before passing on to his assault on Bengal, after which, and in conclusion, he dies. Except for a brief hint of broader social disruptions in the twelfth century, political and military leaders are the only agents in Ansari's history.

The author makes a claim for his authority to write this history in the volume's table of contents, where each author's qualifications are listed. His reads "Lecturer in History, S.M.D. College, Punpun, Magadh University, Bodh Gaya," thereby associating him with the discipline of history in Bihari institutions of higher learning. The inclusion of his essay in a general history of Bihar sponsored by the state government of Bihar (which also controls almost all universities and colleges in the state) adds weight to his claim to authority in the eyes of many readers. This may be furthered by the choice of English as the medium of expression for all the essays in the collection. English is often the preferred language of Indian scholarship.

Ansari relies on various sources to verify his historical claims. The seventeen pages of his essay are peppered with 123 endnotes. The vast bulk of these cite more than forty textual sources (mostly scholarly journals),[82] which usually refer, in turn, to yet other texts, as well as inscriptions and oral narratives. In his treatment of these sources, Ansari reveals some of the rules implicit in his discipline. For one, each described event must be substantiated by more than one source when available. Thus, he doubts the claim of the author of the *Riyāḍu's Salāṭīn* that Qutbaddin Aibak had summoned Bakhtiyar Khalji to his court in 1198 because this "is not supported by any other source."[83]

Ansari becomes particularly vocal about the veracity of his sources when he considers the damages inflicted by Bakhtiyar Khalji on the Buddhist monasteries that the general overran. He doubts the claims made by the contemporary Muslim historian Minhaj regarding the number of non-Muslims killed, suspecting this figure as "exaggerated in religious zeal."[84] Later, he disqualifies a series of Tibetan historians in their accounts of the destruction of monastic libraries when he writes, "We must make allowance for the subjective, exaggerated and unscientific treatment of historical facts at the hands of the Buddhist monks."[85] Whether we agree with Ansari or suspect that his is the prejudiced view, his language re-

82. Most notably, *Journal of Bihar and Orissa Research Society, Journal of Bihar Research Society,* and *Indian Historical Quarterly.*

83. Hasan Nishat Ansari, "Early Muslim Contact with Bihar and Invasion of Bakhtiyār Khaljī" in *Comprehensive History of Bihar*, vol. II, part I, Syed Hasan Askari and Qeyamuddin Ahmad, eds. Patna: Kashi Prasad Jayaswal Research Institute, 1983, p. 36.

84. Ibid., p. 37.

85. Ibid., p. 40.

veals the same call to balance and objectivity that the editors of the series invoke in the beginning of each volume with the quote from the *Rājataraṅgiṇī*. Authority, they imply, can be best claimed by those without vested interest, and verification can best be provided by disinterested sources in agreement with other sources.

Ansari does refer, at times, to oral narratives and grades them according to historiographic notions of veracity. He describes "local traditions" depicting the hostility of a minor ruler to a "saintly" Muslim that led to the military defeat of the ruler. Although he devotes more than half a page to this account, Ansari concludes, "This old traditional account cannot be considered as a piece of sober history because it is not confirmed by any contemporary source."[86] "Traditional account" must be a euphemism for oral narrative, as Ansari associates this account with no written text. Once again, we see the distinction between good or "sober" history and bad history as being defined by the veracity of a narrative's sources. For Ansari, oral narratives are apparently less trustworthy than written ones.

The author also makes use of material evidence in qualifying his narrative, although only to substantiate the claims of written sources. Regarding the question of where Bakhtiyar Khalji was buried, Ansari mentions that contemporary historians say little and that "oral tradition" indicates Biharsharif town. Yet material remains are not enough necessarily to substantiate the oral claim. He writes, "The exact traditional site can be located even now. A large domed mausoleum, still extant in the same locality, is said to contain the remains of Bakhtiyar. No tablet with inscriptional record could be traced thereon, probably because it was lost long ago."[87] Although physical traces exist in the place associated with the conqueror via oral narratives, the lack of written evidence preempts any claim of conclusive proof in Ansari's eyes.

Thus, in terms of transmission, authority is granted to a written text over an oral text or a relic. Ansari and the other essayists of the six-volume *Comprehensive History of Bihar* establish their own works within a creeperlike discourse whereupon they graft their claims onto those of others. Ansari's essay sets its roots among the historians preceding him by as many as 700 years and as few as 8. Through the formalized standards of historiography that, the general editors at least, consider to be uniform over a span of eight centuries, most historians today imagine that they can assess the authority and veracity of previous historiographies and incorporate them into their own recollections. The changes in historiographic method reflect changing interests among the groups that they serve. In this way, for instance, subaltern historians of India critique previous forms of historiography and adopt new methods to serve the interests of postcolonial, educated Indians seeking to remember the events of imperialism within a framework that recalls the lives of the colonized, not simply the colonizer. A historiographic technique by which the colonizer remembered his or her agency in colonization becomes adjusted to serve the interests of some of the descendants of the colonized to reconstruct a memory of their predecessors' agency.

86. Ibid., p. 34.
87. Ibid., p. 46.

Ultimately, then, we can see how historiography relies on the inscribing practices (using Connerton's parlance) of those in the past to provide sources that can verify the claim of those in the present as they, in turn, inscribe their testimony of group memory. Although the "externalized" words of historians' books might not fade as readily as an individual's memory, they always remain at the mercy of individual and group interest and interpretation. We may have the exact words of James Mill's *The History of British India*, but most of us interpret this inscribed memory in a much different way than Mill's contemporaries were likely to do. Curiously, many of us read and remember Mill's narrative today as part of our ongoing group process of reevaluating authority and verification within our system of group memory. We consider his work with less of an interest in *what* he remembers than in *how* he remembers it. Yet that memory—both of the events described and the way in which he describes them—continues through the efforts of the publishers, librarians, and readers who have made new editions possible 150 years after first publication.

In summation, this chapter has mapped the territory of this project. First, the village has been chosen as our focus only with the understanding that it is (1) often taken as central for the self-orientation and self-identification of local residents and (2) but one of many alternating frames of reference available to any individual. Second, Paul Ricoeur has provided the tools to examine the narratives by which residents emplot themselves in time and, as other scholars have added, in space. He demonstrates how individuals associate with groups with which they share a common interest and interpretation of the past. Third, to create an analytic field wherein to examine narratives of various styles without disrespecting their truth claims, we refine a theory of group memory from the works of Maurice Halbwachs and Paul Connerton. Fourth, a comparison of four variants of the raja-*brahm*-sultan story reveals the techniques by which they each make truth claims regarding a common past event by using trope-specific rules of transmission, verification, and authorization. These techniques also include omission, if a narrative fails to meet the ruling criterion for truth. Fifth, then, we see that narratives, with habit and ritual, create a mnemonic map of cultural and geographic features that demonstrates how places, objects, and, most important, area residents are meaningful through their connection to important events and people of the past.

The next two chapters demonstrate the ways in which multiple pasts create multiple identities. Five sets of the most commonly told narratives of the Arampur area are considered regarding the variety of their expressions. Each set includes examples of narratives and counternarratives, each of which reflects how different groups intersubjectively construct identities for themselves relative to others through a group memory of past events. We shall see how "Hindu" and "Muslim" are but two group identities among others, including those associated with village, class, caste, gender, family, region, and nation. Individuals can use narratives of the past to either associate or disassociate one group from another and, in so doing, reconstruct their society and their place within it.

4

Ocean of the
Strands of Memory

The previous chapter showed how narratives can be compared to one another as group memories. It provides the necessary theoretical foundation for the next two chapters, which analyze a variety of local narratives and demonstrate the contextual and multiple nature of the identities that inform them. Here I attempt to portray some of the group identities to which individuals in the Arampur area refer (implicitly or explicitly, for themselves and for others) when they narrate their memories. As the personal expression of an individual narrator, each memory may reflect some of the multiple group identities with which the narrator associates. In the social context in which they are formed and expressed, these memories often negotiate conflicting or contradictory memories offered by family members, neighbors, or strangers. The five narrative themes considered demonstrate some of the primary identities to which residents allude, show how they vary in form according to context, give examples of countermemories, and reflect the recrystallization of individual identities according to social context.

Salman Rushdie adapted the descriptive title of Somadeva's twelfth-century Sanskrit classic, *Kathāsaritsāgara* (*Ocean of the Rivers of Stories*), for his novel *Haroun and the Sea of Stories*. In turn, we borrow Rushdie's description of the invisible, oceanic moon *Kahani* (Hindi and Urdu for "story") from this fantasy to depict the ocean of memory that engulfs all cultures.

> So Iff the Water Genie told Haroun about the Ocean of the Streams of Story, and even though he was full of a sense of hopelessness and failure the magic of the Ocean began to have an effect on Haroun. He looked into the water and saw that it was made up of a thousand thousand thousand and one different currents, each one a different colour, weaving in and out of one another like a liquid tapestry of breathtaking complexity; and Iff explained that these were the Streams of Story, that each coloured strand represented and contained a single tale. Different parts of the Ocean contained different sorts of stories, and as all the sto-

ries that had ever been told and many that were still in the process of being in-
vented could be found here, the Ocean of the Streams of Story was in fact the
biggest library in the universe. And because the stories were held here in fluid
form, they retained the ability to change, to become new versions of themselves,
to join up with other stories and so become yet other stories; so that unlike a
library of books, the Ocean of the Streams of Story was much more than a store-
room of yarns. It was not dead but alive.[1]

Appropriating Rushdie's image, we can visualize the ocean of group memories
in which interconnected and overlapping pools of narrators relate what they
consider to be nonfictional depictions of the past. The following makes use of
Rushdie's metaphor with the term *memory* often replacing *narrative* in reference to these depictions.

Because of the power of group memories in the construction and reformu-
lation of societies, social agents contrive to harness and/or adapt them to their
goals. The greater the popularity and uniformity of a particular memory, the
more effectively it can serve to establish, express, and maintain a group identity. Observe the efforts of national governments in the United States and India
to educate their citizens through narratives of national struggles for independence from Britain. The more the population at large appropriates these narratives and identifies with them personally, the stronger the national identity
can be forged. Within each of these countries, then, a nationalist group memory
acts as a type of current, composed of multiple strands of single stories (e.g.,
the Bunker Hill battle and Jallianwala Bagh massacre; Washington's patient
winter encampment and Gandhi's nonviolent Salt March). This current moves
forcefully among the other group memories in the society (e.g., the enslavement of African Americans and the violence of some Independence fighters),
influencing, and being influenced by, them. In the ocean of group memories,
currents—some more powerful than others—absorb some memories while
subverting others (e.g., Jefferson's slave ownership was until recently forgotten, and the violence following Gandhi's first noncooperation campaign is
mostly overlooked).[2]

There are parallel currents and crosscurrents and countercurrents. Each is
susceptible to the influence of human intention and, at first glance, seems more
like its land-borne counterpart. Human effort may attempt to redirect rivers
with canals, control their motion with levees, check their power with dams,
and divert their energies with bypasses. But the current of popular memory
has its own momentum that can resist such impositions, as demonstrated by
the resiliency of the name St. Petersburg among the citizens of the erstwhile
Leningrad against generations of Soviet revisionism.

However, the dynamic of group memory ultimately acts less like a river and
more like Rushdie's sea of stories. A river runs along a single, well-defined, and

1. Salman Rushdie, *Haroun and the Sea of Stories*. New York: Penguin, 1990, pp. 71–72.

2. See Shahid Amin, *Event, Metaphor, Memory: Chauri Chaura, 1922–1992*. Delhi: Oxford
University Press, 1995.

two-dimensional course and simply conjoins with the streams and rivers that it encounters. Although each community may define itself as distinct from others, none exists entirely in isolation. Each dwells within a broader ocean that brooks no definite boundaries as outside influences interlope. Within the sea of Indian memories that resides, in turn, within the global ocean of humanity's memories, the Arampur nexus has its own pool of narratives comprised of the different strands of individual memories. But some streams within this pool are larger than others and may become, through either direct or indirect human direction, powerful currents that influence the direction of other narrative streams—absorbing some in confluence and submerging others that resist. Although memories such as the narrative of the raja, *brahm*, and sultan reflect an influential stream in the Arampur area, more powerful currents propelled by regional and national agents affect the course of that stream, deflecting part of it away and absorbing another part through its inertia. These waters are deep and the streams convoluted, partly because of the complex nature of the identities that they manifest.

Although sometimes impelled by larger forces, narrative strands often express some element of the narrator's identity. Individual narratives often refer to interests shared with a group with whom the narrator associates himself or herself. In fact, the expression of these interests through narrative helps make a group identity coherent. Yet, an individual's identity is always in a state of flux and affected by external conditions. While one of the multiple identities that compose a person may manifest itself near the surface of social interaction, other dimensions and the narratives associated with them remain more submerged—still potent but less visible. The outsider can operate as a snorkeler at best, skimming the surface, only glimpsing some of the undercurrents, yet discerning some of the group identities that the individual strands of memories suggest.

Overly reductionistic scholarship has assumed that the currents of narratives that seem strongest and run closest to the surface (e.g., politically motivated and religiously chauvinist narratives) speak for all Hindus and Muslims. Excessively deconstructive research focuses so myopically on the differences among individual narrative strands that larger streams and currents are neglected in part or entirely. Here, I attempt to steer a middle course that recognizes that, first, no major stream of memory runs without resistance and, second, countercurrents often share common elements of the mainstream and, thus, may suggest some common identity. To ignore this would be to settle for a two-dimensional depiction of identity that admits to little depth in the individual and ignores how different identities are continually rearranged in terms of prominence. The recent, violent turbulence on the surface of India's sea of stories (where, for instance, memories of the Hindu avatar Ram and the Muslim emperor Babar have led some to stir colliding narrative currents into powerful whirlpools) has attracted deserved attention. However, greater depths underlie this surface, and important currents flow, collide, and abide there.

We will examine the manner in which Arampur residents use narrative expressions of group memory to formulate and describe identities for themselves and others. Residents make these identifications most obvious when they refer to "we people" as *ham log* in Hindi, Urdu, and Bhojpuri and "those people" as *wo log* in Hindi and Urdu and *u log* in Bhojpuri. As we shall see, self-identification usually involves some measure of negative identification: defining the member through juxtaposition with the nonmember. The following narratives demonstrate the many group identities available to individual Arampur residents, the manner in which residents employ narratives to express group memories that help define these identities, and the ways in which narratives change in response to different social contexts. Such changes prompt a dynamic, fluid recrystallization of individual identity through a readjustment in which a person forefronts certain group identities while de-emphasizing others.

To portray this dynamic, we will analyze various versions of five narrative topics in this and the following chapter. First, in a return to the raja-*brahm*-sultan narrative considered in the previous chapter, group identities of religion, education, village, *muhalla*, and gender are considered. Second, a narrative of how a set of Hindu and Muslim families—the Vaīs Rājpūts and Diwan Khans—descends from two brothers demonstrates family, village, class, and religious identities. Third, debating narratives regarding the origin of Naugrah village reveals class, caste, and religious identities. The next chapter considers more institutionalized narratives and identities. First, narratives associating the raja to two dead yet active healers—the *brahm* and a Sufi—evidence the promotion of a common area identity through narrative and ritual. Second, narratives of *Āzādī* ("Independence") that the government aggressively advances through mandated school texts display the divergence between popular memory and government promotion in the creation of nationalist self-identification through narrative and ritual among area residents.

Before continuing, it is necessary to invoke the warning of Bipan Chandra mentioned in the introduction regarding the language of communalism. He cautions that many contemporary writers adopt communalist assumptions in the course of arguing against communalists and, in doing so, become hostage to communalist rhetoric. With this in mind, two points need to be made regarding the present project. First, following my experience among the residents of the Arampur nexus, it would be disingenuous of me to deny that people often refer to one another and themselves according to labels of religious identity. Those scholars who would do a disservice to their subject because we cannot hope to better understand communalist tensions by pretending that it is simply the invention of a few political elites—important as their impact past or present might be. Whatever the origins of communalist discourse, we begin here with the fact of its currency in everyday conversations and attempt to understand it relative to the larger context of local discursive practices.

Second, there exists the threat of exaggeration through examination; that is to say, by focusing on the place of religious identity in respect to other identities among Arampur residents, we will necessarily magnify communalist discourse disproportionate to its frequency in everyday discussion. I have chosen the following narratives because they are among the most commonly used, but I have selected particular versions to analyze in detail to demonstrate how even blatantly communalist discourse often admits to other, shared identities. So the prevalence of communalist language in these examples should not be taken as representative of their prevalence in everyday interactions but rather as a necessary tactic in the process of their detailed analysis. In the course of my project, I must, too, rely on the general labels of "Hindu" and "Muslim" but do so only with the dual understanding that, first, local residents occasionally identify themselves and one another through these categories and, second, these are never monolithic or primary at all times for any individual.

The Local Raja, the Vengeful *Brahm*, and the Delhi Sultan

The narrative and counternarrative of Lakshmi Devi and Majun Khan that we analyzed as we examined various elements of oral narrative in chapter 3 allow also an insight into a variety of group identities, both shared and disparate between them. Illustrative of the dynamic examined earlier, the public context of Lakshmi Devi's narration provided the opportunity for others to agree and object according to their views, thus creating consensus and conflict in memory and interpretation.

The most obvious explanation for at least part of the difference between the narratives of Lakshmi Devi and Majun Khan rests in the religious identities of the two narrators. Lakshmi Devi is one of many thousands of devotees to the *brahm*, and she expresses her respect for his powers in her narrative, crediting him with the downfall of a mighty raja. Majun Khan, like many (but certainly not all) local Muslims, is skeptical concerning the powers of the *brahm*. He attributes the fall of the raja to the invasion of the armies of the Delhi sultan, whose massive mausoleum attests to his power. As a reflex of his identity as a Muslim, Majun Khan is proud of the triumph of the Muslim sultan over the Hindu raja, an event that some Hindus argue led to the decline of a once wealthy Arampur.

Common among residents of the area is the idea that Arampur suffered a traumatic decline after a period when it thrived with tremendous wealth and spread expansively beyond its present boundaries. In discussions about this past and contemporary communal tensions, many local Hindus point (often literally) to the several examples of architecture from the era of the conqueror Sher Shah Suri found in the area surrounding Arampur[3] as unfortunate memorials of this Muslim conquest and the subsequent devastation of the area hundreds of years ago. When they narrate the story of the raja's fall to the sultan's armies, they add that the whole of the once glorious town of Arampur—which is said

3. See Catherine B. Asher, "Sub-imperial Palaces: Power and Authority in Mughal India" in *Ars Orientalis*. vol. 23 (1993), pp. 281–302.

to have once boasted huge neighborhoods, numerous silversmiths and gold-smiths, and incredible wealth—was laid waste by the conquerors, who, they usually note, were Muslims. Meanwhile, some local Muslims speak of the period of "Muslim rule" as the time of "our government," citing with pride the Red Fort, Taj Mahal, and Qutb Minar as the monuments of that rule.[4] Many Muslims interpret the emperor's mausoleum and the dozens of tombs it houses as a memorial to the *shahīd* or martyrs of the battle against the raja, who, they commonly emphasize, was Hindu. Majun Khan made a similar communal gesture when he contrasted the "history" of Bakhtiyar Khilji's defeat of Raja Vicitra with "what the pandit folk say . . . to make money." Such cases express a definite communal identity among some residents that allows *only* a Hindu or a Muslim identification.

And so, we must first consider religious identity as one component of self-identity among many area residents. It must be pointed out, however, that here "religious identity" does not mean an identity based solely on a group's behavior toward and beliefs in superhuman agents. A great many Arampur residents identify themselves as Hindu or Muslim without associating themselves with any of the practices or ideas of those two groups. Rather, they understand themselves as Hindu or Muslim in a broad social and cultural way, sharing an affiliation with others who have what might best be described as a similar sensibility.

Not uncommonly, local narratives reflect dissension about the "native" character of Muslim identity itself. In contrast with those who point proudly to the architectural monuments of Suri and Mughal rule as the relics of an Indian Muslim order, others take them as traces of the looting and devastation that occasionally accompanied the invasion of foreign Muslims. Whereas many Muslims take special pride in the Mughal dynasty as the zenith of Indian civilization, some Hindus consider it the destructive force that wrestled India to the vulnerable nadir that invited British incursion. And so, the polemic of Muslim-as-Indian opposite Muslim-as-foreign-invader arises. Reciprocally, these narratives implicitly construct a Hindu identity. Although local narratives take for granted the notion of Hindu-as-Indian, they may raise the issue of Hindu-as-misbeliever or Hindu-as-sophisticated-native, depending on the narrator.

Often, these narratives borrow from those provided in schools by both textbooks and lectures. A teacher in Arampur Girls Middle School elaborated for his class on a common Hindu sentiment regarding "Muslim invasions," while referring to one of the few passages in the Standard VII social studies textbook regarding Bakhtiyar Khilji. The passage reads, "In order to set his sights on Indian rule, [Muhammad] Ghuri appointed Qutubuddin Aibak, and army commander Bakhtiyar Khilji conquered Bihar and Bengal" [H].[5] The teacher

---

4. In an interesting nod of agreement as to the grandeur of these edifices but without relinquishing the theme of Hindu sophistication and Muslim devastation, a few local residents explained that buildings like the Taj Mahal were actually built by Hindus, as we shall see later.

5. *Madhyakālīn Bhārat.* Patna: Bihar State Textbook Publishing, 1994, p. 45.

pointed west toward Punjab and Afghanistan as he added extemporaneously that Muslims (specifically "Turks" and "Afghans") came to loot the rich country of India. As part of this, he explained, Muhammad Ghuri stripped the gold roof of the Somnath Temple in Gujarat while Bakhtiyar Khilji (pointing to the nearby mausoleum) took Bihar and Bengal. In so doing, he cast "those-Muslims-as-foreigners" (i.e., Turks and Afghans) as the despoiler of "we-Hindus-as-sophisticated-natives" (as evidenced by the implied expertise of the Somnath Temple's creators). The looting of Somnath Temple commonly acts as a seminal event in the narratives of those making this point, as was further demonstrated by Surya Pandey when, during his description of his forthcoming *itihās* (history) of Shastri Brahm, he explained that the Gujarati temple was destroyed by "invaders"—that is, "Muslims"—and rebuilt by "Indians."[6]

Schools promote identities not only through textbook and lecture narratives but also in decoration. The teaching staff of Arampur Middle School have hung a variety of pictures in their office, including prints of Independence leaders Mohandas Gandhi, Bhagat Singh, and B. R. Ambedkar posing with Jawaharlal Nehru and Rajendra Prasad. Alongside teaching posters of "The Life of the Aryans" and "Indus Civilization" and a dilapidated world map hang pictures of the gods Vishnu and Shiv, and a large framed picture of goddess Saraswati— set behind glass and adorned daily with a fresh garland—dominates the longest wall. Conversely, in the main room of the Urdu Middle School in Kendra, teachers have hung pictures of Nehru, the Kaaba in Mecca, the Prophet's Mosque in Medina, and Husain's bloodied horse at Karbala, among maps of India and the world. In other words, the predominantly Hindu teachers of Arampur Middle School have chosen images of domestic, Hindu gods and national heroes associated with a nationalist narrative and identity, while the predominantly Muslim teachers at the Urdu Middle School have chosen primarily Middle Eastern Muslim images associated with Muslim narratives and identity to complement the image of one of India's foremost Independence leaders.

Local Muslims, at times, refer to the arrival of Muslims in South Asia through narratives focused on Middle Period Muslim rulers (e.g., Sher Shah Suri and Babar). Many of these leaders fought their way eastward and established the foundation of Indian Muslim culture, for which the Taj Mahal is considered a particularly proud symbol. Local Sufis and *shahīd*s may also be tied with this migration if associated with Arabia, a connection that is taken as emblematic of their religious learning and spiritual powers (as we shall see later in the case of Asta Auliya). Only one man recalled in my presence a family memory of emigration from outside India (in this case, Afghanistan). In contrast, members of Naugrah's Khan family—which traces its descent from the conversion of a Rājpūt in a narrative that is considered in the next section—often recall

---

6. For a broader discussion of how the Somnath Temple figures into communalist imaginations, see Peter van der Veer, *Religious Nationalism: Hindus and Muslims in India*. Berkeley: University of California Press, 1994, pp. 146–152.

the name of the village in Rajasthan from which they say their descendent and his brother derived. For this family, the arrival from outside the nexus remains an emigration from *inside* India, while their ancestor's conversion is often considered as his self-transformation from Hindu-as-misbeliever to Muslim-as-believer, all the while assuming him to be Muslim-as-Indian.

A member of this family expressed this sentiment one September day. While relaxing in the men's quarters of his Naugrah home and in the company of some of his relatives, I asked Hatif Khan why his family converted to Islam, and he answers, "They liked it. They got tired of wondering which god was most powerful" [U]. Although the repercussions of this converted family's identity are explored in depth later, it serves well here to demonstrate the distinctions that are often made between Hindu-as-misbeliever and Muslim-as-believer. In many such instances, local Muslims jokingly portrayed Hindus as religiously ignorant.[7] Hatif Khan uses this narrative theme, therefore, to depict his family's regional presence as the result of domestic migration that led to economic development and local conversions prompted by religious awakening. Contrast this to many Hindu chauvinist narratives that depict the contemporary Muslim presence as the result of foreign invasion that led to domestic decline and conversion motivated by religious opportunism. Many Muslims and Hindus use narratives, then, to prove that the perceived distinction between Hindu and Muslim systems of belief and practice are not merely one of kind but of type (superior/true/positive versus inferior/false/negative).

It would be misleading to portray the identities local to Arampur without examining the prevalence of Hindu and Muslim religious identifications. But I hasten to point out that the differences that these labels mark are not always acrimonious: *awareness of difference does not necessarily signal a context of conflict*. Although many local narrators make note of the Muslim identity of the emperor and the Hindu identity of the raja and the *brahm*, this is often a gesture not of recrimination but simply of difference. While describing the Muslim celebration of Baqar 'īd and the lack of Hindu participation, a Muslim resident of Arampur passed off the difference with the phrase, "*Āp apnā dharm hai*" (To you your own religion) [U], perhaps invoking the passage from the Quran, "To you be your way, and to me mine" (109:6)[8] or the sentiment of the Bhagavad Gita regarding the personally distinctive nature of *dharm*. Similarly, while narrating the events of Independence and Partition, Ravan Tripathi explained that, despite religious differences between Hindus and Muslims, there exists no division among them as Indians. "Both are but one. One brother became a Mussalman and believed in another *dharm* so it is his freedom to do

7. Matters of theology can be used to unfavorably distinguish not only Hindus from Muslims, of course. One day a young Muslim man approached me in the hopes of finding someone whom he presumed Christian and, thus, theologically deficient. "Who was the father of Isa (Jesus)?" he asked suspiciously, expecting me to say "God" and thus be guilty of *shirk*, believing that God has peers.

8. A. Yusuf Ali, trans. *The Holy Qur'ān: Text, Translation, and Commentary*. Brentwood, Md.: Amana, 1983, p. 1800.

pūjā with purity (*pak*). I believe in a separate *dharm*, that is my freedom. But in the national interest, protection is needed for both" [H]. Although some residents make extreme efforts to deny communal division and portray a *bhai-bhai* (brotherly) relationship between Hindus and Muslims, it is important to note the manner in which residents usually accept differences in religious identity without taking them as differences in national identity.

This leads us to turn our attention beyond the identities of *Hindu* and *Muslim* to the shared identities that the interaction between Lakshmi Devi and Majun Khan demonstrates. After Lakshmi Devi initially expressed an identity associated with her state when she forcefully declared of her family, "*Ham log Bihari hai*" (We people are Bihari), she demonstrated an identity of belonging to the village of Arampur through her narrative of the local raja, the vengeful *brahm*, and the Delhi sultan. To that end, this narrative serves as a unifying theme among many, if not most, residents of this village. Almost everyone in the village knows this story, and a great many versions exist. But almost every version includes the Hindu raja who lived in a large fort in Arampur's northern end, the Brahman who was the raja's priest and advisor, the wrongful destruction of the Brahman's house at the instigation of one of the raja's wives, the Brahman's suicide by starvation in protest of the injustice he suffered, the death of the raja, and the eventual creation of a temple to the Brahman (now *brahm*). How the raja dies varies among residents. Some (like Lakshmi Devi) impute the vengeful *brahm*, others (like Majun Khan) credit the contemporary sultan of Delhi or another Muslim conqueror, and yet others combine the two by explaining that after the cremation of the Brahman, he went as a *brahm* to Delhi to enlist the help of the sultan. One might expect that Hindus would believe in the spiritual power of the dead Brahman and that Muslims would not. Yet, Hindus can be found among the detractors of the *brahm* and Muslims among those seeking his help. Local beliefs involving Shastri Brahm, therefore, can be more a matter of personal choice or family tradition than religious identity per se.

In terms of the ocean metaphor, the stream comprised of raja-*brahm*-sultan narrative strands (such as Lakshmi Devi's and Majun Khan's) may diverge into separate streams that are, in turn, influenced by larger (perhaps national) currents of communal invective in contexts of communal tension. Yet, despite the contestation between Lakshmi Devi and Majun Khan, they share a common belief that dramatic events in the past involving a local raja, his wronged Brahman, and the Delhi sultan had a dramatic impact on the village of Arampur. Disagreements regarding the powers of the *brahm* and the identity of the mausoleum's internee notwithstanding, no one suggested to me that these characters never existed or that Arampur never played an important role in the political past of the region. Even though Majun Khan disagrees with Lakshmi Devi, he joins her in pointing out (literally and figuratively) a narrative of past events, thus mapping an orally transmitted memory of the past onto the everyday map of Arampur (see map 3). The vigor with which Majun Khan contests Lakshmi Devi's narrative displays the importance of this memory for him and his concern for its proper transmission. Ultimately, then, what these two share is an identity of we-of-this-nexus that emplots itself in time and space through the common, however varied, narration of the raja-*brahm*-sultan story.

Rushdie's observation concerning the fluidity of narratives—their "ability to change, to become new versions of themselves, to join up with other stories and so become yet other stories"—helps us understand the appropriation of one narrative strand to serve a number of identities within the same individual. A number of times, a resident of the mostly Muslim neighborhood of Loharani in Arampur village stopped me, pointed to an overgrown pile of unremarkable rubble in a nearby field, and asked if I knew what it was. "It is the cremation site of Shastri Brahm," the self-appointed informant would say, showing pride that it was in "our Loharani." Although the cremation site plays a very small role, if any, in most narrations by Arampur's inhabitants regarding the raja, *brahm*, and sultan, many residents of this one Muslim neighborhood seize the opportunity to associate themselves with a narrative that helps define Arampur as a significant place, past and present. In so doing, they identify themselves with their neighborhood (i.e., we-of-Loharani) through a narrative that simultaneously associates them with their village (i.e., we-of-Arampur), demonstrating how the residents of this neighborhood share an identity that overlaps with those of local Hindus, even if they do not share in the belief that the *brahm* has spiritual powers. In many such cases, recitation of the narrative associated with the relic of the cremation site cannot be considered a statement of belief in the powers of the *brahm*. It acts as an affirmation of local territorial identity, not as a confession of faith.

However, this association of relic and narrative with a shared local identity is not automatic, as is demonstrated by the limited awareness among the residents of Swami Sarai of a substantial mausoleum abutting part of their village. Most of the entirely Hindu population were unable to explain what the relic was or with whom to associate it besides "Muslims," although some of the Harijans who lived in the *camṭol* (Camār quarter) bordering the building could name it as the tomb of Badal Khan. However, quite a number of Muslim residents from both Arampur and Naugrah could identify both the structure and its occupant. Perhaps because Badal Khan is understood to be an army commander who accompanied Bakhtiyar Khilji, he finds a place in memories of Muslims from more distant villages more readily than in those of the all-Hindu population of Swami Sarai. After all, many of the Diwan Khans among these Muslims spin a personal narrative strand from a larger family narrative stream when they recollect how members of their family, such as Badal Khan, emigrated to the area while serving Bakhtiyar Khilji. They see various surviving monuments as traces of both their progenitor's arrival and the grandeur of Indian Muslim rule.

Gender also provides some of the unique color to the strand of Lakshmi Devi's narration and demonstrates another dimension of her identity. Significant among the elements unique to this variation of the raja-*brahm*-sultan narrative is her treatment of the two female characters. Although residents commonly include the rani in the story as the inciter of the raja's jealousy, few explain that her anger at the Brahman derived from his suggestion that the raja remarry for the sake of having a son. Contemporarily, this remains an option for those local Hindu and Muslim men who have not had a son but who do have the resources to support more than one wife. As a woman, Lakshmi Devi demonstrates her sympathy for the rani with this detail that mitigates the condemnation that the audience might otherwise feel toward this spiteful woman. Although nexus residents often include the rani in the narrative, they less often incorporate the compassionate daughter who serves the dying Brahman by offering him sherbet and, thus, becomes the sole member of the family not to be felled by his vengeance. Compassion, caretaking, and devotion offer some of the few avenues for women to obtain salvation in a world in which their agency is severely restricted (for most lower-class women) by lack of economic means and (for sequestered upper-class women) by lack of public access. In these ways, Lakshmi Devi expresses her faith as a devotee in the *brahm* and her sentiments as a middle-class, lower-caste woman. Note, however, that Lakshmi Devi presents not an explicitly self-labeled Hindu identity but, rather, an implicit identity as a devotee of Shastri Brahm. Although most such devotees are Hindu, they also include Muslims and Christians.

Among these devotees are the self-described survivors of Raja Vicitra's family, who live in Ishwarpur some 10 kilometers distant from Arampur. Although their versions of the raja-*brahm*-sultan narrative do not vary greatly from those of most Arampur area residents, these memories support a unique family genealogy with different territorial associations relative to Arampur memories. While the memories among the raja's family express a devotion to Shastri Brahm shared by many nexus residents, ritual differences mark a distinction in identity. An examination of a narrative common to Arampur and Ishwarpur residents shows how group memories are meaningful only within particular social contexts, so that similar narratives do not necessarily engender similar identities. This demonstrates how group memory differs from narrative as an activity. Two narratives may appear the same if structurally similar, but group memory involves an entire dynamic that encompasses social, religious, and historic as well as narrative factors.

One late November morning, I managed to find a ride to Ishwarpur. Arampur area residents often describe this village as the home of the descendants of the raja's daughter who had escaped her family's destruction through her act of kindness to the dying Shastri Pandey. Passing a large, two-storied concrete building atop a small rise to the side of the road leading to this large village, I ask a fellow passenger what it is and am surprised to hear him name it as Raja Vicitra Mahāvidyālay (Raja Vicitra College). My astonishment grows out of a sense that, although a central figure in the group memories of Arampur residents, the raja remains an ethically dubious figure who would hardly merit commemoration through the naming of a college. But, sure enough, a sign worked into the protective metal grille atop the building's main entrance proclaims this as the college's name, with the additional message "Established 1979" indicated below. Later, as I walk through a bazaar in Ishwarpur bathed in the warm sunlight of a cloudless winter sky, a young man stops me to engage in conversation. As a crowd gathers quickly and draws a curtain of dust around us, I ask how the college got its name.

First man: "Other people can say."

Second man: "Raja Vicitra was a raja in Arampur earlier. That's where Shastri Brahm is. Have you been there?"

Me: "Why was that name given to the college?"

Third man: "*Baṃs log yahāṁ hai* (His descendants are here). They named the college. Nehru College in Kendra is named after Jawaharlal Nehru, and so it is with Raja Vicitra College. You've been to Arampur?"

Me: "What is there?"

Fourth man: "A *brahm* temple—Shastri Brahm."

Me: "Why is it special?"

Fourth man: "*Bhūt-pret* (ghosts and spirits) are exorcised there and children prayed for."

Me: "What is the connection between there and here?"

Third man: "Many Rājpūt-Ṭhākur people are from there."

Fourth man: "The temple is very old."

Me: "How old?"

Fourth man: "Six hundred or seven hundred years old. There is Mundeshvari Temple. Here is the path [points westward]."

Me: "Why is Raja Vicitra famous?"

Fourth man: "He was a raja."

Fifth man: "Raja Vicitra was a raja in Arampur. Shastri Brahm was his *purohit* (sacrifier). It was his fort."

Fourth man: "It is an old fort."

Fifth man: "It is an old fort and Shastri Brahm was his *purohit*, his guru. The raja of Ishwarpur and his family are here—Somavahan Thakur."

Fourth man: "The family comes from Suryavahan Thakur."

Fifth man: "The family comes from Suryavahan Thakur. There is a book in English about this."

Me: "When was it written?"

First man: "In the time of the British. Suryavahan Thakur lived in the time of the British." He then asks a question of another bystander before adding, "Lalita Thakur was in the third *sīṛhī* (generation)."

Third man: "If you go to other places, you will see *aitihāsik* (historical) things."

Second man: "In 1947 we got our Independence."

Fifth man: "The English period ended. Then there was no raja."

Me: "Did Raja Vicitra live here?"

Third man: "No. He lived in Arampur fort, which you saw."

Second man: "No, Suryavahan Thakur came here."

Me: "From Arampur?"

Second man: "Yes."

Me: "Why?"

Third man: "Shastri Brahm made a curse and so they came here."

Second man: "Out of fear."

Sixth man: "The principal of Raja Vicitra College [points northward] is Virendra Thakur. He will show you. In another village, Dr. Vajra will tell you about it."

Me: "How do they know?"

Seventh man: "It is their family. They have got the 'history.'"

Me: "Which family?"

Fourth man: "*Ham log* (we people)."

Second man: "Krishna Thakur is the brother of Lalita Thakur. He can tell you the whole story. He is the son of Krishna Thakur" [points at fourth man].

Me, to fourth man: "How do you know about this?"

Fourth man: "*Purāṇa log* (old people) say so—*buzurg* (venerated people)."

Me: "Is the story true?"

Fourth man: "Yes."

Second man: "Yes."

Me: "How do you know?"

Fourth man: "It is our family—old people say so."

Second man: "Go to his [the fourth man's] place and you will see pictures of Lalita Thakur and Suryavahan Thakur, but not any picture of Raja Vicitra."

The fourth man, in his forties, identifies himself as Indra Thakur and invites me to his home. As I accompany him, he says: "In the time of you people, we were rajas. Then when that ended we became farmers. The government doesn't pay attention to us. Raja Vicitra is our greatest *buzurg.*"

This moment of recollection among various Ishwarpur residents looks familiar to other recollections we have already examined. As in previous examples, the public act of recollecting is participatory—in this case directly involving eight men. Through agreement and debate, they fashion a roughly consensual narrative for their audience that includes not only the person to whom they directly address the story in answer to his questions (me) but also, implicitly, those who stand around listening and observing. Although the narrators made authoritative claims for their stories through a text (the book in English) and people (the college principal and the doctor), their principal claim to veracity (and the primary medium of transmission and authorization) comes through an association with old people who "say so." Furthermore, narrators mapped the memories onto their territory through pointing and referred also to places of significance with which they take pride because of an association with their own identities. Finally, they offered traces, in the forms of family portraits and an abandoned fort, as evidence.

Notably different from Arampur memories, however, is the smooth segue in the Ishwarpur example from the time of the arrival of Raja Vicitra's descendants to the British period. In Arampur, the raja-*brahm*-sultan narrative may signal the beginning of both Shastri Brahm devotion and a local Muslim presence, but, for most people, it marks the end of the raja's rule and Arampur's prestige. Although it may connect the residents now with their village then, the intervening time remains little more than a protracted lapse. Significant events (such as Independence) surely occurred during this intervening period, but they exist in the memories of residents as disconnected episodes rarely associated with the raja, *brahm*, or sultan. In contrast, both Indra Thakur and, later, his father, fluently narrated how "the English period" and the period "now" follow the time of Raja Vicitra's rule in Arampur and his descendants' arrival in Ishwarpur.

Two factors contribute to this perceived continuity between the time of Raja Vicitra and the present among the Thakur family (and perhaps among other residents of Ishwarpur). First, the Thakurs maintain their family lineage as a continuous bridge between "now" and "then." As Ricoeur indicated (see chapter 3), lineage works as a tool to overcome the disparity perceived between lived time and cosmic time. Certainly, Arampur residents make their own bridge of identification with the past through the use of Ricoeur's other tools—calendars and traces. However, few I interviewed could recollect the names of ancestors beyond two generations.[9] The Thakurs, by contrast, maintain the memory of many more ancestors, partly because the claims of legitimation for their local rule and landowning rely on an accurate lineage. Second, whereas the British made seemingly little impact on Arampur because their local presence was, for the most part, limited to the somewhat distant administrative center at Kendra, in Ishwarpur the British supported Ṭhākur claims to local control even when this family's rule had degenerated into little more than a glorified *zamīndārī* ("landlordship"). Hence we see the warm memories of the Thakur family for British rule and the unhappy comparison with the government now which, even if it pays only lip service to the ideals of land redistribution, demonstrates far less support for large landowners than did its colonial predecessors.

Not only does the Thakur family trace its lineage back to Raja Vicitra but also they trace their devotion to Shastri Brahm (a.k.a. Shastri Pandey) via the raja as well. Indra Thakur demonstrates this as we stop on the way to his home at a Jagganath temple that he said Suryavahan Thakur had constructed. I ask him and his two relatives who join us there whether they went to Shastri Brahm's temple.

> *First Thakur:* "Yes."
> *Me:* "Do you do *pūjā?*"
> *First Thakur:* "Yes."
> *Me:* "Do you take *prasād?*"[10]
> *First Thakur:* "Yes."

---

9. When I asked women this question, many asked whether I meant the names of the ancestors of their natal home or of their marital home and demonstrated an ability to recollect both. This demonstrates yet again how the dynamic of women's memories and identities differs from men's.

10. A gift empowered through proximity with a superhuman agent.

Second Thakur: "But we do not eat it."

Me: "Why not?"

Indra Thakur: "The *itihās* is like this. Raja Vicitra and his rani destroyed the house of Shastri Brahm and he got angry. He made a curse that 'I will become a *brahm* and destroy your family so that no one will live.' So the raja fled."

Me: "Where?"

Indra Thakur: "Another village. . . . Then those people came here, to Ishwarpur. They said, 'We will build a new fort.'"

Me: "Was that Raja Vicitra?"

Indra Thakur: "No. He died right there [points southward]."

Me: ". . . So why don't you eat the *prasād* of Shastri Brahm?"

Indra Thakur: "*Prān lete*" (It kills).

First Thakur: "*Nās-chati*" (Destruction and harm).

Me: "From Shastri Brahm?"

Second Thakur: "Shastri Brahm put a curse on Vicitra Raja that the *vaṃś* will not continue from a boy, but only from a girl."

Me: "Why only from a girl?"

Second Thakur: "Since there was no boy, it continues from her."

Indra Thakur: "The Raj Kumar family is Raj Kumari."[11]

Me: "Are you from this family?"

First Thakur: "Yes."

Indra Thakur: "We have seven houses. Ishwarpur is the 'head office.'"

Indra then went on to name the other six villages in which the extended family of the Raj Kumari resides.

As in the previously described conversation with Lakshmi Devi, Indra Thakur responded to a question regarding the current worship of Shastri Brahm with a narrative ("history") describing the Brahman's close relationship and falling out with Raja Vicitra. Although these two narrators described roughly similar accounts that imply their shared devotion to Shastri Brahm, their ritual practices reflect a difference in their identities as devotees. Through the act of accepting but not eating the *prasād* of the *brahm*, the Thakurs remember their ancestor's fatal association with Shastri Pandey and his role in the genesis of Shastri Brahm. In further deference to the curse, most Thakurs abstain from drinking the water of Arampur village as well. In this case, conspicuous nonaction works as commemorative action, a form of Connerton's "incorporating practices."

Not only do the Thakurs use this narrative to posit Ishwarpur at the center of a constellation of seven villages and the setting for a shared family identity but also they make it the basis of a village identity claimed on behalf of all Ishwarpur residents. When we reached his home, Krishna Thakur, Indra's father, explained that Thakurs had founded Ishwarpur. Still later, Indra guided

---

11. The suffix *ī* feminizes the name.

me through a tour of the ruined, moated earthen mound, which, like the one in Arampur, served as their well-fortified home when they were the local rajas. There we met Chedi Pandey. He explained that his family, descended from Shastri Pandey and serving as the current *purohits* for the Thakurs, migrated from Arampur to Ishwarpur with the Rājpūt family. Indra Thakur then claimed that all the residents of the village—"Harijan, Nāī, Baraī, Dhobī, Darzī,[12] and Muhammadan too, all"—arrived with them. As we shall see next in the Rājpūt and Paṭhān narrations regarding Lakshman and Loka Singh, such memories serve the landed interests of village elites. While, in this case, the memory also serves the interests of at least one Brahman family in explaining and maintaining its client relationship with the Thakurs, it may also be undercut by crosscurrents or countercurrents of narratives from economically and socially subordinate groups. Meanwhile, while assuming a common village origin and identity, Indra Thakur defined the village according to caste composition. He demonstrates the fluidity of multiple identities by including these groups in his notion of "we-of-this-village" while simultaneously separating "we-of-our-caste" from "those-of-other-castes."

What remains clear throughout is the unique role that the raja-*brahm* narrative plays among the Thakurs of Ishwarpur despite its similarity to versions told by Arampur residents. Although the dynamics of constituent participation and physical mapping remain consistent among these two groups, different issues of social context and group identity mold divergent identities that are marked, in part, through ritual commemorations of nonaction.

A Tale of Two Villages

The narrative concerning Lakshman and Loka Singh demonstrates a shared class and family identity of two groups of landowners, the distinct religious differences between them, and the particular caste differences between not only them but also others in their villages. This narrative, told by some of the residents of the neighboring villages of Naugrah and Swami Sarai, also expresses their effort to associate themselves with the constellation of villages surrounding Arampur by grafting the story of their family onto the central story of Arampur.

One evening, I sit with Waliuddin Khan and some of his relatives in the men's quarters of their family home in Naugrah. While waiting for nightfall, when they would break their Ramẓān fast, Waliuddin Khan mentions Baba Singh of neighboring Swami Sarai. I ask him how long he has known the octogenarian Singh and he replies, "How long?! In the time of Alauddin Khilji there was Lakshman Singh and Loka Singh. They were two Rājpūt brothers. They lived in Rajasthan. Raja Vicitra lived here. The raja had to give *jizya*[13] tax. Baba Singh

---

12. Castes previously known, respectively, as Untouchables, barbers, betel leaf sellers, clothes washers, and tailors.

13. A tax levied by Muslim rulers upon non-Muslim subjects.

and we people were one: we were Rājpūts in Bakhtiyar Khilji's time. The emperor sent his two commanders in chief here. When no tax was sent, a war began. Raja Vicitra was defeated. News was sent to Alauddin but he did not come. *Dillī bhī hai dūr* (Delhi is still far off).[14] The emperor said that this area was too far away, so he gave it to the two brothers. Loka Singh was the older brother. He thought the emperor was well off and that his was a great religion so he converted (*mazhab tabdīl kīyā*)—he changed his *dharm*. Lakshman Singh did not change his religion. Those people (*wo log*) are from Lakshman [gestures toward Swami Sarai with his hand]. We people (*ham log*) are from Loka Singh. Because he converted, we are no longer Rājpūt but Paṭhān.[15] But we are still one. This is only true of Swami Sarai and three other villages. If someone from Naugrah meets someone from Swami Sarai, it's remembered that relations are still close. There is some difference in religion but, still, we are one. If a child was born in Naugrah, those people used to send money" [U/E].

Through his narration, Waliuddin Khan primarily intends to promote a shared identity between his family (Paṭhāns who claim the conferred status of *Dīwān* or minister of state) and that of Baba Singh (Rājpūts of the Vais *gotra* or subcaste). By claiming common descent and describing the conversion of one brother, he recalls a time when his and Baba's families were united while, simultaneously, acknowledging the present division of religion. This memory, shared and communicated as well by the Rājpūt members of this extended family, integrates the two sets of landowners (whose lands adjoin one another's) through a narrative that depicts the common origin of their land (as the emperor's gift) while acknowledging that the two groups cannot be integrated on the level of caste. When asked whether the two families could intermarry, Waliuddin Khan replies in the negative, saying that it is a matter of caste, but made a quick reaffirmation of the closeness of the two groups, caste notwithstanding: "But we feel closer to them than we do to Anṣārīs[16] of this village and other Mussalman. I am a Muslim and the Anṣārī is a Muslim, but I have more love for these people [motions toward Swami Sarai]. *Ye prem kī bāt* (This is a matter of love). It is the same for them with other Hindus" [U/E]. After the conclusion of this conversation and as night falls, one of the sons of Baba Singh arrives to share the meal breaking the fast. As he joins the others in eating from the shared dishes of heaped food, he emphatically declares to me (unaware of the preceding conversation), "*Ye hī merā parivār hai*" (*This* is my family) [H].

As the self-professed male descendants of the brothers repeatedly made a point of attesting, despite the passing of hundreds of years, the men of the two sides of the family consider each other "brothers" to this day. This encourages invitations to one another's weddings, gift exchanges, and visits of Vais Rājpūt men

---

14. A rephrasing of the confident reply given by the Middle Period Sufi Nizamuddin when asked why he did not appear worried that the Tughlaq ruler Ghiyasuddin was marching on Delhi to punish him for ignoring his summons. The ruler miraculously died later just short of his destination.

15. A Muslim caste associated with the tribes of Afghanistan and the Hindu Kush.

16. Anṣārīs are a Muslim caste of lower social status than Paṭhāns.

to the homes of Diwan Khans on the Muslim festival of 'Īd-ul-fiṭr, when it is traditional for family and friends to visit one another. Both Vaīs Rājpūt and Dīwānī Paṭhān residents of the two neighboring villages often interpret the narrative as a lesson in intercommunal harmony. The familial identity (we-descendants-of-Lakshman-and-Loka-Singh) among them overlaps and subverts Hindu and Muslim identities. The narrative can also be interpreted as reinforcing a common class identity among the two groups. Although both of these Rājpūt and Paṭhān families often refer to their villages as though they are the sole inhabitants, in fact each village is comprised of several castes. Waliuddin's comment, "If someone from Naugrah meets someone from Swami Sarai, it's remembered that relations are still close" is not meant to include the numerous non-Rājpūt and non-Paṭhān caste members of these two villages. The Rājpūts and Paṭhāns remain by far the largest landowners of their villages and the most economically and politically powerful inhabitants. Thus, the narrative reflects their sense of appropriation, ownership, and domination of the villages. Each sees their family as synonymous with the village.

Yet, we cannot overlook the fact that the same narrative has countercurrents of interpretation that can undermine the Hindu-Muslim *bhai-bhai* or brotherly interpretation. Some of these countercurrents stem from identities rooted in religious tradition and turn on the interpretation of whether the original Diwan Khan converted out of convenience or conviction. On the one hand, some of the Hindu Rājpūts argue that their converted great-great granduncle sold out his faith. In regard to their Muslim Paṭhān neighbors, they suggest, "We are brothers, but we Rājpūts did not sell our religion for land." On the other hand, some Paṭhāns emphasize that this convert chose Islam once he saw the "truth" in it, implicitly criticizing Hinduism. They insinuate, "We are brothers, but we chose the true religion." In times of tension regarding water rights, land boundaries, or other issues, it can be expected that the overlapping identity of family will be subverted by a religious identity that is communally exclusive (i.e., we-Hindus-as-native versus those-Muslims-as-sellouts or we-Muslims-as-believers versus those-Hindus-as-misbelievers).

This is a strategy found among many aggressive Hindu nationalists and zealously pious Muslims (as well as among many other religious militants elsewhere in the world), who define an orthodox and orthoprax identity according to their visions of a universal ideal of belief and/or practice. During protracted conflicts among groups that define themselves along religious lines, shared identities and local beliefs often give way to radicalized notions of what a "proper" Hindu or Muslim should believe and practice as defined by bellicose groups. In such circumstances, local religious communities may turn to more centralized, perhaps national institutions for identity and direction. The evolution of powerful parties that attempt to harness (if not create) currents of religious and national sentiment to political ambition has quickened the pace of religious nationalism begun in the nineteenth century.[17] Dependent on an

17. Van der Veer, pp. 106–137.

exclusive identity based on an us-them dichotomy, such currents deploy markers of orthodoxy and orthopraxy to delimit and control the group's self-definition. In contrast, many Arampur Hindus and Muslims demonstrate faith in the local belief in the ghost of the dead Hindu Brahman, Shastri Brahm, or in a Sufi's interdiction with a deity without reflex to a notion of exclusive religious identity, as we noted earlier in regard to Lakshmi Devi.

Recent reform and revival movements in north India reverberate in the Arampur area. Many Muslims recall an earlier time when they participated more completely in such "Hindu" holidays as Holī and Dīwālī. But as Hindu-Muslim tensions have risen in north India, more Muslims embrace the exclusionist religious identity promulgated by Islamic revivalists who allege that such participation is un-Islamic. Some local Muslims seemed to be caught between the ideal of intercommunalism and the criticism leveled by conservative Muslims when they would emphatically tell me that they participate in Hindu festivals yet were conspicuously absent.[18] Stuck between his fondness for ideals of intercommunal fraternity and fear of criticism from fellow Muslims, Hamzah Ansari persistently claimed to participate in Hindu festivals yet would seldom be seen doing so. Indeed, the reflex to an austere, noncelebratory ideal provides a convenient avenue of supremacist critique for some Muslim groups. A number of years ago, the residents of Arampur's Qasbah neighborhood prohibited Naugrah's Muslim residents from participating in their Muharram procession because of a ruckus that the latter were alleged to have instigated. Stung by the rebuke to this day, the Naugrah Muslims keep their distance from the mournful participants entirely, criticizing the procession of the *ta'ziya* as un-Islamic.[19] Yet, still some Muslims do participate in Hindu holidays and, among those who do not, many attempt to avoid seeming antagonistic to the religious lives of their neighbors, at least in public. During the Holī season, I asked Muslim residents whether they joined Hindus in the game of throwing brightly colored water on one another that typifies this springtime revel. Almost all said no, although most gave roundabout excuses that avoided any criticism of the festival. One man explained that Holī fell on Friday and so Muslims could not play because they had to participate in the *jum'a namāz* (Friday prayers), the weekly prayers for which most Muslim men assemble in

18. For a penetrating treatment of the debate regarding "non-Muslim" elements in the beliefs and practices among Indonesian Muslims, see John Bowen, *Muslims through Discourse: Religion and Ritual in Gayo Society*. Princeton: Princeton University Press, 1993. Bowen's depiction of the "traditionalist" and "modernist" sides of this debate usefully reveals the complexity of both these terms and their underlying social conditions.

19. Nita Kumar describes how Muharram and 'Īd Milāud-ul-Nabī reveals divisions of social and religious propriety among Muslims. In the course of observing these holidays, Anṣārīs disagree with Wahhabis and Deobandis about the Islamic propriety of certain behavior; Sunnis contest Shiite claims; the rich censure the poor. Each *muhalla* (neighborhood) competes with the other through decorations and the processions. See her "Work and Leisure in the Formation of Identity: Muslim Weavers in a Hindu City" in *Culture and Power in Banaras: Community, Performance, and Environment, 1800–1980*. Berkeley: University of California Press, 1992 (1989), pp. 158–162.

the village's main mosque. When I pressed the issue, asking whether they had celebrated Holī in other years when it did not occur on a Friday, he relented and responded with a touch of irritation that they did not "because we are Mussalman."

According to popular accounts, tensions have also increased with regard to the space that villagers share. Two of the newest temples in the area are Hanuman temples. Many Muslims allege that one of these was deliberately and provocatively situated along the river near the collection of Muslim tombs that includes those of the general Bakhtiyar Khilji and the Sufi Usman Koti. Many local Hindus claim that the broken remains of a Hanuman *mūrti* were discovered in the river, evidence of a temple broken by the Muslim invaders, and rightfully restored. It is probably no coincidence that these local temples, dedicated to one of the dominant figures in the *Rāmacaritamānas*—a central devotional book for both locals and the BJP, VHP, and RSS—have risen at this time. Currently, Hindu nationalists have tried to stir Ram devotionalism into a national whirlpool of chauvinist sentiment and disrupted the current of secular nationalism.[20]

Other contestations of space highlight a struggle over the definition of communal identities. Certain local residents attempt to define sites as "Hindu" and "Muslim" through narratives that reflect the supposedly essential quality of those identities. Perhaps following national leaders, some local Hindus construct narratives and point to local relics as evidence of we-Hindus-as-sophisticated-natives and those-Muslims-as-invaders even while others plead tolerance.

Watching the cremation of a Harijan whose family could not afford to transport him to Banaras for the ritual, a sadhu, Dinanta Tirth, and his son, Shivaji, talk with me one evening. As the corpse slowly broils beneath the mound of dried cow dung patties and the few logs of wood that the low castes could afford, Shivaji, a Rājpūt from Malik Sarai, asks in Hindi if I know about "the tomb," as he points toward that of Bakhtiyar Khilji. He explains that in "the Hindu period" the tomb was a temple. When I query how he knows about this, he says that the sandstone material and lotus adornments used in the construction of the tomb were the same as those used by Raja Vicitra to construct his fortress. When I ask whether the lotus figures on the Taj Mahal means that it had been a temple as well, he replies, "I'm not very knowledgeable, but I read a book which said that the Taj Mahal was really the Raj Mahal. The Mussalman came here and destroyed so many Hindu buildings. They gave money to Hindus to become Mussalman. Look, between that village [points at Naugrah] and ours [points at Swami Sarai] there were two brothers: Lakshman Singh and Loka Singh. Alauddin Khilji brought them to Delhi. He said, 'If you become a Mussalman then you can get good work and a *sūbedārī*.'"[21]

---

20. For a portrayal of the current surge of Hanuman temple renovation and construction set within the long history of Hanuman devotion, see Philip Lutgendorf, "My Hanuman Is Bigger Than Yours" in *History of Religions*, vol. 33, no. 3 (1994), pp. 211–245.

21. An appointment as governor of a province.

The older brother became a Mussalman and got a Delhi *dīwānī*[22] —he became Diwan Khan. They came to fight the raja. . . . Diwan Khan gave his brother a village. You can ask them; they say that they come from Hindu culture. They are a 'mini-Pakistan' for us."

> At this point, Dinanta Tirth protests, "No."
>
> His son continues, "They are not educable."
>
> *Dinanta:* "That is not *itihās* (history)."
>
> *Shivaji:* "They disturb Hindus wherever they are."
>
> *Dinanta:* "If it is always 'Hindu-Mussalman this, Hindu-Mussalman that,' then the reason for the differences between us is that *ham log nahiṁ jānte* (we people don't understand [one another])."
>
> *Shivaji:* "Mussalman are killing Hindus everywhere."
>
> *One of the Harijan bystanders:* "That is not true."
>
> *Dinanta:* "The problems are due to misunderstandings. There are different paths but they lead to the same place. Imagine that you want to go to Jagahpur. So you can go on that path [points in an arc eastward]. I can go on this path [points on an arc northward]. This is what is called *māyā*."[23]

Shivaji's argument demonstrated a certain trajectory of reasoning. First, he claimed that a famous place commonly associated with a Muslim (i.e., the tomb of Bakhtiyar Khilji) actually was built by a Hindu raja in a "Hindu period." Second, through reference to the authority of a book, he made a similar claim for a space commonly emblematic of India and Muslim history (i.e., the Taj Mahal). Third, Shivaji referred to a group of local Muslims and depicted their transition from Hindu-thus-Indian to Muslim-thus-foreigner through the narrative of their ancestor's conversion of convenience and their current condition as an alien and enemy state within India (i.e., "mini-Pakistan"). As such, they continue the violence against Hindus begun by Muslims-as-invaders under the more contemporary form of Muslims-as-internalized-invaders. Fourth, Shivaji casts them on the poorer side of another common identification often used to deride groups considered unsavory: educated versus uneducated. Ultimately, then, Shivaji tried to prove that all is not as it seems. The good is the product of we-Hindus-as-sophisticated-natives. Conflict is the product of those-Muslims-as-invaders. The space where the two might overlap (i.e., Muslim-as-sophisticate) is erased by claiming the evidence of such (i.e., Bakhtiyar Khan's tomb and the Taj Mahal) is not as it seems (i.e., "Hindu," not "Muslim"). This strategy has been adopted by P. N. Oak's school of revisionist history, which has published such books as *The Taj Mahal Is a Hindu Palace* and *Agra Red Fort Is a Hindu Building*.

Significantly, Dinanta protested his son's views by denying not the communal identities but, rather, the particular characteristics ascribed to them. Implicitly recognizing both the commonality and the corrosive effect of the Mus-

---

22. A ministerial office.

23. The Hindu concept that the world as perceived by the senses is temporary and illusionary.

lim-as-invader idea, he dismisses such characterizations as the fruit of misunderstanding between the members of the two religious traditions. Satadal Dasgupta, whose work we examined in chapter 2, strove to show how groups integrate their identity at the level of *gram, thana,* and the like. Shivaji's rhetoric, however, strives for the *disintegration* of a Muslim Indian identity—alienating Muslims from India as a homeland and portraying them not only as outsiders to India but also as a threat.

In summary, the narrative of the two brothers provides the basis for both separate village identities and a shared family identity. The Paṭhān residents of Naugrah often refer to their village as though they are the sole inhabitants. Their narrative of its founding by Diwan Khan (born Loka Singh) establishes their family as the village originators and owners in the same way that the Vaīs Rājpūts claim Swami Sarai as their own. In other words, this narrative not only reflects how their local family identities have become conflated with their village identities but also acts as a vehicle for this end. Bound by common concerns for family identity and landowning validation, the various strands of individual narratives unite into parallel streams of Dīwānī Paṭhān and Vaīs Rājpūt memory. Crosscurrents of communal tension always linger, although they remain fairly insignificant until divisive issues regarding land or water rights split and submerge the Paṭhān-Rājpūt stream of family narrative. Narratives of group memory, then, express communal identities—both assumed for oneself (e.g., Muslim-as-believer and Indian-as-Hindu) and projected onto others (e.g., Hindu-as-misbeliever and Muslim-as-sellout)—which replace fraternal identity (i.e., we-descendants-of-Lakshman-and-Loka-Singh). This process works with others as well through both rituals and beliefs that can support either antagonistically communal identities, fraternally communal identities, or entirely noncommunal identities.

New Village/Stolen Village

Despite Dīwānī Paṭhān and Vaīs Rājpūt rhetoric, they are not the only caste groups to inhabit their respective villages. Among Naugrah and Swami Sarai's populations, nearly 10% and more than 15% are Scheduled Castes alone, respectively.[24] Inhabitants belonging to these groups often identify their subaltern caste group with their village through their own narratives that self-consciously subvert the narratives of the economically dominant castes. At first glance, these would seem to express a set of antagonistic, communalist dualities such as Muslim-as-foreign-invader versus Hindu-as-native and Muslim-as-landowner

---

24. Current census surveys do not report any caste figures except for Scheduled Tribes and Scheduled Castes. These labels derive from the British-devised system of caste categorization, still in use in contemporary India, which ranks and classifies castes according to their presumed social status as (from highest to lowest) Forward Castes, Other Backward Castes, and Scheduled Castes. Members of tribal groups comprise the category of Scheduled Tribes.

versus Hindu-as-oppressed. However, further analysis will demonstrate the complexity of the identities with which some of the subaltern castes understand themselves and their neighbors. Herein we find identities nested within identities and identities that can assume a label in some contexts and then define themselves with an opposite label in another.

This complex dynamic becomes clear in Naugrah's Chamtol, as one of four Harijan[25] men lounging on hemp-strung *cārpāī* calls to me from beneath the open-walled, thatched roof, where they take shelter from the April sun. After asking if I had met with another Harijan of their neighborhood with whom they knew I was to share a meal, Asvagriva Ram asks suddenly, "Will you write *garīb kā itihās* ('a history of the poor')?" [H]. I reply that if he would tell me, I would write it.[26] "Look at this poverty," he says, referring to the neighborhood around us—dried mud–walled homes in various states of repair, open drainage, and a montage of farm animals. I ask why it was like this, and he answers, "They came from a village in another *thānā* (police district). Before, the village was all Hindu. We all had our land taken away by force. Look at these children," he says as he points to some who stand in grim, gray clothes nearby. "They have only food." When I ask who had come from that village, another of the men, Dasvan, answers simply, "Khan."

> *Ekavir:* "Mussalman. They came and everyone fled."
> *Nanda:* "There were fifty houses before and then everyone fled."
> *Dasvan:* "After one or two days everyone fled."
> *Ekavir:* "Koiri[27] had land, but they all fled."
> *Dasvan:* "If we go to the police station [to file a grievance], maybe no one will listen."
> *Me:* "Even now?"
> *Dasvan:* "Yes."
> *Ekavir:* "*Naugrah* means 'nine houses.' All of them were Hindu."
> *Dasvan:* "After this everyone fled."
> *Me:* "But *Nanda* said that there were fifty houses here."
> *Ekavir:* "They grew from nine to fifty."
> *Me:* "Where did those who fled go?"
> *Ekavir and Dasvan together:* "To the mountains—here and there" [gesticulating with widely flung arms].
> *Dasvan:* "They went to Jagahpur and Bari."

25. Gandhi coined the euphemism *Harijan* (Children of God) in an attempt to provide Untouchable low-caste Hindus with a more positive identity. Although some resent this label today, many low-caste nexus residents use it in reference to themselves. None use the term *Dalit* (oppressed, crushed) preferred by many national leaders of this group.

26. Remembering Narayana Rao's earlier point that many Indian oral traditions refer to a written source as a claim to authority, even when the existence of such a source is doubtful, we note that in this conversation, Chamtol residents look to an outsider to produce a written source which they do not have otherwise. Personal conversation, September 27, 1996.

27. Included in the Other Backward Castes group.

Ekavir: "This was all a *bastī* (settlement)."

Me: "How much land did you used to have?"

Ekavir: "Everyone had fifty *bīghā*s, one hundred *bīghā*s, twenty *bīghā*s.[28] Today this group has nothing and it's *that* group which has everything."

Me: "When did this happen?"

Ekavir: "Old men—men with beards [strokes an imaginary beard]—they can say. What can we say?"

Dasvan: "Those people eat water buffalo. *Ham log* (we people) drink milk. We don't eat water buffalo."

Nanda: "They eat cows, water buffalo, and oxen."

Typical of many north Indian villages, the Harijans of Naugrah live in a *muhalla* known in Hindi and Urdu as a *camṭol*, isolated at the southern extreme of the settlement. Although fairly removed from the main avenues of the village, Chamtol residents know the comings, goings, and business of many in the area—especially strangers. So the four men relaxing under the roof knew not only of the meal that I was to share that day with one of their neighbors but also of my ongoing conversations with the Diwan Khans regarding their past. Perhaps knowing that I had been talking with the wealthy of their village, Asvagriva asked me if I would write the history of the poor, thus evidencing one dimension of his identity, that of an impoverished person. The narrative that he used to explain this poverty establishes a duality between two sets of identities. On the one side are his ancestors, the original inhabitants of the village known for its nine houses, whom he typifies as "Hindu." Juxtaposed with these are the outside interlopers whom he and the others identified interchangeably as "Muslim" and "Khan." Although not explicitly linked with the stories of the two Rājpūt brothers or the raja, *brahm*, and sultan, this collaborative narrative echoes the themes of a Muslim invasion that displaced Hindu inhabitants. The identities of Hindu-as-native and Muslim-as-invader find yet another expression.

But the characterization of these two identities that follows the narrative makes their juxtapositioning more extreme. The description of "those people" as consumers of beef and of "we people" as those who do not radicalizes the Muslim-as-invader into Muslim-as-antipode. That is to say, the commentary of Dasvan and Nanda describes *Muslim* not only as non-Hindu and nonnative but also as the *exact opposite* of *Hindu*. Subsequent conversation proves even more demonstrative of this point, following my question of why some nearby children were not in school. In the meantime, an audience of neighbors slowly increases the number of observers and participants.

Dasvan: "They are too poor. Their father cannot buy the books."

Ekavir: "If a boy goes to study, they will not let him and will ask, 'Why do you want to study?'"

---

28. "A measure of land (the official or *sarkārī bīghā* equals about five-eighths of an acre; a *kaccā bīghā* varies from a quarter to a third of an acre)." R. S. McGregor, ed. *The Oxford Hindi-English Dictionary.* Delhi: Oxford University Press, 1993, p. 738.

Me: "Who would do this?"

Ekavir: "*Gāṁv vāle—Paṭhān log*" (Villagers—Paṭhān people).

Me: "What about the Anṣārīs?"

Ekavir: "When the Khans came, they told others, 'Mussalman live here so come along.'"

Me: "When did this happen?"

Dasvan: "At the time of Congress."

Ekavir: "No."

Nanda: "At the time of the English."

Dasvan: "No. During the time of the zamindars."

Ekavir: "No, when the raja was zamindar."

Me: "Who was the raja?"

Ekavir: "Before there were Rājpūts here, then the Mussalman looted the area. The Mussalman cut the *cuṭṭī*."[29]

At this comment, everyone, children and adults alike, laughs.

Me: "What is the joke?"

Ekavir: "They cut here [pointing to the back of his scalp] and there [pointing to his penis] and became Mussalman."

First newcomer: "When we cut an animal's throat, we cut once. They cut back and forth" [demonstrates with his hand].

Ekavir: "*Ḥalāl*"[30]

Me: "Why do they do it that way?"

First newcomer: "*La ilāha illā-llāh*[31] they say as they cut" [All laugh].

Me: [Referring to a settlement physically discontinuous from Naugrah whose residents often claim to be a separate village, although officially it remains part of Naugrah] "Is Namazgarh part of Naugrah or not?"

Dasvan: "There is only one village."

Me: "Why is it separate?"

Dasvan: "Hindus who eat fish live there."

Me: "Why is there a division?"

Dasvan: "We are separate. We have separate *pān-khān* (customs of eating)."

Me: "Is this a *ṭola* (neighborhood)?"

Dasvan: "This is Chamtol because Camārs[32] live here."

Me: "Who are the others who live in Naugrah?"

Dasvan: "Hindus and Mussalman—two *jāti*s (caste groups), but no names for their *ṭol*s."

29. The long, thin strand of hair remaining at the back of the scalp after a Hindu ritual shave of the rest of the head.

30. Rules of purity according to Islamic law.

31. The Islamic profession of faith (*kalima* or *shahāda*): "There is no god but God."

32. A Hindu caste associated with the ritually defiling work of leather crafting and, therefore, considered among the lowest status of Untouchable groups. Today, many members prefer the caste name Mochi.

Second newcomer: "Mussalman are *faqīr*. He is Telī, Ahīr, Bind [pointing to three different men in the shelter]. All are Hindu. I am a Camār. Mussalman pray in a mosque, Hindus in a temple."

Once again in this conversation, these residents of Chamtol referred to a narrative in their answers to my questions regarding their social condition while also casting the Diwan Khans of the village as both oppressors and antipodal characters. So, when asked why some children stood watching us instead of studying in school, Dasvan explained that they were too poor to afford books, and Ekavir elaborated that the Pathāns prohibit them from studying. Because the Ansārīs depend on the Pathāns, who own the carpet-making enterprises and agricultural land on which they subsist, Ekavir might have seen them and his group as similarly subservient to the Pathāns. Instead, however, Ekavir opts to align the Ansārīs with the Pathāns as Muslims by connecting their arrival to the narrative of Muslim invasion and settlement of the village. In other words, although cognizant of a division within the category Muslim-as-invader, in this conversation Ekavir prefers to depict the Ansārīs and Pathāns as members of this same category instead of contrasting Ansārīs-as-oppressed with Pathāns-as-oppressors.

The Chamtol residents, after a brief debate involving the assertion and correction of the group memory in regard to the dating of the Pathān invasion, then took the opportunity to characterize their oppressors as those-Muslims-as-antipode. With the assistance of two of their neighbors who joined the conversation in its middle, the residents contrasted their behavior and beliefs with those of Muslims—Pathān and Ansārī alike. These speakers ridiculed the Muslim rites of male circumcision, animal slaughter, and reciting the *shahāda*. They cast these activities as markers of difference, just as some Muslims do when they joke about Hindu cow reverence, *mūrti* worship, and polytheism.

Yet, as the dialogue continued, these Harijans reveal more complex dimensions of their identities that problematize any simple understanding of "Hindu." When asked about a separate settlement to the south of Naugrah (whose residents often declare themselves an autonomous village), Dasvan distinguished its residents as a different kind of Hindu (i.e., those who eat fish), distinctive in their different dietary customs (i.e., *pān-khān*). When queried about his neighborhood, Dasvan described it as Chamtol because (we) Camārs live there and portrayed the other residents of Naugrah as "Hindus and Mussalman—two *jātis*, but no names for their *tols*." At this turning point in the conversation, then, some of the discussants depicted Naugrah as a village of three *jātis*: Camārs, Hindus, and Muslims. Each has separate *tols*, but only Chamtol has a specific name. The second newcomer reinforced this point by distinguishing between Muslims (as *faqīr*), Hindus (such as the Telī, Ahīr, Bind among us), and Camārs (himself). This stands in significant contrast with the notion of Camārs included among we-Hindus-as-natives who once occupied Naugrah before the coming of the Pathāns. Ekavir had described this period in terms of his village's residents: "All of them were Hindu." The contrast that Ekavir,

Dasvan, and Nanda had depicted earlier between we-Hindus-as-native and those-Muslims-as-invaders (including themselves, as Camārs, in the former group) in their narrative of the past shifted when the discursive context changed, focusing on the present composition of the village.

This particular shifting of self-identification most dramatically demonstrates our thesis that individuals live with multiple group identities, any one of which may be forefronted in one social context and backgrounded in another. In the first half of this conversation, Ekavir, Dasvan, and Nanda forefronted their identities as we-Hindus-as-natives in their narrative of those-Muslims-as-invaders who seized their village and wealth. The change in discursive context (which included the development of a larger and more diverse audience) inspired a change in their self-identification to we-Camārs in juxtaposition to those-Hindus and those-Muslims. In other words, these speakers can at one time consider their identity as *Camār* to be nested within the larger identity of *Hindu* while, in another context, *Camār* stands outside *Hindu*. The participants' identities recrystallize in different forms around different issues. In regard to the loss of village and wealth to the Muslim invaders, some of Naugrah's Camārs find common cause with other local non-Muslim castes and thus formulate an all-encompassing identity of *Hindu*. However, in regard to the physical plan of their village, in which caste groups live in segregated neighborhoods, the participants' identity reorients around the issue of spatial exclusion. This particular issue casts *Camār* as other to *Hindu* because of circumstances that led their *muhalla* to be labeled according to its low-caste occupants, although Naugrah has no other neighborhood, besides Namazgarh, with a distinguishing name.

Just as economic oppression leads the Camārs of Naugrah to integrate their identity with the other non-Muslims of Naugrah as we-Hindus-as-natives and we-Hindus-as-oppressed, so ritual exclusion disintegrates this identity and creates one of we-Camārs-as-excluded relative to those-Hindus-as-excluders. The unscheduled castes in a number of villages exclude Camārs and other Harijans from participation in various rituals. During Kālī Pūjā, Hindu men and boys run through their village settlements and circumambulate the field boundaries before joining women and girls from the village at the Kali temple or *Kālīsthān* (Kali shrine) on the village's eastern extremity. There they conclude the *pūjā* with the sacrifice of animals through either their physical release or their death. In many villages, Harijans must execute their ritual either the day before or the day after. They also face everyday discrimination. Some Harijans complained that the Brahmans who tend the Shastri Brahm temple ban their entry because of their caste. Many slip in anyway in pursuit of their devotions.

Hindus, Harijans, and Muslims often understand this exclusion to be the result of upper-caste allegations of ritual impurity regarding Harijans. "We are thought to be *gandā* (dirty)," said one Camār member of Naugrah's Chamtol in reference to upper-caste attitudes to his caste. Although few Camārs do leatherwork, other castes often associate them with this "traditional" task, considered degrading by many. One of his neighbors added, "Those who have the sacred thread [mimics a Brahman winding it around his ear as is customary before bathing or defecating] want to be *pāk* (pure)."[33] The first explained that despite his family's change in profession, the family name carries the stigma of leatherwork.[34] The Harijan caste identity can find itself either in league or at odds with those whom Harijans identify as Hindus—sometimes finding themselves included while at other times not. More broadly, the identity of *Hindu* disintegrates in electoral politics, in which the media and general opinion predict the impact of "vote blocs" such as Harijan, Brahman, Ṭhākur, Yādav, and Muslim. But, of course, the identity of *Muslim* disintegrates in various social contexts as well.

This disintegration among Muslims becomes apparent particularly in terms of status and occupational groups. Although some Muslim residents protest against any notion of division among the *umma* (the community of Muslims), many more refer to the difference between and within two particular sets of Muslim groups. The first set consists of three endogamous groups often described as "forward castes." These include Sayyid, Shaikh, Mugal, and Paṭhān. *Sayyid* refers to descendants of the Prophet Muhammad through Fatimah and Ali. *Shaikh* is an honorific term for a respected man with political or spiritual authority. *Mugal* implies descent from the formerly ruling Mugal dynasty. *Paṭhān* suggests a lineage stemming from Afghanistan.

The second set of Muslims, described as *birādarī*s (brotherhood, kinsfolk, community) include exogamous groups delineated by occupation. As mentioned in chapter 1, many of these groups changed their titles as part of a series of movements among Hindu and Muslim low castes to improve their social status at the turn of this century. The weavers abandoned the self-referential title *Julaha* for *Anṣārī*.[35] Many of these new names derive from historically special status groups in the *umma*. In the example of the Julaha, this group's adopted name derives from *Anṣār*, the Prophet Muhammad's name for the believers in the city of Medina, the first community to adopt Islam outside his native Mecca. Similarly, *Quresh* is the name of the Prophet Muhammad's tribe

33. Residents who identify themselves as "Hindu," "Muslim," and "Harijan" can be found who accuse members of the other groups of exclusion on the basis of purity. "Because of *chūt* (defilement)," one Muslim resident said, "Brahmans and Kṣatriyas will not eat with Mussalman or Harijans." Some Hindus make the reverse charge against Muslims while many other Hindu and Muslim residents explain that this was something of the past.

34. In an attempt to escape the stigma of their caste name, many Harijans not only change that name but also convert to other religions, most notably Christianity, Islam, and Buddhism. For example, a Harijan in Tamil Nadu adopted Islam and changed his name from S. Ramachandran to A. Rehamatullah. He explained, "[High-caste Thevars] never called me by my name but my caste. Now they cannot do that." V. R. Mani, "Caste Oppression Forcing Harijans to Convert to Islam" in the *Times of India*, New Delhi (August 9, 1994), p. 8.

35. Nita Kumar, *The Artisans of Banaras: Popular Culture and Identity, 1880–1986*. New Delhi: Orient Longman, 1995 (1988), p. 153. Kumar also provides a brief yet excellent insight into the commonalties and conflicts between Anṣārīs and other Muslim "lineages" or castes in "Work and Leisure," p. 153.

from which Muslim butchers derive *Qureshī*, their self-appropriated title. Other groups retain occupational titles that they share with Hindus who do the same work, such as the Dhobī clothes washers and Telī oil pressers. In all, residents identified fifteen groups from both sets, often referring to each as a *jāti* or "caste." When first asked, many Muslim residents explained that members of this large set of Muslims could intermarry. When pressed, however, they admitted that the Muslim groups of the lower-status set could not marry into the higher one. "In Bihar and Uttar Pradesh, there is no intercaste marriage," one Muslim told me before employing a common explanation for the divergence between ideals and realities, "This is because of illiteracy."[36]

Of course, these examples of endogamous, exogamous, and occupational groups are but some of the ways in which the identity of *Muslim*, understood as a caste name by many residents, fractures into subgroups. Overall, although the importance of caste for Indian identity formation has been a topic of ongoing debate in Western scholarship, we can see here that caste *can* become the ascendant identity for an individual, depending on personal disposition, social context, and contemporary circumstances. In other words, it would be best to understand caste not as the essence of an individual but as one particle of association among many particles which, together, comprise the atom of the individual's overall identity. Caste, like all of the other constitutive particles, has no fixed place or dominance within the atom but reorients itself relative to the atoms around it in response to the changing circumstances of its environment. Each atom exists in a dynamic situation that changes according to its association with surrounding atoms and molecules. Just as electricity may cause a crystal's atoms to realign into another molecular configuration, social dynamics may *prompt* the individual (who has volition, whereas an atom does not) to reassociate with another group or groups.

At times, circumstances may even induce the individual to orient herself or himself toward two identities at the very same time. One instance of this can be found during the biannual *pūjā* to the protective *pret* of Malik Sarai. Like many protective guardians of north Indian villages, Di Baba used to sit at the perimeter of the inhabited part of Malik Sarai. However, this village has expanded recently to the point that various castes have spun off neighborhoods unattached to the central village, like moons evolving out of the spare mass of a planet and settling into distinct orbits of their own.

As others sitting with us in Arampur Bazaar busied themselves in conversation one evening, I ask the young Mahagriva Singh about the *piṇḍa*[37] sitting atop a meter-high, cubelike platform on the path leading west from the central portion of Malik Sarai to outlying neighborhoods and villages. "I heard

---

36. In Uttar Pradesh, a representative of the Backward Muslim Morcha ("Front") has complained about discrimination by high-caste Muslims and warned than many lower castes were in danger of conversion by Christian and Buddhist missionaries. He added that they sought common cause with Hindu low-castes. "BMM's Threat to Defy 'Fatwas'" in the *Times of India, Lucknow* (July 21, 1994), p. 7.

37. A cone or mound of clay, stone, concrete, or other material used for the veneration of a deity.

that he was a Yādav caste and someone killed him. He became a type of *pret* who used to cause problems. So he said, 'If you do *pūjā* to me, I won't trouble you.' So his is the *mūtri* there—it is not a *mūtri*, it is a stone. It is not in the shape of a *mūtri*." I ask how he knew about this. "I do not know all about it. Someone in my *jāti* killed him—I don't know which house he was from" [H].

This *pūjā* that Di Baba demanded reaffirms simultaneously both village and caste identities. When asked who does *pūjā* to Di Baba, Mahagriva responded that one or two families of one caste are deputed to do daily *pūjā* to him. However, he added, the whole village of Malik Sarai, including Mahagriva's family, does *pūjā* to him once every 2 years during the Hindi month of Sāvan on the same day as Kālī Pūjā. At that time, all the villagers bear the responsibility for the ritual, with Mālī caste members bringing the fruit, Gaḍerī members providing the requisite sheep, and every adult male offering at least two rupees for expenses.

Meanwhile, a commonly known narrative reaffirms the centrality of the village to the *pūjā*, while it also marks the disparity of power often involved in caste differences. Upon my asking how Di Baba died, Mahagriva explains: "The reason, as I heard it, was that he was a servant for a landowner. There was some *sindūr*[38] on his clothing. The landlord thought that it was from one of the women [of his house]. This was not the case, but he killed him anyway." Mahagriva's narrative demonstrates the disparity in social status and power that allows the imagined possibility of Rājpūts—his caste—to commit a capital crime without consequence against a member of a caste that he would consider "lower" or "smaller." The narrator identifies himself according to caste and village affiliation while acknowledging a social order wherein the wronged may find judicial satisfaction only through powers provided postmortem through a superhuman agent. The lesson of this narrative is not lost on the less privileged castes of Malik Sarai, whose versions may vary in every manner but in the caste affiliations of the characters.[39]

Whereas Mahagriva Singh discerned from the memory of Di Baba a particular conclusion about the place of his high-status caste in his village, a member of a low-status caste of the same village interprets the narrative—and his identity—in a very different way. Kalikan Gond's home stands opposite the *piṇḍa* of Di Baba in the Gond caste settlement created just 4 years ago. It straddles the old boundary of the inhabited core of Malik Sarai. When he invites me into his house for water as I passed one day, I take the opportunity to ask him about the *piṇḍa*. "That is Di Baba," he replies. "Who is that?" I query. "*Devatā*—if there is a problem, he brings results." When asked if he had been

---

38. A red powder used, among other purposes, by women to trace a line in the part of their hair to mark their married status.

39. Diane Coccari explores similar issues of village and caste identity in her "Protection and Identity: Banaras's Bīr Babas as Neighborhood Guardian Deities" in *Culture and Power in Banaras: Community, Performance, and Environment, 1800–1980*, Sandria Freitag, ed. Berkeley: University of California Press, 1992 (1989), pp. 130–146.

a person, Kalikan answers, "Before." I then asked if there was a story behind him, and Kalikan's father replies in Bhojpuri as his son translates into Hindi: "He lived here. Some people took him into the jungle and killed him. Then they made a *sthāpan* ('established place') and did *pūjā* there." I ask him to explain further. He continues, "When some Rājpūts went to the jungle to hunt birds, they killed him."

Me: "Why?"

Kalikan's father: "They thought mistakenly that Baba was a bad person."

Me: "And after that?"

Kalikan's father: "They knew they'd made a mistake when *sindūr* began to appear on the heads of Rājpūt women without them putting it there."

He goes on to explain that every *qom* (community) in the village still does *pūjā* to Baba, whom he identifies as Yādav in caste "like Laloo," referring to Bihar's scandalous erstwhile chief minister.

As so commonly happened, Baba Singh (Mahagriva's father) offered yet another dimension to the issue at hand, demonstrating that shared family, caste, and village identities do not necessitate a common interpretation of shared memories. One day after talking with his son about Di Baba, I ask him about his village's guardian. This venerable man, who had immediately upon my arrival in the area taken it upon himself to teach me everything possible about the locality—from the story of Shastri Brahm to the way to call chickens—sniffs disapprovingly at the question. "He protects the village," he replies in Hindi.

Me: "Who is he?"

Baba: "It is only a belief."

Me: "Do you believe it?"

Baba: "No."

Me: "How do you know about him?"

Baba: "I do not know. He is very old. The world advances, so these things disappear. Shastri Brahm was nothing before."

Me: "Since when has Shastri Brahm been growing?"

Baba: "A long time. In the last twenty years a lot has happened."

Me: "How old is the temple?"

Baba: "Less than twenty years old."

Me: "Why did it grow?"

Baba: "Faith—blind faith."

Me: "Do you believe in Shastri Brahm?"

Baba: "No."

Me: "Do you believe in Di Baba?"

Baba: "No one knows the story—'he said and he said'—it's only like that."

Me: "How do you know about it?"

Baba: "*Apne, apne viśvās*" (To each one's own belief).

In his own way, Baba Singh demonstrated a crucial point for the issue at hand: no identity is monolithic. Baba Singh mildly resented what he perceived to be my expectation that he would believe in the power of Di Baba, or any *pret* for that matter. Certainly, his understanding of himself as both a Rājpūt and resident of Malik Sarai does not require belief in Di Baba, yet his final sentence recognized that this belief belongs to him through his community *and* that he reserves the ability to disregard that belief without eschewing his identity. Furthermore, he implicitly affirmed the dynamic nature of memory and identity when he refused to embrace a faith story concerning caste and village that his own son accepts while continuing to share the same family, caste, and village identity as Mahagriva.

Group memories, then, operate in a dynamic fashion, mediated through the intersubjectivity of individual interactions within multiple, shifting social contexts. Composed of myriad strands of individual narratives, they nevertheless may coalesce into powerful streams that challenge and, at times, subvert alternative narratives. However, like the identities that they often serve and express, each strand or stream never stands in a vacuum but, rather, moves in everchanging relation and tension with others. Individuals live with multiple identities and so can never be reduced to any one group association. Instead, they maneuver among multiple associations, some of which may be at odds with others. Through social interaction, individuals may conform to, complement, or challenge the group memories narrated by others. Whatever the result, the process expresses the identities invested in the issues. Without denying the prevalence and pungency of religious identities among many Arampur residents, we have seen how unsatisfactory depictions of the nexus would be without an appreciation for the dynamic quality of their multiple identities, as expressed in their narrated memories. With these examples of individual narrations in place, we turn to examine in the final chapter more institutionalized expressions of group memory and the identities that impel them and that they foster.

5

Institutions of Integration
and Disintegration

The Healing Sufi, the Exorcist *Brahm*, and the Arrogant Raja: Authority and Efficacy among the Dead

> Why bump your head on the ground,
>   why bathe your body in water?
> You kill and call yourself 'humble'—
>   but your vices you conceal.
>
> What's the use of ablutions, litanies, purifications
>   and prostrations in the mosque?
> If you pray with a heart full of guile
>   what's the use of *Haj* and *Kaaba*?
>
> Twenty-four times the Brahman keeps the eleventh-day fast,
>   while the Qāzī observes the Rāmzan:
> Tell me, why does he set aside the eleven months
>   to seek spiritual fruits in the twelfth?
>
> Hari dwells in the East, they say,
>   and Allah resides in the West,
> Search for Him in your heart, in the heart of your heart:
>   there He dwells, *Rahīm–Rām*!
>
> All men and women ever born
>   are nothing but forms of yourself:
> Kabīr is the child of *Allah-Rām*:
>   He is my Guru and my Pīr.[1]

Typical of the iconoclastic songs of the Middle Period devotional poet Kabir, these lines mock certain Hindu and Islamic traditions and those who unreflectively follow them. Kabir rhetorically questions Brahmans who keep

1. Charlotte Vaudeville, *A Weaver Called Kabir: Selected Verses with a Detailed Biographical and Historical Introduction.* Delhi: Oxford University Press, 1997, pp. 217–218.

135

their fasts and facetiously derides Muslims who practice *namāz*, the basic daily prayer, for only bumping their heads on the ground. He eschews mortal gurus and Sufi *pīrs* (spiritual teachers) for the one, authentic spiritual guide. True faith, Kabir argues, cannot be found in external places, practices, or teachers but only within the devout heart. Yet, Kabir's portrayal of his belief in "Allah-Rām" (and, obviously, that name itself) derives from and is expressed in language that comes from Hindu and Islamic traditions.

Although relatively few in the contemporary Arampur nexus consciously model their religious lives via Kabir's caustic critique and unique synthesis of Hinduism and Islam, a great many exercise their religiosity in ways quite dissimilar from the portrait of Indian religions drawn by many scholars. Just as Kabir ignored orthodoxy and orthopraxy in his search for a mystical experience of the god he commonly called Ram, many Hindus and Muslims throughout north India pursue their personal ends outside the narrow religious categories that these scholars depict as Hinduism and Islam. Too many scholars see Hindus and Muslims as inhabiting religious worlds of discrete practices and beliefs and little overlap, without properly recognizing the intercommunal nature of so much of popular north Indian religiosity. As with our understanding of Kabir, whose unique religious vision cannot be entirely understood apart from its Hindu and Islamic context, we must recognize the traditional sources of current practices and beliefs *and* the manner in which many nexus residents borrow freely from these sources and their lexicons without regard for their supposed religious identities as Hindu or Muslim. This is particularly true in the folk practice of visiting sites associated with the healing dead.

Previous scholarship has identified certain tombs and temples throughout South Asia that have become centers of spiritual healing through their association with the personality, space, and power of certain "dead" individuals. Devotees often learn of and communicate these elements through narratives describing events in the life, death, and afterlife of the healer. These narratives demonstrate that the veneration of dead healers draws from and belongs to more than just one tradition. To explore the tradition-specific and intercommunal aspects of religious healing in India, we will examine the group memories surrounding the temple of a *brahm* and the tomb of Sufi in Arampur. Then, we will analyze the uses of narrative by local residents to describe both the authority and the efficacy of the powers that they seek to access. Whereas the narrative components that demonstrate authority often ascribe a particular religious identity to the Sufi or *brahm*, the narrative elements that depict the efficacy of these men commonly reflect the intercommunal nature of their various sites of healing.[2] In other words,

---

2. All of the dead healers in and around Arampur were men. However, examples of dead female healers exist in other regions. For example, see Paul Courtright, "The Iconographies of Sati" in *Sati, the Blessing and the Curse: The Burning of Wives in India,* John Stratton Hawley, ed. New York: Oxford University Press, 1994, pp. 27–48. Although numerous, large monuments to women who committed *sati* stand at one end of Arampur, I neither saw nor heard of anyone worshiping there, as Courtright describes in regard to Rajasthan. Also see Diane Coccari, *The Bir Babas of Banaras: An Analysis of a Folk Deity in North Indian Hinduism.* Ph.D. dissertation, University of Wisconsin–Madison, 1986, pp. 117–126.

local narratives demonstrate both the authority and the abilities of these dead healers and, in so doing, express the multiple identities of local residents and devotees. It is a crucial element of the social dimension of death in this area that beliefs, practices, and narratives regarding the dead who heal work to affirm both inclusive and exclusive religious identities, as well as intercommunal local identities.

Ignoring the busy traffic of the bazaar, Surya Tiwari sits on the porch of his family home and describes for me the local centers of spiritual healing among the many temples and tombs in his village of Arampur. Above, on the wall behind him, a painted advertisement encourages pilgrims to enlist the services of his brother, who works as a priest in the nearby temple of Shastri Brahm, as his father and grandfather had before him. Surya narrates the origins and development of this temple, which attracts devotees from far beyond the borders of his native Bihar. Yet, despite its considerable powers, he explains, this *brahm*, or vengeful Brahman ghost, has limitations. "Any Muslim who is not buried after death can seize a Hindu (for example, someone going to the toilet). They can cause the person to go nude, be crazy, or act like a Muslim by doing *namāz* or *wuzū*.[3] These people can come to Shastri Brahm's temple and be judged [diagnosed], but they are then sent to the places said to control *jinn* because there is no system to control *jinn* in this temple. So they are sent to a Muslim saint's tomb where there is *jinn* control, or the Muslim ghost is asked what it wants since it's possible that the *jinn* will take that and abandon the person."

I leave the conversation wondering whether spiritual healing practices had long been divided along such communal lines or whether the recent national tensions exacerbated by Hindu and Muslim chauvinists had penetrated even the realm of the dead, such as *bhūt-pret*[4] and *jinn*.[5] Only later do I realize that my question was shortsighted. It relied too much on the descriptions of Surya Tiwari and those others who declare the religiously exclusive character of religious healing sites. I had failed to appreciate the narratives of yet other devotees that imply the intercommunal nature of these sites. More precisely put, when the Hindus, Muslims, and Christians who frequent these sites describe the authority of a Sufi or *brahm* to heal, usually they refer to an exclusive religious identity for these dead healers. Yet, when these supplicants depict his ability to heal, they portray the multiple identities associated with the dead healer, as well as those of the devotees themselves. Commonly, area residents make these claims to authority and efficacy through narrative and, in so doing, create an intercommunal public sphere.

An important shared factor among the healing *brahm* and Sufis of Arampur is that they are dead. Stuart Blackburn has observed, "As a source of Indian

3. Muslim daily prayers and ritual ablutions, respectively.
4. A general term for ghosts and spirits that are often malevolent. Both terms derive from Sanskrit roots: *bhū* (becoming) and *pre* (to come forth).
5. Entities mentioned in the Quran as created from fire that become, in South Asia, synonymous at times with ghosts of the dead.

religious thought, death is probably unsurpassed."[6] Of course, death becomes primarily important insofar as it affects the living, and one way in which the dead do so—for many Hindus and Muslims—is through healing. Many believe these dead individuals act as animated agents who can affect, for good and ill, the health of the living. If, as Blackburn argues, death plays such a central role in much of Indian religious thought and behavior, it is partly because it denotes neither the end of life nor its opposite but, rather, acts as a milestone in an individual's life. This milestone marks the appropriation, for some, of remarkable powers that can influence the lives of others in the community in which they formerly resided. A wide variety of the dead actively inhabit the Arampur area. We might roughly divide them between those socially incorporated and those who are not. Among the latter that residents identify are the *bhūt, brahm, pret, Paṭhān, Sayyid, jhureyal, pahalvān,* and *jinn* that roam the area or inhabit solitary places like trees or graveyards. Anyone who bothers them—intentionally or not—may become possessed or otherwise troubled. The socially incorporated dead include the various *ḍīh bābās* that protect the entrances to villages, Shastri Brahm, Sufis, and *shahīd* (Islamic martyrs).[7] A key difference between the two groups is that, whereas the former are seldom associated individually with any particular place, the latter have shrines (*sthān*), temples (*mandir*), courts (*dargāh*), or tombs (*mazār*) dedicated to them, where devotees can propitiate them.

Because these sites are often established by local devotees at places associated with the life or death of the active dead, they act not only as locales for devotion but also as spatial and temporal markers for the current community. Such sites serve as spatial intersections between the life of an individual healer and a local community. Meanwhile, annual festivals at these sites, often commemorating the death and expanded empowerment of the healer, create a temporal intersection. With their time fixed on a community's annual calendar, these festivals relate the mortal life of the healer to his continuing presence in the community. A date, perhaps associated with a singular event in the mortal life of the healer (e.g., his death), becomes an annually repetitive holiday observed by and demonstrative of the continuous community. These temporal and spatial elements as manifested at the places associated with dead healers establish them as a permanent part of the social order that they had been on the verge of departing.[8] As such, they reflect the nature of that order.

6. Stuart Blackburn, "Death and Deification: Folk Cults in Hinduism" in *History of Religions*, vol. 24, no. 3 (1985), p. 255.

7. Residents often conflate Sufis with *shahīd*.

8. Maurice Bloch and Jonathan Parry, "Introduction" in *Death and the Regeneration of Life*. New York: Cambridge University Press, 1982, pp. 32–38. Also, Blackburn, pp. 270–274. It is useful to observe that the socially unincorporated dead become dangerous as they assert themselves in the lives of the community by causing illness or possession. Living members of the community may opt to create a shrine for them and propitiate them, should they become too unmanageable, thus settling them back as a recognized part of society, as we shall see accomplished successfully in the case of Shastri Brahm.

Before a community establishes such intersections between itself and a healer, however, it must first recognize the healer's authority and efficacy to heal. We shall explore the ways in which residents do this through narratives about two local healers in order to demonstrate how group memories of dead healers help mold both communal and intercommunal social contexts for the living. First, an examination of the authority invested in local healers reflects how they can represent traditions uniquely Hindu or Islamic. Second, an analysis of the efficacy that devotees ascribe to these healers will reflect the intercommunal dimensions of both devotional and healing practices *and* the village environment. We will detail in each consecutive section how the *authority* to heal (that creates a socially sanctioned potential for power following certain conditions of the person's life, death, and afterlife) differs from the *ability* to heal (that demonstrates, through anecdotes, the publicly recognized actualization of this authorized power). As manifested through expressions of group memory, both dynamics result in the construction and affirmation of an intercommunal public sphere.

If we can briefly define *authority* as "the social sanction to exercise power," then the event of death becomes, when socially recognized in particular ways, an important step in gaining the authority to heal. Both Hindus and Muslims believe that death can initiate or further the empowerment of a person as a healer. Of course, death alone does not sanction a healer because, otherwise, all the dead would be considered capable of healing the living, and this is not the case. Among the additional criteria by which devotees judge a healer's credentials, we discover the differences in authority ascribed to Hindu and Muslim healers. A more detailed examination of two examples of these healers, Shastri Brahm and Asta Auliya, will illustrate this point.

For most residents of Arampur, no one among the empowered dead commands more respect than Shastri Brahm. For at least a century, pilgrims from across north India have traveled to Arampur village for the sake of worshiping and petitioning him. Large numbers of pilgrims, if they do not come from the city itself, make use of Banaras as a transportation hub to reach the cobblestoned main street of Arampur. A walk of 20 minutes brings them through the busy central Bazaar of the village, where residents of the surrounding area come to buy merchandise, sell grain, drink tea, eat snacks, and trade gossip. If they do not stop first to obtain the help of professional Brahmans such as Surya Tiwari's brother, the pilgrims soon reach the end of the street, which is overshadowed by a mammoth, open gateway at the edge of a large, eroded mound of earth. This is all that remains of the once proud fort of the local ruler Raja Vicitra.

A path leads the pilgrims through this heavy sandstone portal, past merchandise-ornamented shops, to the mound's rounded top, over which the tall white steeple of Shastri Brahm's temple towers. After ringing the bells hanging above the temple entrance, the pilgrims join others either in the large courtyard dominated by an expansive shade tree or within the much smaller inner temple, where Brahmans direct the proper offering of prayers and gifts to the small stone that is Shastri Brahm's *mūrti* (embodiment). The courtyard seldom empties entirely of people. Devotees, most of whom are women, beseech this ghost of a Brahman for various favors, among them the healing of mental instability, spirit possession, and various physical illnesses. Many of the devotees suffering possession rely on the powers of exorcism practiced by the professional Brahman men who work at the temple. Some arrive with their own *ojhā* (exorcist), who may be neither Brahman nor male.

In either case, the exorcist positions the client, surrounded by the family members and friends who brought him or her, in the courtyard facing Shastri Brahm's *mūrti*. This proximity to the *mūrti* may cause the possessing spirit to induce its host to tremble, shake, gyrate, weep, sing, and/or shout. The exorcist attempts to speak with the spirit, often physically provoking its attention by prodding the host with a short stick. "*Bhūt bole!*" (Speak, ghost!), the exorcist commands. "Who are you? What do you want?" He warns the ghost that it is in the *darbār* (royal court) of Shastri Brahm. When the exorcist thinks that he or she understands the nature of the possessing spirit and what needs to be done to extricate it from the client, the exorcist commands it to say and accept that Shastri Brahm is *mālik* (lord). If the spirit finally affirms this (it may take a while if it resists), the Brahman leads the victim to the *mūrti* and the sacrificial fire pit so that the proper offerings can be made.[9] Small, engraved marble tiles comprise much of the temple's floor, each attesting to the devotion and thanksgiving of one of Shastri Brahm's supplicants. Outside the whitewashed walls of the temple, short, semispherical *piṇḍ*s make a similar witness.

The narratives of authority and efficacy by which devotees explain the importance of the temple of Shastri Brahm portray this temple as a locus of personality, space, power, and the past. The variations among these narratives demonstrate the variety of perspectives among the devotees who tell them, and the endurance of the core elements of the basic story suggests the narrative's local importance. Although stories about how Shastri Brahm came to be a powerful healer told by contemporary residents of the Arampur area differ in various details (including or excluding a range of characters and events), they all share elements which remain completely consistent with a version told to a British visitor to Arampur more than a century earlier.

Communal Authority

As we sit with another member of his household in the shade of a thatch canopy overlooking the family fields, Usman Khan explains his story of Shastri Brahm in his native Urdu:

---

9. A compelling examination of similar spiritual interrogations among Indian charismatic Catholics can be found in Mathew N. Schmalz, "Sins and Somatologies: Sexual Transgression and the Body in Indian Charismatic Healing." Paper presented at the annual American Academy of Religion conference, San Francisco, November 1997.

He lived in the time of Raja Vicitra. Arampur is a very historical place. Shastri Brahm was Raja Vicitra's guru. Raja Vicitra was a Rājpūt[10] and Shastri Brahm was a resident of [another village]. His house was tall and a light shone from it. One day the rani saw this and asked people whose light it was, then ordered the house to be destroyed. And so it was. Shastri Brahm was troubled and began to fast. Raja Vicitra explained to Shastri Brahm that he would make an even better house for him and that he did not know what the rani was doing. But Shastri Brahm did not believe him and died by his own hand.

Like most other Muslims of the area, Usman Khan concluded his narrative of Shastri Brahm's life with his death. However, most Hindu residents extend this narrative with a final story that gives testimony to the *brahm*'s powers. For them, the narrative does not conclude until Shastri Brahm, as a ghost, goes to Delhi and leads the sultan's army back to Arampur to precipitate the raja's ultimate demise. At first glance, it would seem as though the omission of these postmortem activities reflects Usman Khan's doubts or disbelief concerning the powers ascribed to the dead Brahman, both at the time of the raja's defeat and currently. Throughout his narrative, however, he referred to Shastri Brahm in the polite, plural third person of Urdu, in contrast to the informal, singular third person with which he referred to the raja. Although Muslims with a strictly orthodox theology may be unable or unwilling to acknowledge any authority by which a dead Hindu—or any dead person—can hurt or heal,[11] many accord some of the dead with the possibility of power and, so, talk about them with cautious deference. Less doctrinally constrained Muslims and most area Hindus accept the power of Shastri Brahm based on their respect, if not for his authority, then for his efficacy—a point that we develop later.

Within the realm of authority, we observe a strict distinction among Muslims and Hindus based on their religious traditions. Blackburn notes that the power of the deified dead in folk Hinduism derives from the nature of their death. They must have died a premature, unjust, (preferably) violent death.[12] Blackburn emphasizes that the deification of the Hindu dead in no way depends upon the moral stature of the deceased. Indeed, we find that devotees to Shastri Brahm emphasize not his life but the suicide he felt compelled to perform because of the unjustified crime of jealousy committed against him by the rani and/or raja.[13] The authority imparted by this type of death is dem-

---

10. A Hindu high caste associated with the Kṣatrya or warrior/king class of society.

11. For example, a Pakistani Shii pamphlet instructing Muslims on the facts of death and funerals cites several Quranic passages regarding the condition of the dead between the time they die and are resurrected. It adamantly concludes, "The above mentioned verses are sufficient to refute the claims of the so-called spiritualists and occultists to [sic] who pretend to talk with the dead." *Death and Death Ceremonies.* Karachi: Peermahomed Ebrahim Trust, 1972, p. 47.

12. Blackburn, p. 260.

13. It will be instructive to watch what possible devotions and powers will be associated with Bishop John Joseph, the late Catholic Bishop of Faisalabad who, on May 6, 1998, committed a similar type of suicide in protest of the discrimination suffered by Christians in Pakistan.

onstrated in a variety of ancient Sanskrit and modern texts that many Hindu devotees refer to as evidence of the *brahm*'s authority. These include *purāṇas* and books seldom, if ever, seen and said to be in the care of special Brahmans in places away from Arampur.

Arampur is also home to healers less famous than Shastri Brahm. Local residents associate the nearby tombs of *shahīds* and Sufis with the healing powers that these men are said to have exercised in their lives. Many of the Hindus, Muslims, and Christians who visit these sites describe through narratives the powers of the healer to whom they entrust their well-being. Whether these supplicants believe that the Sufi performs the healing himself or acts as an intermediary for Allah varies according to the individual. Whichever the case might be, the concern for and evaluation of authority and efficacy remain equally important. In the increasingly polarized climate of Indian religious politics, we might expect that such narratives would reflect an exclusive religious identity of the site, its healing practitioners, and its devotees. This is, indeed, the case for many of the narratives that depict the authority by which the dead can heal. The divergent stories of Shastri Brahm commonly depend on a common trope in Hindu folklore of the Brahman who dies an unjust death and returns as a powerful spirit. Similarly, the narratives of the Sufi Asta Auliya often rely on the Islamic folklore trope of the Sufi who clears the jungle and civilizes its residents—a theme we explore in greater detail later.

Among the dozens of tombs of Sufis and *shahīds* local to the area, the *dargāh* (or shrine) of Asta Auliya or, as he is popularly known, Makhdum Sahib stands among the most important. Situated on the edge of Arampur on a well-developed path leading from the nearby Bazaar, this Sufi's whitewashed tomb rests atop a raised concrete platform surrounded by a low wall that is itself set within an enclosed garden of untended plants and trees. Faded banners, waiting for the next '*urs*[14] celebration to be changed, hang from the large tree that shades the tomb. To the left of the eastern gate into the garden is a small, open mosque. Because the *miḥrāb*[15] of the mosque looks immediately over the Sufi's tomb, those praying inside face not only distant Mecca but also the tomb outside. Above the garden gate entrance, an inscription provides Asta Auliya's full name and the spiritually significant number 786.[16] A home just east of this compound houses the current *faqīr*, who, as a blood descendant of Asta Auliya, is said to continue his powers.

Asta Auliya draws devotees daily. Men and women can be found, at any time between morning and night, bowing or kneeling before the tomb, hands pressed or spread wide with palms up in the fashion of a Muslim prayer form, *du'ā*.

---

14. The annual celebration of a particular Sufi's death day.

15. The niche in a mosque's front wall that indicates the direction of Mecca and, thus, prayer.

16. The number inscribed on the Sufi tomb, ٧٨٦ (786), probably derives from *abjad*, a numerological science, which attributes a number to each letter of the Arabic alphabet; 786 is the *abjad* equivalent of the *bismillāh* (the prayer, "In the name of Allah"). However, most Muslim residents whom I asked about this did not recognize it as such and usually guessed that it represents the Sufi's death date.

Occasionally, a family arrives with a disturbed member who they hope and pray can be relieved of her or his confounding *bhūt*s, *pret*s, or other malicious, marauding entities. As at Shastri Brahm's temple, some of these distressed people arrive in ropes or even chains, bound by their family to prevent them from harming themselves or others. Unlike the temple, no professional intermediaries work at this or any of the area *dargāh*s. Suppliants make their requests directly to the dead healer. Very often, a devotee comes to make a prayer in front of the tomb and then places a bottle of water or oil on the tomb's raised floor or tall walls. The devotee expects the Sufi's power to energize the liquid so that it can be used as a remedy for some family member's physical ailment, whether it is sickness or infertility.

When asked about Asta Auliya, many local residents describe his sanctity according to established patterns of Islamic religious authority. They may claim that he belongs to either a familial or educational Sufi lineage; that is, they may describe his connection to a Sufi *silsila* or chain of teachers, either by claiming that his father and/or other ancestors were important Sufis or by describing him as the student of a famous Sufi teacher, like the nationally renowned Muinuddin Chishti of Ajmer. They may also relate his travels to and studies in Arabia, particularly Mecca. His authority may further be demonstrated through the common South Asian Islamic trope that describes the spiritually powerful and religiously devout Sufi who clears the jungle for civilization and converts nonbelievers to Islam.[17] Like the colored bottles of water carefully perched along the sides of Sufi tombs, the Sufis themselves absorb power through their association with important places (such as Mecca) and/or the *silsila* of family or teachers who are markedly Muslim. As discussed in chapter 3, lineages allow those of the present to find their place in time and to access what has long passed—in this case, the considerable power of the *silsila* originator. In the minds of their clients, this power authorizes the properly sanctioned dead to heal according to some understanding of Islamic traditions.[18]

Salman Alam alludes to some of these claims to authority when, during the carnival atmosphere of the '*urs* or death celebration of Asta Auliya, he answers my question as to where the Sufi had come from. "Either from Ajmer or Pakistan," he replies. When I ask where in Pakistan, he continues,

Near Lahore. Others came with him. The ruler of Arampur was Raja Vicitra. Islam was not common then. Raja Vicitra did not think that Asta Auliya was powerful so he decided to test him. A living woman was sent to Asta Auliya, who was told that she was a dead Muslim servant and that *jināzī kī namāz* (funeral prayers) should be said for her. Asta Auliya said "no," but he was pressured to

17. Richard Eaton, *The Rise of Islam and the Bengal Frontier, 1204–1760.* Delhi: Oxford University Press, 1994, pp. 207–219

18. The development and role of authority within institutional Sufism has recently been examined by Arthur Buehler in his *Sufi Heirs of the Prophet: The Indian Naqshbandiyya and the Rise of the Mediating Sufi Shaykh.* Columbia: University of South Carolina Press, 1998. Buehler, too, notes the importance of genealogy.

agree. He told Raja Vicitra that the woman would die as a result of the prayers. The raja told him to go ahead. . . . The woman, who was alive, had been sent a *kafan* (burial shroud) by the raja. Asta Auliya told people to line up for the prayer and did the *namāz*. The woman died. Asta Auliya was a powerful man. The body of the woman was put in a grave that is there today. The woman was a *ṭawā'if* (dancer or prostitute). Her tomb is right in front of where Asta Auliya's is and was oriented north-south. But when he died, it changed direction by itself.

Indeed, today the tomb attributed to the *ṭawā'if* stands unusually skewed southeast-northwest in contrast to the surrounding Muslim tombs, which are all oriented north-south.

Salman's narrative accomplished a number of general descriptive tasks. It tied Asta Auliya with Raja Vicitra as an important local entity through a proud association with one of Arampur's most famous figures. Despite his renowned injustice against Shastri Pandey, residents speak of the raja with a pride that reflects their lofty regard for their village and its legendary past grandeur that he embodied. The narrative implied the importance of both Asta Auliya's devotees (because of their faith in a Sufi spiritually powerful enough to foil the politically dominant Raja Vicitra) and Arampur's residents (because their village includes a powerful Sufi within its boundaries). It is worth noting that Salman's story does all of this without explicit communal exclusivity. None of the many devotees, either Hindu or Muslim, who provided me some version of this narrative made any mention of the raja or the woman as being Hindu. The narrators' intentions seemed more focused by the trope of the humble spiritual leader who overpowered the proud political leader, a theme common to Sufi narratives throughout the world.[19]

More specifically for our concerns, Salman Alam's narrative established the Sufi's authority. First, it associated him with Ajmer and Lahore, both homes of important South Asian Sufis such as Muinuddin Chishti and Ali ibn Usman al-Hujwiri. Second, the narrative strengthened this authority with an allusion to the Sufi's Islamic character, suggesting that he arrived in the Arampur area because "Islam was not common then." Third, it furthers this notion as it demonstrates the spiritual and compassionate powers of Asta Auliya (a.k.a. Makhdum Sahib), who attempted to avoid the lethal result of the raja's deviousness but exercised his powers when left without an option. Globally, many Muslims celebrate Sufis who live lives of compassion, but they seldom expect

---

19. This theme has already arisen in Hasan Nishat Ansari's essay, examined in chapter 3. Other scholars have explored in more detail the role of devotional narratives that juxtapose Sufis and political leaders. These include Michael Gilsenan's treatment of Lebanese *shaykhs* in his *Recognizing Islam* (New York: Pantheon, 1982); and Clifford Geertz's depiction of Sidi Lahsen Lyusi in *Islam Observed: Religious Development in Morocco and Indonesia* (Chicago: University of Chicago Press, 1968). It is useful to contrast these portrayals with the somewhat different pattern of Sufi and state interactions described by Sarah Ansari in *Sufi Saints and State Power: The Pirs of Sind, 1843–1947.* Cambridge: Cambridge University Press, 1992.

them to be passive. When facing an injustice against other Muslims or Islam, Sufis are expected to act decisively, as Asta Auliya did.[20]

Narratives such as those of Usman Khan and Salman Alam depict a disjunction at several points between the separate authority of Shastri Brahm and local Sufis to heal. While the devotees of Sufis in Arampur emphasize the nature of the Sufi's life that is usually described as devoted to religious learning and compassionate acts of healing and/or teaching, devotees ascribe power to the *brahm* according to the manner of the *brahm*'s death. Further, devotees commonly refer to the Sufi's knowledge and veneration of the Quran and other Arabic religious books, whereas the quality of Shastri Brahm's scholastic or devotional life seldom, if ever, arises.

Consistent with broader Hindu cultural expectations, only three elements of Shastri's life determine his authority to heal: he was (1) a male (2) Brahman who (3) died an unjust death. The implied basis of a *brahm*'s authority to heal, therefore, does not derive from the manner of his life, as with Sufis, but rather the nature of his death. Many Hindu traditions pay great attention to the successful migration of the dead away from the society of the living into *pitṛ lokā* (the realm of the ancestors) until reincarnation returns them to the realm of the living. Sanskrit texts such as the *Garuḍa Purāṇa* detail the nature of this passage. In separate works, David Knipe has explored contemporary rituals performed to both facilitate this passage[21] and cope with the dangerous consequences of untimely death.[22] Although the *manner* of a *brahm*'s life might not matter, his social status (as a male Brahman) most certainly does. Inversely, devotees prove the Sufi's authority to heal with reference only to the integrity of his life, not his inherited social position. Consistent with general Islamic ideals, a person obtains religious stature through the equal opportunity to truly submit—to be true Muslims— that Allah grants all believers regardless of class, age, or gender.[23] Classical Islamic

---

20. An almost identical narrative, but associated with the Chighti *shaykh* Muhammad Qajim Nanatauwi, can be found in P. Lewis, *Pirs, Shrines, and Pakistani Islam*. Rawalpindi: Christian Study Centre, 1985, p. 33. Biographies about local Sufis often explain their appropriation of spiritual powers as a result of their retreat into the forest. Although no one made such a claim for Asta Auliya (other than his arrival in the jungle as a proselytizing civilizer), such elements comprise parts of the narratives of two other dead Sufi healers—one in Arampur and another 5 kilometers nearby.

21. David Knipe, "*Sapindikarana*: The Hindu Rite of Entry into Heaven" in *Religious Encounters with Death: Insights from the History and Anthropology of Religion*, E. Reynolds and E. Waugh, eds. University Park: Pennsylvania State University Press, 1977, pp. 111–124.

22. David Knipe, "Night of the Growing Dead: A Cult of Vīrabhadra in Coastal Andra" in *Criminal Gods and Demon Devotees: Essays on the Guardians of Popular Hinduism*, Alf Hiltebeitel, ed. Albany: State University of New York Press, 1989, pp. 123–156.

23. "The Believers, men and women, are protectors, one of another: they enjoin what is just, and forbid what is evil: they observe regular prayers, practice regular charity, and obey God and His Apostle. On them will God pour His mercy" (Quran 40.71). Although ideally true and the famed examples of such female figures as Rabiah of Basra notwithstanding, the comparative lack of female Sufis, living or dead, demonstrates the gendered limits of this notion in the public recognition and celebration of particularly devout Muslims.

thought pays little concern to "bad deaths" like Shastri Brahm's. The *shahīd*, who certainly suffers an untimely death, proceeds immediately to the paradisiacal Garden and so does not threaten the living in any way. Despite some discrepancies between the Quran and Ḥadīth, the general understanding in these foundational texts of Islamic belief is that most of the dead remain in or near their graves awaiting the Day of Judgment, their contact with the living limited to the medium of dreams.[24] But these understandings changed over time as some Muslims came to accept the ability of dead saints to intercede on behalf of the living.[25]

All of these differences, therefore, clearly demonstrate that the *brahm* and Sufis do indeed appear to be religiously defined and communally distinct in the context of authority. Ultimately, we see that a religious community recognizes religious power within and according to the parameters that its tradition allows. One way in which Hindus and Muslims portray a dead healer's authority in regard to these parameters is through narratives that use tropes specific to their respective traditions. As they tell or accept such stories while in the company of others from their religious community—whether in the home, place of worship, or tea stall—they assert their membership in that community.

Yet, to halt our analysis here would be to ignore a social dimension of Indian religious life in which the common worship of the dead unites the living beyond the confines of communal boundaries through intercommunal activities, perspectives, and identities. Almost to the same degree that devotees recognize and refer to specifically Hindu and Muslim traditions while describing the authority of dead healers, they ignore communal differences while portraying the effectiveness of these men.

Intercommunal Efficacy

If we return to Salman Alam's narrative, we notice that the elements that demonstrate the Sufi's efficacy, in juxtaposition with those proving his authority, do not rely on any specifically Islamic character. We have already noted that Asta Auliya showed his compassion, when he attempted to avoid harming the woman, and his stridency, when he exercised his powers when left without an option—powers effective enough to kill her. Significantly, Salman's story avoids explicit communal exclusivity. None of the many devotees I interviewed, either Hindu or Muslim, who provided some version of this narrative made any mention of the raja or the woman as being Hindu or Muslim. Presumably, the fact that the raja sent her supposed corpse for burial instead of cremation implies that she was Muslim. Even if this is the understanding of Arampur residents, they made no indications in their narratives to me that the point is

---

24. Jane Idleman Smith and Yvonne Yazbeck Haddad, *The Islamic Understanding of Death and Resurrection*. Albany: State University of New York Press, 1981, pp. 47–61.

25. Ibid., pp. 183–190.

important. No one hinted at any injustice served upon the woman by the Hindu raja because she was Muslim. And, although residents widely recognize the raja as having been Hindu, no narratives suggested that the outcome was especially deserved because he was Hindu or would have been any different had he been Muslim. This feature becomes all the more significant when we consider that local Muslims could have remembered Asta Auliya's success against the Hindu raja as the victory of a warrior Sufi against a non-Muslim. Arampur residents identify various tombs in the area as belonging to *shahīd*s (Islamic martyrs) and *gāzī*s (victors against non-Muslims), popular figures in hagiographic folklore and literature.[26] Yet, no one suggests such an identity for Asta Auliya.

A similar intercommunal dynamic operates in narratives regarding Shastri Brahm. The lengthy and detailed version that Surya Tiwari shared illustrates this dynamic well. While providing a protracted history of Arampur stretching from Gupta rule (circa fourth century) to the local victory of a king in 1180, Surya explains further in a fluid mix of Hindi and English:

> So [that king] picked Arampur fort as his new capital and built a seven-story tall fort. He buried his [wealth] there. Three or four generations later Raja Vicitra . . . ruled. Shastri Pandey was his priest and chief minister. After twenty-two to twenty-five years without issue from his first wife, he consults Shastri Pandey concerning a pure Hindu son for the future. . . . Shastri Pandey suggests a second wife and this angers the first who then tries to create friction between the king and priest. She convinces the king to be against the priest. As a result, Shastri Pandey's house was damaged. . . . The king also took back the villages given by the king's ancestor to the priest's family. Shastri Pandey became angry and said that he would have no peace until he defeated the king. So he sent his family away. . . . Shastri Pandey went to see the king but was refused. So Shastri Pandey entered the fort through the moat canal and commenced to do a *dharnā* (fast). He said he would do an . . . indefinite . . . hunger strike while awaiting the king's return of his property. Otherwise, he would destroy the raja, the fort, and [the raja's] family. On the twenty-second day Shastri Pandey died and became a *brahm* or Brahman ghost. Accidental deaths lead to *brahm* or *brahmaṇapret* (spirits of Brahmans).

Surya Tiwari continues:

> The raja began to have more problems. He sought relief through *tāntrik*s (practitioners of tantra) but with no success. Before a visit by Shastri Pandey's grandson, Sudarshan, a mysterious incident happened. There was an attempt to bury Shastri Pandey's body, but local tradition holds that it turned to stone. Many priests were asked to come from Banaras and asked how to do *śrāddh* (the Hindu ceremony for the recently deceased). Some suggest doing a *samskār* (a Hindu rite of passage) with a priest using a *putlā* (human image) made out of grass. Shastri

---

26. Richard Eaton, *Sufis of Bijapur, 1300–1700: Social Roles of Sufis in Medieval India.* Princeton: Princeton University Press, 1978, pp. 19–37.

Pandey's grandson and his family priest go to Manikarnika Ghat (a cremation site in Banaras). All see Shastri Pandey there in human form . . . while others prepare the funeral pyre. They were scared. Shastri Pandey said that he would not be happy until the raja was dead or had quit the fort. The raja didn't believe the story. People saw Shastri Brahm from Banaras to Arampur.

In Delhi at this time was the Muslim dynasty of Mubarak Shah. The raja paid the sultan of Jaunpur protection money. Meanwhile, the Delhi sultan was thinking of taking Jaunpur in July or August 1427 or 1428. During the planning, a simple Brahman—Shastri Brahm—said that the ruler of Jaunpur would fall if the Arampur raja was defeated. No one in Delhi knew who the simple Brahman was. He came in a dream to the [Delhi] sultan to assure him. . . . On October 1427, after five days [of fighting], the [Jaunpur] ruler's forces ran away. All the Hindu rulers were defeated along the way . . . the Delhi Sultan remembers Shastri Brahm and constantly thinks of him. As he does so, invisible powers increase through nonhuman inspiration. A three-day battle occurred, and the Arampur raja was destroyed. Mubarak Shah looted the fort. He made someone who was . . . not a pure Rājpūt into a small king or *jāgīrdār*[27] of Arampur after giving Mubarak Shah a lot of the loot.

Yet the *jāgīrdār* began to feel a shadow in the fort and suffered from Shastri Brahm's curse for one week or a month. An astrologer or demonologist explained that the soul of Shastri Brahm is present. It is necessary to make complete satisfaction of Shastri Brahm's revenge. Adhinath and other Brahmans from Banaras came to question Shastri Pandey's soul. They promise to establish him as a *brahm*, and the residents and king will establish a home for him and worship him as a god in exchange for the end of the curse. Shastri Pandey's soul was ready, so Shastri Brahm was established in a room in the fort. A *yajña* (sacrifice) was done in the fort, and this was the first day of the worship of Shastri Brahm in the form of Lord Shiva.

At first glance, the story seems anything but noncommunal. Surya made great effort to explicitly identify certain figures as either Hindu (Shastri Pandey, Raja Vicitra, the *jāgīrdār*, and other Hindu rajas) or Muslim (Mubarak Shah and the Jaunpur sultan). He describes the lineage to which Mubarak Shah (not to be confused with the Arampur Sufi of the same name) belonged as a "Muslim dynasty" and the rulers whom Mubarak Shah defeated on his drive toward Arampur as "Hindu kings." As one of the most formally educated individuals from Arampur, Surya has read many Indian textbooks and Western histories that depict South Asia's political history as a competition among various Hindu and Muslim factions. His narrative reflects the overall picture that these texts often paint of the slow yet inevitable conquest of "Hindu kingdoms" by "Muslim invaders." Yet, despite this obvious attention to religious identity, he portrays Shastri Brahm's powers as indiscriminately applied. Note that Shastri Pandey, transformed by death into Shastri Brahm, acted against not only Raja

---

27. The holder of a government grant to own land and villages.

Vicitra (who craved a "pure Hindu son") but also the *jāgīrdār* who is "not pure Rājpūt" in revenge for their respective infractions (damaging his house and looting the fort). Meanwhile, he aided without prejudice the Muslim sultan of Delhi in his campaigns against the Muslim sultan of Jaunpur, the Hindu raja of Arampur, and the Hindu kings unfortunate enough to stand between these two. In summary, Surya Tiwari (and most other Arampur residents) narrated a memory about how Shastri Pandey came to be a *brahm* that demonstrates the efficacy of his powers for or against individuals without regard for their religious identity, *despite the obvious concern on the part of the narrator to identify them in this way.* Not only does Surya Tiwari's awareness of religious difference not necessitate communalist antagonism but also it reflects the perceived reality that Shastri Brahm aids those who respect him no matter what their religious identity. This allows for an intercommunal identity among his devotees.

Significantly, the power of seemingly disempowered spiritual figures to successfully wrestle with political and social figures finds a parallel in both religious traditions. In the realm of efficacy, we notice interesting parallels between the narratives concerning Shastri Brahm and Asta Auliya. Although the authority for his powers derive from specifically Hindu traditions, Shastri Brahm's abilities are demonstrated in a narrative in which he destroys a Hindu raja through an alliance with a Muslim sultan. This notion of the humble spiritual person overpowering the proud political leader is a theme common not only to Sufi narratives throughout the world but also to many oral and written narratives in north India that depict animosity between Brahmans and Ṭhākurs (lords of the land).[28] Brahmans often overcome the Ṭhākurs' economic and political power through the exercise of their spirituality in ways similar to Sufi victories over abusive rulers.[29] Therefore, the independent efficacy of this *brahm* and Sufi of Arampur is demonstrated through their confrontation with the local political leader, whose religious identity plays no part in the outcome.

It is consequential that both narratives depict their protagonists as proving their efficacy through conflict with Raja Vicitra. Each vies proudly for a place in popular memory through an association with the raja, perhaps the most widely remembered figure in the area. In turn, each narrative implies the importance of the devotees of both Asta Auliya and Shastri Brahm because of their faith in a man spiritually powerful enough to foil the politically dominant Raja Vicitra.

But doesn't Surya Tiwari's initial comment about Shastri Brahm's inability at "*jinn* control" seem to suggest that efficacy *is* tradition specific? When he acknowledged that professional Brahmans at Shastri Brahm's temple could

---

28. Perhaps the fact that both the generic terms *darbār* and *dargāh* used for the *brahm*'s temple and the Sufi's shrine, respectively, can also mean "royal court" also reflects this power struggle.

29. Diane Coccari, "The Bir Babas and the Deified Dead" in *Criminal Gods and Demon Devotees: Essays on the Guardians of Popular Hinduism*, Alf Hiltebeitel, ed. Albany: State University of New York Press, 1989, p. 254.

diagnose a person's possession as caused by a Muslim ghost or *jinn* but that the *brahm*'s powers could not exorcise it but a Muslim saint could, was he not admitting that the religious association of a ghost disables Shastri Brahm's efficacy? Simply put, the Hindu *brahm* seems to exercise no authority over a Muslim ghost.[30] What would seem to reflect the tradition-specific nature of efficacy, however, actually demonstrates the intercommunal nature of efficacy within the limits of tradition-based claims to authority. But how?

Although Shastri Brahm may not be considered effective against Muslim ghosts, we must consider first that devotees of area Sufis never suggested that a dead Muslim healer could not be effective against a Hindu ghost. This one-sided limitation reflects the lopsided activity of local Hindus and Muslims at the *brahm*'s temple and Sufi shrines. Whereas most Hindus show little hesitation to seek healing or exorcism at a site associated with a Muslim healer, many Muslims consider it inappropriate to request help at a Hindu temple. As many Indian Muslims hew a course of greater conservative orthopraxy in response to national communalist politics and international revivalist movements, they refuse (increasingly, I suspect) to accept (or, at least, admit) the authority of Hindu spirits.[31] Just as Hindu residents of Arampur will as likely accept the authority of a dead Sufi as that of a *brahm* because doctrine constrains them less, so, too, the Hindu ghosts who afflict them. But Muslim ghosts, like their premortem coreligionists, are more likely not to accept the authority of Hindu healers. In this way, then, traditional notions of authority do limit the realm of an individual healer's efficacy according to the religious identity of the healer and the afflicting ghost.

This demonstrates that the issue of authority exists within a large context that determines the relative characteristics of the various members in the community of the dead. The question of a Hindu ghost's efficacy over Muslim ghosts derives from a vast domain in which different powers, both malevolent and benevolent, are ascribed to spirits of deceased humans, depending on their place in life and manner of death. No nexus resident suggested that rancorous spirits had any religious preference regarding whom they possessed or otherwise afflicted. Although some ghosts do prefer certain victims (such as *curail*, ghosts of barren women who attack pregnant women out of envy), most spirits of the dead—whether Hindu or Muslim—seemingly pounce on the living

---

30. This dynamic is reported in other areas as well. Parry refers to the issue of authority when he writes in regard to Banaras: "[Hindu guardian spirits] do not, however, have jurisdiction over Muslim spirits; and here the exorcist (whatever his religion) will enlist the help of a Muslim *Sayyad*, or one of the *Panchon pir* (the five Islamic saints)." Jonathan P. Parry, *Death in Banaras*. Cambridge: Cambridge University Press, 1994, p. 231.

31. This increasing concern for orthopraxy among many Muslims does not limit itself to criticism of "Hindu" practices alone but also the practices of other Muslims that seem unacceptable. A large number of local Muslims, with the complaint that it was "un-Islamic," refused to participate in the annual Muḥarram commemoration, although many admitted that in previous years they had. The rise of Hindu revivalist groups such as the RSS and VHP may be creating a similar dynamic among increasing numbers of Hindus.

without regard for their religious tradition. Although Muslim ghosts may not accept Shastri Brahm's authority, the fact remains that Hindu ghosts afflict Muslims as well as Hindus and that members of both communities, despite the resistance of more orthodox Muslims, can be found seeking respite at Shastri Brahm's temple. The point can be made once more that recognition of religious identity does not necessarily denote conflict but, at times, only an awareness of difference.

Finally, although neither Shastri Brahm nor Asta Auliya nor most of the several other dead Sufi healers local to the area originated from the area, it is significant that their presence acts as a significant source of local pride for Arampur residents. Almost all Hindus and Muslims of this large village and the many surrounding villages know their stories and respect their powers, even if they do not personally rely on them for healing. Local residents interweave the memories of these important healers into the narrative of the area itself. Beyond their demonstration of the healers' authority and efficacy, narrators at times promote their pride of belonging to a village with such important and effective powers. In this manner, these villagers—both Hindus and Muslims—often use these narratives to forefront their shared village identity while de-emphasizing their religious, caste, and class identities.

Constructing and Affirming an Intercommunal Public Sphere

Although Arampur's neighbors are acutely aware of their communal differences, they share a common public sphere in their village. The group memories regarding local healers, the daily rituals that attempt to access their healing powers, and the ceremonies that ritually commemorate them at Shastri Brahm's temple and Asta Auliya's *dargāh* play a role in the integration of villagers into a common identity as residents of Arampur and devotees of one or both of these healers.

Scholars have rightly made much of the interreligious communion that Sufis—both living and dead—have generated across South Asia since the first large-scale arrival of Muslims at the turn of the first millennium. From the role of Sufis in creating an Indo-Islamic culture in thirteenth-century Bengal as described by Richard Eaton[32] to the intercommunal healing services provided by the female *pīr* Amma in modern Hyderabad as analyzed by Joyce Burkhalter-Flueckiger,[33] Sufis have played a prominent part in forging a foundation of common memory, ritual, and identity among Hindus and Muslims.[34]

32. Eaton, *The Rise of Islam and the Bengal Frontier, 1204–1760.* Delhi: Oxford University Press, 1994.

33. Joyce Burkhalter-Flueckiger, "Religious Identity at the Crossroads of a Muslim Female Healer's Practice." Paper presented at the annual South Asian Studies Conference, Madison, October 1996.

34. See also S. A. A. Saheb, "A 'Festival of Flags': Hindu-Muslim Devotion and the Sacralising of Localism at the Shrine of Nagore-e-Sharif in Tamil Nadu" in *Embodying Charisma: Modernity, Locality, and the Performance of Emotion in Sufi Cults,* Pnina Werbner and Helene Basu, eds. New York: Routledge, 1998, pp. 55–76.

One occasion demonstrated the shared devotional space that Asta Auliya's *dargāh* affords. While sitting with Druma Yadav, Rati Khan, and other members of Rati's Diwan Khan family—all residents of Naugrah, the village neighboring Arampur—I ask about a recently discovered temple near Shastri Brahm's temple. Some Arampur residents recently began excavating this hitherto forgotten temple from beneath a building atop the mound of Raja Vicitra's fort. One member of Rati Khan's family answers, "The temple surrounded by the pipal tree is a Shiv temple."

A second Khan family member adds, "That is nothing to us. We must keep our hearts clean."

> *Druma Yadav, in Hindi:* "A pandit lived there, and a raja too. Then it was destroyed. Before, there was an *akhāṛā* (wrestling ground) there. When they were removing soil there, they found the Shiv *mūrti*."
>
> *Me:* "Is that true?"
>
> *Druma:* "Yes. To the east of Arampur is a village where my *birādarī log* (caste folk) have a neighborhood. Makhdum Sahib is a great *buzurg* (venerable person). He is above everyone. No temple or mosque is greater than that one."
>
> *Me:* "Who was he?"
>
> *Druma:* "A *faqīr* (Muslim ascetic)."
>
> *Me:* "Why was he famous?"
>
> *Druma:* "There are so many temples and mosques but none are as great as he is. There is Bhagwan and Shankar and there is Allah, and *nabī rasūl*[35] (Muhammad). *Cāroṅ mālik* (All four are lords)."
>
> *Second Khan:* "Allah is Lord of all."

Once again, a local resident responded to a question regarding an Arampur site with a narrative memory (i.e., the pandit and raja) and, in so doing, successfully negotiated a common ground between his Hindu beliefs and the Islamic ideas of his Muslim neighbors (i.e., the Khans). He accomplishes this in three ways.

First, despite the conflicting beliefs of some of his Muslim landowning neighbors (or, perhaps, because of them), Druma, a Hindu fieldworker, successfully shifted the conversation away from the potentially troublesome topic of the new temple to Shastri Brahm's temple. Then, he maneuvered the conversation to focus on the *dargāh* of Makhdum Sahib (i.e., Asta Auliya) before suggesting common cause with these neighbors through a statement of theological fraternity. What might seem to be a haphazard connection between the temples and the *dargāh* is quite intelligible to residents in the area fluent in the memories that connect the derelict fort, Shastri Brahm, and Asta Auliya to Raja Vicitra. Despite the class and religious differences between them, Druma and the Diwan Khans can share a local identity through their mutual group memory of the area's most renowned figures. This strategy of narrative association lends some of the local significance of the raja-*brahm*-sultan story to less-known group

---

35. The Islamic term for a messenger from Allah who brings a divine book.

memories and identities, such as those surrounding Asta Auliya. Devotees of Asta Auliya, by narrating stories that depict his involvement with the raja, graft their identity as the Sufi's devotees onto that of being Arampur residents to the exclusion of communal, caste, and class identities.

Second, Druma created a common ground with the Khans when he alluded to the current power of the Sufi. Although the second Khan family member, not brooking the idea that Allah has any peers, rebutted Druma's claim that Bhagwan, Shankar, Allah, and Muhammad were all lords, he did not contradict Druma's lengthier comment regarding the efficacy of Asta Auliya. Druma praised the Sufi's grandeur in the present tense, clearly claiming that his power survived his death and resides still in his *dargāh*.

Third, we take note how Druma, a resident of a village adjoining Arampur proper, made a personal connection both to the Sufi and to the Arampur area. Although he could have simply started talking about Asta Auliya, Druma initiated his conversation with reference first to his fellow caste members and then to their neighborhood in a village just opposite from the *dargāh* in Arampur. In so doing, he revealed the interrelatedness of his caste, area, and devotional identities. The manner in which Druma effortlessly transposed the *dargāh* as a metonym for the Sufi demonstrates that Druma's regard for the Sufi is tied inexorably with a specific local place. For Druma, the *dargāh* is the locus of the Sufi's powers in life and afterlife; for others, it is the Arampur area itself wherein these powers are associated. Salman Alam's earlier narrative demonstrated how the Sufi became associated with the place of Arampur through his triumph over Raja Vicitra, who is often attributed with the creation of a monumental and successful Arampur. Yet, other residents associate him with Arampur by depicting him as the founder of the village. They narrate how the Sufi cleared the jungle, established Arampur, civilized its *janglī* inhabitants, and brought Islam to many of them.

At times, efforts by devotees in the Arampur area to associate the person, power, place, and the past of Asta Auliya with the Arampur area may lead to a conflict of group memories. A discussion between the current *faqīr* and three other Arampur residents led to an impasse after a check of a marble engraving affirmed for them that Asta Auliya had died circa 1384 C.E.[36] One person claimed that Arampur did not exist when Asta Auliya first arrived in the area, that he had civilized the *janglī log*[37] (uncivilized people), and that Raja Vicitra had flourished before his arrival. Another person argued that it was impossible for Raja Vicitra to have lived before Asta Auliya because Bakhtiyar Khilji had arrived at the time of the raja, and the Sufi—not the Delhi sultan—was the first Muslim in the area. Eaton's work on thirteenth-century Muslim expansion into Bengal has recognized the prevalence of this trope of Sufi as jungle clearer and civilizer.

---

36. As concluded from their reading of the 786 engraved in Arabic numerals mentioned earlier.

37. Literally, "jungle people."

In popular memory, some [Muslim holy men] swelled into vivid mythico-historical figures, saints whose lives served as metaphors for the expansion of both religion and agriculture. They have endured precisely because, in the collective folk memory, their careers captured and telescoped a complex historical socio-religious process whereby a land originally forested and non-Muslim became arable and predominantly Muslim.[38]

In the case of the conversation in front of the current *faqīr*, debate ensued when the story depicting Asta Auliya in the familiar role of jungle clearer and civilizer could not be accommodated within the narrative associating this Sufi with Arampur's most famous son. These men wrangled with their memories to produce a uniform group memory to suit their identities as both devotees of Asta Auliya and residents of the Arampur area, while also insinuating how the manner of the Sufi's life led to his authority to heal.

In conversation with a group of Diwan Khans in the home of Rashid Khan opposite Naugrah's Jama' Masjid, Rashid wove a thread from the story of Asta Auliya into the fabric of his family narrative. Having invited me into the men's quarters of his house, Rashid offered a *cārpāī* for me to lounge on, sent for tea, and sat with me and a number of his relatives in conversation within the cool darkness of the dried mud–covered walls. When I asked him about the name of his village, Rashid answered with a version of the narrative of Lakshman and Loka Singh settling Swami Sarai and Naugrah, a familiar story in the Arampur area (see chapter 4). When I asked what the reason was for Loka Singh's conversion, Rashid responded, "Loka Singh met the man who is buried in the *dargāh* on the east side of Arampur. He liked what he had to say and became a Mussalman" [U]. Note the contrast between this narrative, which depicts the Sufi's teaching as persuasive enough to inspire someone to change religions, and the notion argued by some area Hindus that Loka Singh converted for the sake of a land grant. These different views reflect a larger debate wrestling with the question, "Why did some indigenous Hindus decide to convert to a 'foreign' religion?" Significantly enough, the views here assume most Indian Muslims as native in lineage, even if not in belief and practice, in stark contrast to the identification of those-Muslims-as-foreigners.

These narratives about Asta Auliya establish not only the well-known story of his life but also his postmortem effectiveness as a healer and his identity as an area resident. The annual *'urs* pays homage to both and shows that an intercommunal devotional identity and a public sphere form not only through discourse but also through ritual. Like the previous stories, this ritual couples the dead healer with place and power. Because tradition regards the death of a Sufi as the rending of the final veil separating him or her from Allah, residents of the Arampur area and devotees even from outside the state celebrate the day of Asta Auliya's death, venerating his past life and present efficacy. Pushcart merchants position their vehicles, laden with fruits and sweets, along footpaths

---

38. Eaton, *The Rise of Islam and the Bengal Frontier*, pp. 207–208.

near the *dargāh*, while itinerant merchants display their wares on spreads of cloth. Children shoot balloons with a small air rifle. In two huge cauldrons, cooks prepare the free community meal for all who wish to partake.

After sundown, a small group of men perform the evening *namāz* in the mosque. Then a group of devotees, evenly divided between women and men, gather on the eastern side of the tomb and begin the long process of offering coins, incense sticks, and platters of food. Individuals and groups of devotees offer *cādars* (a tomb-covering sheet), which young men attending to the tomb spread carefully along the length of the barrow. Often these are given in fulfillment of a vow. The long chains of fresh flowers that commonly accompany these *cādars* may be devoted by individuals, families, or whole *muhallas* ("neighborhoods"). Most *muhallas* in Arampur are populated by one or a few specific castes and, therefore, are religiously distinct. Yet, *muhallas* of both Hindu and Muslim castes send their men with one or more *cādars* as physical evidence of their respect for the Sufi and their unity as a *muhalla*. When the offerings have been completed, a group of about fifty men cover their heads with whatever they have available and gather on the tomb's eastern side to offer *du'ā* under the leadership of the contemporary *faqīr*. Finally, the offerings presented earlier to the tomb are returned to their owners, who identify the changed and charged substances as both *prasād* and *baraka*.[39] Throughout the *'urs*, Hindus and Muslims of all castes and classes intermix, converse, and pray together. This and other religious celebrations provide the rare moments when village men and women freely mingle in public. Many are drawn by the *melā* atmosphere of eating, shopping, music, and socializing. Others combine these activities with their devotional practices. Whatever the case, the *'urs* of Asta Auliya and some of the other major Sufis in the area provide an opportunity for area residents, regardless of identity, to celebrate the personage collectively. They express their pride in both him and their home territory in a space that is defined by narratives as significant, shared physically in ritual once a year, and, through the gift of *muhalla cādars*, connected with the rest of Arampur.

Area residents take a similar pride in their spatial association with Shastri Brahm. Any resident can point out the local places associated with the *raja-brahm*-sultan memory, including Raja Vicitra's defunct fort, Shastri Brahm's active temple, and Bakhtiyar Khilji's mammoth mausoleum. But most indisputably will see Shastri Brahm as the most important feature of both the narrative and the area. The raja may be considered the architect of many of the oldest and most notable features in the nexus, and the sophistication of the sultan's mausoleum has attracted the attention of national and international scholars since the days of British rule. However, the primary site associated with the raja—his fort—serves now only as the setting for the *brahm*'s temple, while the Suri-era tomb of the Sultan has no greater significance for residents than as a picnic place. Clearly, these centuries-old sites have remained associated with the raja and sultan only through their connection with the contempo-

---

39. Both terms, the first from Sanskrit and the other from Persian and Arabic, denote "blessing."

rary, though dead, healer—Shastri Brahm. Oral and written narratives, whether told in family homes and tea stalls or read in the *Brahm Prakās*, reinforce these associations. Like his *dargāh* in regard to Asta Auliya, the temple often acts as a metonym for Shastri Brahm in people's conversations. Like the Sufi, the *brahm*'s renown as a famous character of the past and an effective healer of the present empowers any place associated with his person and power. His temple, situated atop the barren mound where the raja's palace had once stood, is the most obvious locus of his memory. Yet, as described in the previous chapter, some residents in the Muslim-populated *muhalla* Loharani proudly associate themselves with the memory of the pandit when they identify his cremation site in their neighborhood. Again, we note that remembering the life of a dead healer helps affirm an identity among the living that goes beyond—though without denying—the identities of Hindu and Muslim.

Ultimately, which-identity-local-residents-express-when depends on how they want to assert themselves in a particular social context. Some may derisively narrate these stories to mock them and demonstrate their religious chauvinism. However, those who respect the powers of these healers cannot help but express their own multiple identities in their narratives of authority and efficacy. Contemporary Arampur residents explain that Shastri Brahm helped kill a Hindu raja and supported a Muslim sultan despite his personal religious identity. Many of those same residents patronize Shastri Brahm and Asta Auliya with little regard for their own religious identities. These religious identities, themselves, come into question as many self-proclaimed "Hindus" and "Muslims" follow practices and beliefs that borrow from one another's "traditions" as strictly defined by many orthodox and/or orthoprax coreligionists and secular scholars.

Despite the more or less noncommunal nature of the ʿurs of Asta Auliya, some residents have made strident efforts to define rituals as either Hindu or Muslim in order to delimit participation communally. One conversation in particular demonstrated this trend. Ravan Tripathi, Hamzah Ansari, Mahagriva Singh, and Sayyid Nadimuddin gather one night in the office of a doctor adjacent to Arampur Bazaar. Despite their disparate caste and village backgrounds, these young men of middle-class and landowning families became friends while studying at Arampur High School, and together they are an important part of the Arampur cricket team. Conversation centers on the forthcoming Muḥarram commemorations. Doctor Panda explains to me that Muḥarram is observed out of sorrow for the death of Husain. When I ask Nadimuddin whether his family participates, he answers "no," saying that it was neither of any use nor the proper way to express sorrow.

With the doctor nodding his agreement, Ravan, a Hindu, answers the same question by saying, "I used to before, but not for ten or fifteen years due to the split between Hindus and Muslims. It is the fault of both sides" [H]. Hamzah, a Muslim, takes Ravan to task for the latter claim, arguing that as minorities Muslims were less to blame and had always shown respect at temples. Ravan redoubles Hamzah's excited tone as he responds, "Talk of ʿizzat (respect)? How many Hindus do you see at *roza*[40] (mausoleums) and *mazār* (shrines)? There are so many. And how many Mussalman do you see at Shastri Brahm?" Hamzah shoots back, "And what is the percentage of Mussalman in the population?" After a series of increasingly heated exchanges, the ever dispassionate Mahagriva, a Hindu, calmly explains that his family does not participate in the Muḥarram procession because "Mussalman are very wicked." This tongue-in-cheek comment and its accompanying wry smile has its intended effect, and the conversation breaks up into bantering and joking. Belying this interaction of friendly adversity resided memories of shared participation in the past and sensitivity over divisive issues in the present. Waliuddin, in his earlier conversation regarding the family relations between Naugrah and Swami Sarai, subtly noted this change when he said, "If a child was born in Naugrah, those people *used* to send money" (emphasis mine).

There are—despite the effort of some to communalize—shared spaces, sentiments, and rituals that work to counteract the divisive streams of exclusionist and disintegrative activity. Sayyid Afifuddin, a wealthy landlord of Arampur who travels for months at a time through north India giving sermons to Muslim communities, asks me one day for the "history" of Shastri Brahm. Having heard my narration of a story he already knows, he replies, "Those people say that there is *śakti* (power) there for sickness and barrenness. Muslims too [he laughs]. But not everyone believes this. Musa (Moses) went to a mountain and there was a shepherd there. The shepherd wanted to offer milk from a goat to God. Musa told him not to do this. This troubled the shepherd. 'I am poor. What to do?' God asked, 'Musa, why did you say that? I like his offering. *Kis rūp mem yād karte* (People remember God in whatever way they choose)" [U].[41] Sayyid Afifuddin then goes on to narrate stories associated with Jesus Christ as though to confirm for me, whom he assumes to be Christian, that true faith does not necessarily follow what would seem to be the expected paths for most Muslims. Faith, he suggests, can include devotion to a dead Brahman or even to someone who claimed to be the Son of God—two figures in which he certainly held no personal faith. Afifuddin does this without any loss of his own religious identity.

Rituals of family tradition, too, work to counteract the delimiting of exclusive spheres of "Hindu" and "Muslim" devotion, as was demonstrated by the reluctant participation of Sitaram Sharma in his family's commemoration of a local *shahīd*. Surprised to find him away from the small repair shop he operates, I approach Sitaram as he and his young daughter join more than a dozen of their family members beside the large concrete platform of a *shahīd*'s tomb overlooking Rani Sagar. Plainly, this leader of the local RSS *śākhā* (branch) would prefer that I not observe his participation in the honoring of a Muslim and suggests a number of times that I should observe the Kālī Pūjā of a nearby village instead. An older member of the family, after satisfying himself with

---

40. This spelling follows common pronunciation. Platts transliterates this word as *rauza*.
41. A Jewish tradition describes an identical story with a rabbi in place of Musa.

questions about my presence in the area, launches into a narrative explaining how Raja Vicitra built the reservoir for his wife 4,000 years ago. Then, in answer to my questions, he explains that his family arranges and attends this annual *pūjā* in commemoration of the help that the *shahīd* provided a member of their family when he lived "at the time when the reservoir was made" [H]. He distinguishes between his kinsman who had commissioned the *pūjā* as "Hindu by caste" and the *pūjārī* (sacrifier) as "Muhammadan by caste." These two finish positioning a garland of orange flowers and half a dozen *cādar*s atop the tomb's long barrow and light handfuls of incense stuck upright in clumps of clay. Then, nine of those present—Sitaram included—cover and bow their heads before cupping their hands in the manner of the Muslim prayer position of *duʿā* just as the *pūjārī* recites a prayer in Arabic. After the recitation, some present kiss their hands, touch them to their foreheads, and then touch the tomb. Despite his apparent discomfort, Sitaram, who does not hesitate in his criticism of Muslims, participates with his family in this annual event that does not erase the distinctions between its Hindu and Muslim participants yet links them through a shared physical vocabulary of ritual.

Once again, we are reminded of Kabir's religious vision that could transcend the religious categories of *Hindu* and *Muslim* only through the use of language and practices learned through them. Daniel Gold writes that the followers of Kabir and other Sants devoted themselves to their gurus whose "sanctified personality . . . could then serve for some as an object of devotion both readily believable and close at hand."[42] Most residents of Arampur do not have the lofty ideals of Kabir as they, like his followers, seek a more tangible center for their devotional lives. When searching for relief from illness, they may frequent the worship places of one or more dead healers. Although some refer to a healer's tradition-specific authority to justify their faith in his power, others rely on the stories that demonstrate his efficacy and reflect the intercommunal life of the temple, *dargāh*, and village. Generally, then, Arampur residents live interrelated lives with their neighbors—alive and dead—aware of religious differences only within a much larger context of multiple identities, some shared and some not.

Āzādī (Independence)

We have seen how stories about the raja, *brahm*, and sultan act as a socially pervasive and identity-forming narrative current within the pool of Arampur's group memories. Only the theme of India's Independence approaches its commonness and importance. Returning to the metaphor of an ocean of memories, the prevalence and force of this narrative current demonstrate the shared

---

42. Daniel Gold, "Clan and Lineage among the Sants: Seed, Substance, Service" in *The Sants: Studies in a Devotional Tradition in India*, Karine Schomer and W. H. McLeod, eds. Delhi: Motilal Banarsidass, 1987, p. 305.

quality of memory that envelops area residents within territorial identities beyond those of the nexus. In this case, the identity of we-Indians taps into a nationalist narrative of political and cultural self-definition relative to British imperialists and, increasingly, American neo-imperialists. Residents most commonly periodize the past with reference to "the time of the raja," "the time of the English," and "Independence."

Whereas nexus residents usually learn the group memories that we examined previously from local, oral transmissions, they know about *Āzādī* through the additional media of school texts, other books, magazines, newspapers, film, radio, and television. Many of these media are managed by national and state governments and represent their efforts to direct a narrative current serving state and national identities through local pools with the aim of incorporating them into a larger sea of community. In contrast to the widespread knowledge of and interest in the raja-*brahm*-sultan narrative, the depth of understanding of and response to *Āzādī* correspond almost exactly to the level of an individual's formal education. Because of the relative remoteness of Arampur from main lines of communication and the historically minimal British presence in the area, the event seems to have left far less impression in group memories than one might find in Indian cities and places which had greater British involvement.[43]

While most narratives that I heard regarding the raja, *brahm*, and sultan were offered without my prompting, residents seldom narrated the events of Independence. Although they commonly referred to this period, residents usually provided a full narrative regarding *Āzādī* only when I asked them to elaborate on a passing remark they made about "the time of Independence" or when I prompted them with some other deliberate question. Sometimes, as with Santa and Sayyid later, I asked why so many people spoke about *Āzādī*. More commonly, I would ask why the fifteenth of August was so important. In the overwhelming majority of cases, a resident would respond with a phrase very similar to "*Hamārā deś āzādī huā*" (Our country became independent). Often, they would follow this answer with a narrative of variable length.

A conversation with Sayyid Nadimuddin and Santa Singh demonstrates the manner in which formal education can provide a narrative that promotes a singular national identity. Acting as the integrating environment that it is by uniting members of divergent social groups in the common experience of education, Arampur High School brought these two men together as friends during their studies. Although they share a similar economic background, inasmuch as both of their families could spare them from work, send them to school, and afford to pay for college education, they come from divergent cultural backgrounds. Sayyid's family consists of wealthy Muslim landowners who once held the *zamindārī* for Arampur, while Santa's family runs a small shop in Arampur and identifies itself as both Hindu and Sikh.[44] Their response to my

---

43. For a well-analyzed example of memories that link British occupation with local life, see Shahid Amin, *Event, Metaphor, Memory: Chauri Chaura 1922–1992*. Delhi: Oxford University Press, 1995.

44. His is but one of two families in Arampur that identify themselves as Sikh.

question about *Āzādī* evidences a common identity forged in the education that they share with any of the residents of the area who consider it worthwhile and can afford it. As teachers in a privately owned school newly founded by one of them, they have now moved into the position of communicators of this *Āzādī* memory and fashioners of national identity.

A week before the annual celebrations commemorating Indian national independence on August 15, 1947, I sit talking with Sayyid, Santa, and other teachers at their school at the end of the school day. I ask, "Why do so many people talk of *Āzādī?*" Sayyid answers in his native Urdu, "In any country, there is one important day. *Āzādī* Day is ours. Before, the East India Company ruled here." Santa then picks up the narration, using Hindi, "They levied taxes. Our children could not study in schools—just like how it was in South Africa." Sayyid returns, "The *Udyogajanit Krānti* (Industrial Revolution) occurred in England. In India, the English sold cheap cloth. The English could buy it cheaply, but here it was very expensive." Santa adds, "The factories that existed here before the English were closed, and people were killed. Handlooms were destroyed. It became a big problem for India. Also, the first-class compartments in trains were only for the English. Indians could sit only in third and fourth class. Gandhi was removed from a first-class compartment. He was told that *kālā log* (black people) could not stay there." Sayyid continues, interjecting an occasional English phrase: "You [me] got *āzādī* too. So, because of all this trouble, *Āzādī* is very important. The fifteenth of August is a red letter day for India." Santa adds, "*Bhārat Mā* (Mother India) was in prison. England attacked and killed a lot of Indians. In 1757, the first war happened when the English came from Surat to Calcutta. They began to build a fort. Sirajuddaulah said 'no' and a war occurred. The English came in the name of trading."

I asked what happened then.

Sayyid: "They moved from Calicut to Calcutta and maintained an army. They made a fort and a factory. Sirajuddaulah fought them and was defeated. This was the first struggle."

Santa: "There was a lot of trouble for Indians."

Sayyid: "The English killed a lot of us. So it was a happy day when Mahatma Gandhi and Jawaharlal Nehru were national leaders."

Together: "Lakshmi Bai, Subhas Chandra Bose, Bhagat Singh, Kumar Singh, Madan Lal Dhingra, Chandrashekhar Azad, and Nana Sahib were all killed by the British."

Sayyid: "This was the *Svatantratā Senā* (Independence Army). They were freedom fighters. Most of them were between twenty and thirty years old. One was fourteen years old."

Another teacher adds: "He was shot in the mouth" [points to his mouth, tracing the bullet's path].

Sayyid: "General Dyer murdered with bullets. Do you know General Dyer?"

Santa: "There was the Jallianwala Bagh massacre."

Sayyid: "Two thousand died in 1919."

Santa: "Dyer killed them."

Sayyid: "A meeting of *bhārat kī log* (Indian people) regarding *āzādī* was happening in a garden. He arrived with the army and ordered them to fire."

Santa: "Two thousand died."

Sayyid: "Think about it: a bird is caged and struck repeatedly. How will it like it?"

Santa: "Madan Lal could not stand this so he went to England to study and shot General Dyer dead. He was a *bahādur* (hero). After Independence, in the 1971 war against Pakistan, Abdul Habib destroyed a naval vessel. The English took everyone's money, so the wealthy—[momentarily interrupting himself]— Everyone wanted to be in the government. Muhammad Ali Jinnah said, 'Make me prime minister.' Others said, 'No.' 'If you don't give it to me, *ham Mussalman* (we Muslims) will live in a separate place and give it a separate name: Pakistan.' Even today, a lot of people in Pakistan think that Partition was a mistake. A division occurred in the name of religion: Pakistan for Mussalman, Hindustan for Hindus. Abul Kalam Azad was against that. Many went to Pakistan, but many stayed. Jinnah's idea was that Hindustan would be Hindu only and Pakistan would be Muslim only. And what is there in Pakistan today? Look at [the violence in] Karachi. Many of his relatives [pointing at a bystander] went to Pakistan. His father's father didn't want to go and so didn't. Mahatma Gandhi wanted that both sides would live in India. Therefore, Mahatma Gandhi is seen as a great leader."

Sayyid: "He is the father of the nation."

I ask: "What happened in this area?"

Santa: "People were killed here. My great grandfather and father said that when the English lived here there was no work, and we were slaves. His [Sayyid's] father knows about this. The English beat us and killed us."

Sayyid: "Antu Ram was killed in Kendra. Many people died, but I do not remember their names."

When I ask how they knew about this, Sayyid answers, "It is written in books."

Another teacher adds, "There is an *itihās* (history)."

"How do you know that it is true?" I probe.

Sayyid concludes: "Some people are still alive who lived in 1947: they have seen it with their own eyes. My father has talked about it. He studied in Sassaram and saw the English bully Indians."

First, note the initiation of this team narration. As mentioned before, residents make common reference to this narrative second only to that of the raja-*brahm*-sultan narrative. Whereas residents often use their version of the latter narrative to introduce themselves and the Arampur area to outsiders, they far less frequently use a version of the *Āzādī* narrative in that way. Most commonly, "the time of Independence" acts as a temporal marker measuring the relative timing of various events or objects. So, for instance, when I asked Mahan Singh on a different occasion about high-caste attitudes toward Harijans, he first responded with a narrative of society's origin: a man had four sons, one for each *varṇa*. He then added that in Madras the Śūdras were so oppressed that they had to wear a bell around their necks to warn others of their approach. "When did this occur?" I asked. "A long time ago—1935. *Āzādī* hadn't happened yet. Only by law did it change." I asked when the law changed. Mahan Singh answered, "After *Svatantratā* (Independence)." Not only does this anecdote demonstrate the way that *Āzādī* acts as a temporal milestone against which events can be posited but also it shows how Hindi and Urdu speakers interchangeably use the Sanskrit-derived term *Svatantratā* and the Persian-derived *Āzādī* (although the latter is more common). Despite the communal shadow that Partition introduced to the event of Independence, few residents communalize their recollections of Independence to reflect pride in their religious identity or revulsion at that of another. This reveals yet another identity (i.e., we-Indians) that can displace communal identity (i.e., we-Hindus or we-Muslims) within certain contexts.

Narratives about *Āzādī* often follow the pattern of Santa and Sayyid above. The core of this narrative consists of English arrival, Indian oppression, and, finally, *Āzādī* itself. This core expresses an identity of we-Indians in contrast to those-English. Narrators often cast certain Indian characters as opponents to an English rule that is commonly depicted as an enslavement. In this way, the two teachers made mention of a number of figures, beginning with Sirajuddaulah, who stood supposedly for a united Indian resistance. Residents seldom admit to division and competition among Indians during the colonial era. When they do, they usually explain it as the result of the British policy of "divide and rule"—an English phrase referring to British subterfuge to create artificial divisions among supposedly united South Asians. The assumption, then, is that Indians rebelled together against their enslavers. This notion is fostered with the use of *Bhārat Mā* (Mother India) and *sonā ciṛiyā* (golden bird) as metaphors of an oppressed yet united people. Note how the golden bird image may be used not only as the representation of a Hindu India looted by invading Muslims (as seen in the last chapter) but also as a noncommunal India plundered by invading English, depending on the context of the narrator's self-definition. Those who would consider themselves as included in we-Hindus-as-Indians may concede an identity of we-Indians-as-Hindu-and-Muslim in the face of the divergent identity, those-English-as-invaders.

Certain figures play a prominent part in the depiction of the Independence of we-Indians. Residents overwhelmingly mention Mohandas Gandhi in reference to *Āzādī*. Congress leaders Jawaharlal Nehru and Indian National Army commander Subhas Chandra Bose come next, followed distantly by Congress leaders Maulana Abul Kalam Azad and Sardar Vallabhbhai Patel and revolutionaries Chandrashekar Azad and Sardar Bhagat Singh. The figures used to personify those-English commonly include the East India Company and General Dyer, as evidenced in the narrative of Santa and Sayyid.

To the core narrative current of arrival-oppression-*Āzādī*, other narrative strands can be added for the purpose of defining a certain type of Indian identity. At times, narrators depict the Sepoy Rebellion (1857)[45] as a precursor of the more formal Independence movement that developed at the turn of the century. Occasionally, others extend the Independence struggle further back in time when they explain that it began with Sirajuddaulah's conflict with the British in Bengal (1757). Some narrators conclude their *Āzādī* narrative with the British departure and others with the event of Partition, as again in the case of Santa and Sayyid's narrative. The manner in which the narrator depicts Partition often demonstrates an element of her or his identity. In the course of his narrative, Santa made a rough segue from the defiant assassination of General Dyer to Partition. Aware of the communally sensitive nature of the Partition topic and the Muslims present, Santa implicitly compared the assassin Madan Lal with the 1971 Muslim Indian war hero Abdul Habib as a prelude to his narration of the Partition. Next, he suggested that, although the Partition of Pakistan from India supposedly occurred in the "name of religion," Muslims have fought bravely for India against Pakistan. Then, he gently countered the communal reasons for Partition by implying that this political division among the people of the Subcontinent actually derived from British looting that compelled members of the newly impoverished upper class, including Muhammad Jinnah, to seek government positions. Jinnah, then, becomes such a person of displaced wealth motivated by a personal quest for power camouflaged as a call for justice for we-Muslims. Championing a notion of we-Indians that should never have been set in opposition to those-Pakistanis, Santa argued that Partition stands as the last act of the British divide-and-rule policy. He claimed that even many Pakistanis believe Partition to have been a mistake and that Independence leader Abul Kalam Azad (a prominent Muslim who remained in India) protested against the division.

Following these points, Santa contrasted Jinnah's vision of two communal countries ("Pakistan for Mussalman, Hindustan for Hindus") with Gandhi's secular ideal of coexistence and judged Gandhi to be the "great leader." The final piece of evidence Santa utilized in support of the idealized identity of we-Indians-as-all-South-Asians began with reference to his friend Sayyid as one of those-Muslims. He used the example of Sayyid's family to demonstrate how some of those-Muslims became those-Pakistanis, but his ultimate goal was to use Sayyid's father as an example of one of those-Muslims who refused to abjure the identity of we-Indians. Santa, then, aptly showed how communal identities can be mentioned, even highlighted, yet remain subservient in some contexts to another identity, in this case we-Indians.

However, while Santa recognized and attempted to thwart the subversive effect of the communalist narrative current on the secularist nationalist current in India, in another conversation Ravan Tripathi consciously sought to emphasize and promote a communalist countercurrent. While attending Arampur High School, Ravan befriended Santa and Sayyid and remains friends

---

45. Also known as "The Mutiny" and "The First War of Independence."

with them to this day, often drinking tea with them and others in one of Arampur Bazaar's tea shops. One day in his grain store, I asked him why so many people spoke of *Āzādī*, and he responded with a narrative using the familiar pattern of arrival-enslavement-*Āzādī* and the characters of Gandhi, Nehru, and Bhagat Singh, among others. When asked about Partition, he showed how the inclusive identity of we-Indians in an *Āzādī* narrative can be submerged by the overpowering resistance of a countercurrent narrative depicting Muslims as aggressors against all peoples, even themselves.

As he relaxes comfortably against the cushion of his seat, Ravan replies to my question about *Āzādī*:

> Bharat and Pakistan were divided. But this was really an issue between Jinnah and Nehru. In reality, a war between Hindus and Mussalman occurred in India. Actually, there is no internal difference: both are but one. They are two brothers. One brother became a Mussalman and believed in another *dharm*, so it is his right to do *pūjā* in a way that's pure for him. I believe in a separate *dharm*, and that is my right. . . . If at this time Jinnah had become prime minister of Bharat, then Bharat and Pakistan would not be divided today. But Nehru said that he would be prime minister and so the division of Bharat and Pakistan occurred. One other thing: I said that Hindus and Mussalman are but one, from one family. But the thing is [Mussalman] do not live in much peace anywhere. It is believed that wherever they live, they fight there. It is believed that Hindus and Mussalman kill one another but in Pakistan there are only Mussalman— *muhājir* (immigrants) in Sindh . . . there are Afghanis, Punjabis, and Sindhis. There is every kind of conflict among them. They always fight bloody battles. Among those people *dharm* is the most important thing. . . . It is these people's nature. And *ahiṃsā* ("nonviolence") is taught where *ham log* (we people) live.

I asked Ravan who *ham log* were, and he answered, "We whose religious books are the Vedas and *Purāṇas*" [H/E].

Just as we witnessed Ram Nisad use a narrative regarding the East India Company's incursion into India as a stepping stone into a warning of the ongoing Western economic exploitation of India (see chapter 2), so Ravan answered my question with a narrative of Partition that he then used to demonstrate the "inherent" aggressiveness of Muslims. He began his answer to my query with reference to the narrative of Nehru and Jinnah's clash of personal ambitions, much as Santa and Sayyid explained. At the same time, he deliberately strove to make the point that "we-Indians" include both Hindus and Muslims because they are "but one." He used the metaphor of brothers strikingly similar to, and perhaps inspired by, the story of Lakshman Singh and Loka Singh. Yet, in the course of the interpretation of his own narrative, Ravan slowly began to foreground one identity in place of another.

Why did Ravan's views at first parallel but then diverge so radically from the fraternalism of Santa and Sayyid's narrative, suddenly distinguishing an identity for "our (Hindu) people" that is antagonistically set apart from Muslims? The answer resides in the shift that occurred in his immediate primary identity: from we-Indians-as-Hindus-and-Muslims to we-Indians-as-Hindus established in juxtaposition to those-Muslims-as-aggressors. In his response to my question regarding *Āzādī*, Ravan answered from his identity as "Indian" in opposition to the one that he posits on me: "Westerner." He began with a narrative relatively similar to that given by his friends Santa and Sayyid, with whom he shared a government-directed education that uses a nationalist narrative to define an inclusive, noncommunal "Indian" identity. After echoing the we-Hindus-and-Muslims-as-Indians theme of this narrative, Ravan displayed the influence of the Hindu chauvinist politics that he follows with a Partition narrative that absolutely divides South Asia into two religious nations. Ravan relied on an implied narrative of Muslim conflict in all countries and against all peoples, including themselves. In our conversation, he referred to intra-Muslim conflict and expected me to know the example narratives that demonstrate it. This shift began with the carefully anonymous claim, "It is believed that everywhere they live, they fight there," and was soon completed with Ravan's own undisguised claims about "these people's nature." Finally, he defined *ham log* with reference to place (i.e., India), ideology (i.e., *ahiṃsā*), and religious tradition (i.e., Vedas and *Purāṇas*). The incompatibility of the national fraternity of the first narrative and the communal chauvinism of the second reflect two group identities with which Ravan associates: we-Hindus-and-Muslims-as-Indians (as instilled by government education) and Indian-as-Hindu (as promoted by chauvinist organizations). This dynamic of contradiction demonstrates how different identities exist simultaneously in an individual, with a shifting emphasis that varies according to social context. Thus, some narratives show that group identity dominates an individual only at the particular time, place, and social situation of the narration.

Beyond its use by communal chauvinists to demonstrate the barbarism of their religious enemies, Partition got little mention among those with whom I spoke. Two reasons may explain why few residents mentioned Partition in their *Āzādī* narratives (only nine of thirty-two narratives about *Āzādī* collected included an unprompted reference to Partition). First, government programs primarily use the *Āzādī* narrative and celebration in the promotion of nationally unifying identity of we-Indians-as-all-religions. Second, western Bihar suffered a small fraction of the Partition violence and upheaval that devastated Punjab and Bengal. Therefore, the personal memories of the survivors of those years dwell more on the more apparent changes accompanying *Āzādī* than on the less apparent horrors following Partition.[46]

In useful contrast with the lack of discussion regarding Partition is the near total silence associated with a local indigo factory. Located near the slow-flowing and meandering river just west of Naugrah, the extensive ruins of the factory include two long rows of interconnected square tanks, whose cement-lined brick

46. Nita Kumar delves into children's memories of and their education concerning Partition in "Children and Partition: History for Citizenship," Occasional Paper No. 167 (February 1998), Centre for Studies in Social Sciences, Calcutta.

walls admit little decay despite the moderate jungle that has overtaken the area. These facilities, built deeply into the ground, have fared better than the adjoining brick buildings above ground, whose few remains continue to deteriorate into crumbled rubble. Although at the edge of the nexus area, the site is a popular bathing and swimming place for the boys and men of Naugrah. Considering that Gandhi initiated his first campaign against social injustice in South Asia with his 1917 Satyagraha protests against indigo in Bihar's Champaran district to the north of Arampur, we might expect residents to refer to the factory in their *Āzādī* accounts as a symbol of British oppression. Gandhi had responded to the complaint of a Champaran villager to investigate abuses committed by British indigo planters against local fieldworkers, who were often forced to plant the dye-producing crop in place of more practical food crops.[47] Yet, despite the importance of the *Āzādī* memory to so many residents and the centrality of Gandhi in that narrative,[48] only three residents made unprompted mention of the abandoned factory, its proprietress Basanti Bibi, or her derelict house on a rocky promontory nearby.

There is little consistency among those who talk about the factory, as some residents of the nexus display during an evening of conversation in a Bazaar tea stall opposite Arampur's post office. Mahagriva Singh and Balaram Singh of Swami Sarai sit with Majnun Khan of Arampur and a number of residents from Arampur's Qasbah *muhalla* when I ask what the factory was by the river.

Mahagriva Singh: "*Nīl* (indigo) was grown there. I heard that it was in the time of the English. I do not know how it worked."

Me: "How long has it been there?"

Mahagriva Singh: "Three hundred or four hundred years."

Majnun Khan: "No."

Mahagriva Singh: "Yes."

Me: "How long was it open?"

Mahagriva Singh asks the Qasbah residents, who do not seem to know. He prods them: "*Sunī-sunāī!* (Tell the folklore!)"

Qasbah resident: "We don't know it."

Balaram Singh: "Basanti Bibi."

Me: "Who?"

Mahagriva Singh: "She had a bungalow that is now very old."

Me: "Who was she?"

Mahagriva Singh: "*Zamīndār?*" [he asks the Qasbah residents.]

Qasbah resident: "She lived after Bakhtiyar Khan."

47. S. M. Burke and Salim Al-Din Quraishi, *The British Raj in India: An Historical Review*. New York: Oxford University Press, 1996, p. 199. Paradoxically, the English word *indigo*, used for the crop which the British forced so many Indian farmers to cultivate, derives from the ancient Greek *Indikos* ("of India," i.e., the land beyond the Indus).

48. Residents mentioned Gandhi in more than sixty narratives that I recorded, more than twice as many as Nehru, the nearest competitor among modern figures.

Balarama Singh: "She had a *jagīr* ('government-granted estate'). Go to Naugrah and ask the elder people there."

Me: "How do you know about her?"

Balarama Singh: "I do not know the 'history,' I have only heard her name."

Me: "Why do people talk so much about Shastri Brahm, Raja Vicitra, and Bakhtiyar Khan, but not about the factory?"

Balaram Singh: "In the same way that there were emperors after Aurangzeb but people do not know them because they were not famous."

Me: "Did Gandhi come here?"

Balaram Singh: "No."

Qasbah resident: "He went to Champaran."

Like the previous memories considered, these recollections refer to a relic (Basanti Bibi's factory and house), calendar ("in the time of the English" and "after Bakhtiyar Khan"), and authorized transmitters (elder people of Naugrah). Indeed, members of the Khan family in Naugrah were far more likely to refer to the factory than anyone else in the nexus, undoubtedly because they sued to obtain the land on which it stands. One member of this Muslim family narrated how a dead Hindu "guru" guided his paternal grandfather through a dream to burn frankincense as an act of devotion, which, in return, gained a favorable judgment for him from the Calcutta High Court and a stinging punishment for Basanti Bibi from a swarm of bees. (He also identified Basanti Bibi as the local rani who built the water reservoir near Bakhtiyar Khan's tomb that is usually identified as one of Raja Vicitra's work projects, thus illustrating yet again how memories of minor nexus events can be absorbed by the dominant current of the raja-*brahm*-sultan narrative.)

In contrast with the differences among raja-*brahm*-sultan narratives, the debate surrounding Basanti Bibi's memory arises more from the faltering uncertainty caused by little interest than from conflicting opinions reflecting the great significance of the narrative for the community. Overall, narratives of Basanti Bibi and her factory have little currency despite an apparent narrative and physical connection with the popular and rigorously taught narratives of *Āzādī*. Perhaps this is the case because Basanti Bibi, identified by nearly all narrators as an Indian, muddies the preferred distinction between the imperious British and the oppressed Indians. As an Indian who profited from the British introduction of indigo and the harmful effects on Indian farmers, she threatens the unified identity of we-Indians created in juxtaposition with those-foreigners in the context of the memory of the Independence struggle. When I asked him who she was, one resident attempted to racially marginalize her identity with the response, "*Āp logoṁ kī birādārī se* (From your people's community): Anglo-Indian." Although recognizing her Indian birth, this resident suggested that her mixed ethnicity put Basanti Bibi among "my people" (that is, for him, those-foreigners, outside of or, at least, a marginal member of we-Indians). To admit otherwise would be to acknowledge that the boundary between the two groups is not as clearly defined as nationalists prefer. Because the memory of Basanti Bibi serves no local group's interests and, indeed, challenges the imagined unity of we-Indians, she is more forgotten than remembered. Little more than the durability of her abandoned factory remains to challenge the silence.

In some ways more problematic than the memory of Basanti Bibi is that of Gandhi himself. In the overwhelming majority of cases, residents remember him favorably as *rāṣṭrapati* or "the father of the nation." However, a corrosive undercurrent celebrates his assassination without refuting his role in Independence. Through a reinterpretation of the mainstream *Āzādī* narrative, certain organizations advance this seemingly paradoxical view to fashion a group memory serving an Indian national identity defined by interests often at odds with those promoted by Gandhi. Devamitra Pandit and Ganesh Tripathi portrayed this alternate view of Gandhi as we sat talking together in the latter's shop in Arampur Bazaar.

As I converse with them about history textbooks mandated for government schools, the M.A.-educated Tripathi (who identified his mother language as "Devanagari") advises me to go to the family of Satya Pandey for books about "real history." When I ask what the difference was between these books and the textbooks, he replies, "In [the latter] there is no explanation if [the writers] are Mussalman, Brahman, or Kṣatriya. There is no special difference other than this. . . . Different people have different *itihās* ('history'). Maybe Satya Pandey has a different book than [his Brahman neighbor]. . . . You should go to the place run by the RSS in Banaras. There you can get a *Bhāratī itihās* (Indian history)." After Tripathi describes the RSS as "*Hindu logoṁ ko saṅghaṭhan*" (an organization for Hindu people), the formally uneducated Devamitra Pandit adds, "There is a connection between it and *Bhagvān* (God) [points upward], so it cannot be destroyed." Ganesh Tripathi continues, "It could fix the problem in Jammu and Kashmir[49] in twenty-four hours. It is not a political party, it is a *saṃsthā* (association). BJP is the political party; they came out of the RSS." Then Devamitra Pandit reaffirms his previous point, "There is only one VHP in the world. The RSS cannot make a mistake because it's connected with *Bhagvān*." His companion adds, "It is a discipline."

I then ask whether Gandhi's assassin had been an RSS member.[50] Ganesh Tripathi answers, "It supported Nathuram Godse. He wrote *Gāndhī Badhan Kyoṁ* (*Why Was Gandhi Killed?*) in jail. He thought that Gandhi had made a mistake. Gandhiji wanted to give money to Pakistan. He wanted to give to both Nehru and Jinnah." When I ask him what he thought about this, Ganesh Tripathi responds, "The RSS thinks that Mahatma Gandhi was *rāṣṭrapati* (Father of the Nation). He spoke against urinating in trains." When I ask whether Gandhi had made a mistake and whether his death had been a good thing, Ganesh Tripathi answers "yes" both times. Responding to my question about

---

49. He refers to the perennial conflict between India and Pakistan regarding the territorial affiliation of this state, currently inflamed by a battle for secession.

50. Nathuram Godse had quit the organization some years before his murder of Gandhi.

what would have happened had Gandhi survived, Devamitra Pandit says, "The killing would have continued. If Sardar Vallabhbhai Patel[51] had been prime minister in Nehru's time, there would be peace everywhere. There would be no Mussalman." I ask where they would have gone. "Pakistan," he answers, "Patel said, 'You caused Partition, so go to your own place.' There would not be a problem now in Punjab, Assam, or Kashmir." Finally, I ask if it would be good if all Muslims left India. "Yes," Devamitra Pandit replies firmly.

The honorifics ("*jī*" and "Mahatma") with which both men referred to Gandhi demonstrates the nominal regard with which they hold him. Whereas Basanti Bibi's involvement with the British indigo industry can be forgotten or her physical person associated with those-foreigners, the memory of Gandhi perpetuated by both the inertia of his national fame and the nationalism of government-mandated education makes any effort to portray him in a similar way impractical. How, then, can these Hindu chauvinists understand the "Father of the Nation" who accommodated Muslims in a nation which, they believe, should be reserved for Hindus alone? If he does not derive from those-foreigners (British or Muslim) and is, ethnically and religiously, among us-Indians, who is he?

Perhaps through their association with the RSS, these two men have decided that Gandhi's mistaken ideology condemned him to a place outside the appropriate realm of Indian-as-Hindu identity. Because he was not an "other" but, rather, a flawed yet powerful one-of-us, he had to be neutralized/executed by someone of the proper ideology for Indian identity: the Hindu nationalist Nathuram Godse. In their opinion, it is because this ideology had not been fully implemented that the nation to this day remains hampered by the divisive presence of Muslims. Rather than acknowledge the alternative identities (religious in the case of Punjabi Sikhs and regional in the instance of most Assamese), with which some citizens violently assert themselves as not-Indian, Devamitra and Ganesh dismissed these secessionist struggles as not caused by Indians. They collapsed all possible opposition to their notion of a revered national identity into the category Muslim-as-invader. Indian newspapers and magazines often perpetuate this perspective by focusing on the role of the ubiquitous "foreign [i.e., Pakistani] hand" in regional disruptions rather than on the complaints and resistance of regional inhabitants. This perspective represents the hybridization of two views of India advanced by the British—India as originally Hindu and a singular Indian nation—and demonstrates yet another way in which Western epistemology (e.g., historiography) and ideology (e.g., nationalism) have been appropriated by Indian agents in the service of creating native identities.

Using the paradigm of identity formation, we could depict the actual conflict between the British Empire and the Indian nationalists as one between

---

51. (1875–1950) An Independence leader who, as home minister and deputy prime minister, gained the reputation as an "iron man" through his determined and, at times, violent integration of princely states, including that of the Nizam of Hyderabad, into the Federal Republic of India.

two sets of ideological identities. The empire sought to create a unifying identity among the subjects of that empire. To this day, Arampur area residents repeat (sometimes fondly) the popular adage from the British Raj's zenith days, "The sun never set on the British Empire." Indian nationalists, however, attempted to subvert this identity with a nationalist alternative. Of course, to do so required an alternative group memory serviced by a system of narration. They turned, paradoxically enough, to the historiographic tools that they learned through the British educational system imposed on them and accepted by many. The legacy of this conflict remains in the current government-mandated public school system that trumpets a national and state identity at the expense of regional and local identities. The conflict among the nationalists that resulted in Partition can be understood, in part, to be the struggle for an Indian identity. Congress leaders needed to construct notions of Indian identity to counter the idea of empire, but the Muslim League balked at what they considered to be a Hindu-dominant identity. Despite their secular assurances, Gandhi's home rule ideal of Rām Rāj (rule of the god Ram) and Nehru's support for the Cow Protection Act (restricting slaughter for beef, a favorite meal of many Muslims) suggested that their understanding of the Congress-proposed national identity favored Hindus over Muslims as more normatively Indian.

A review of government-mandated textbooks for social studies and history proves how aggressively the government promotes its nationalist *Āzādī* narrative in the effort to instill a national identity in children. The textbook authors lavish overwhelmingly more attention on this narrative and the more prominent figures associated with it than on any other topic (see the appendix for each book's table of contents). In Standard II, the forty-page social studies book, *Nūtan Bāl Samāj* (*A Young Person's Society*), includes one-page biographies of five historical figures, all of whom but one gained prominence in the Independence struggle. The exception is the Buddha. The Standard IV social studies textbook, *Hamārā Deś Bhārat* (*Our Country India*), commits a quarter of its two hundred pages (otherwise concerned with India's natural environment, physical resources, transportation lines, communication systems, and central government) to descriptions of the lives of fifteen of the "primary leaders of India's Independence Movement." The Standard V social studies textbook, *Ham aur Hamārī Duniyā* (*We and Our World*) similarly dedicates nearly a quarter of its text to the Independence Movement, following chapters that examine the geography, natural environment, and cultures of the world.

History classes replace social studies in Standard VI. The course books for this and the next standard deal exclusively with "Ancient" and "Middle Period" history and, so, have little to say about *Āzādī* beyond what is mentioned in the introduction of Western imperialism to Asia. The theme returns, however, in Standard VIII in the textbook *Ādhunik Bhārat* (*Modern India*), which features on its cover an image of Gandhi stooped in the act of collecting sea salt in defiance of the British law prohibiting the Indian manufacture of salt in 1930. Behind him a headline from the *Bombay Chronicle* declares in English:

"Mahatma Breaks Salt Law." The textbook briefly details the beginning of the modern age in Europe before shifting hastily to the arrival of Europeans in India. After narrating the expansion of British rule and the rising Indian resistance, the text concludes with the achievement of *Āzādī* and the establishment of both the constitution and the Republic of India.

Standards IX and X use a two-part textbook collectively titled *Sabhyatā kā Itihās* (*History of Civilization*). It describes the development of and diversity among world civilizations. The Standard IX text covers the prehistoric era to the European and American revolutionary and nationalist movements of the nineteenth centuries. The final standard's text has seven chapters with a total of 186 pages that cover "Imperialism" (48 pages), "Indian Ascendancy" (20 pages), and "India's Independence Movement" (51 pages). Once again, the state-directed narrators of history textbooks devote a quarter or more of their text to *Āzādī*. In half of all the texts within which they will study history—from the Ancient to Modern Periods—local students will encounter Independence narratives. Students are persistently exposed to narratives of and references to *Āzādī* that help forge a nationalist identity meant to transcend diverse identities of religion, caste, and class. The significance of this influence has ignited recent debates in Uttar Pradesh and Bihar, as newly elected governments have attempted to rewrite their state's school books for the promotion of their ideological and social agendas.

Central and state governments commemorate *Āzādī* through nationalist rituals as well as state education. August fifteenth is an annually observed central government holiday, when all public services are closed. Schools often run special programs of nationalist poetry reading and singing. The government-run radio and television systems Akashvani and Doordarshan celebrate the day with various programs celebrating nationalism and patriots. Not uncommonly, residents would respond to my question about the importance of August fifteenth with an additional reference to the annual celebration of Republic Day on January 20, a holiday that commemorates the creation of India's constitution. The central and state governments celebrate both these days as holidays during which public offices close and government-sponsored parades and gatherings occur.

In 1995, two schools in Arampur—Arampur High School and Sayyid's private school—had voluntary programs for students on August fifteenth. Among the government buildings near the bus stand, flag-unfurling ceremonies took place at the block development office, the general hospital, the veterinarian hospital, the telephone exchange, and the *thānā* (police station). In a pattern to be repeated at each one of those occasions, the *mukhya* (head) of each village arrives with some of the other wealthy men from the area, as well as public servants (e.g., inspector of police, block development officer) and a gaggle of expectant young children. With everyone at attention and facing the flag pole (around which a *cauk* or ornamental design has been traced in white powder), the guest of honor pulls the string that bundles the flag atop the mast. With this tug, the flag unfurls and a cloud of flower petals floats to the ground.

Someone cries, "*Bhārat!*" to which the crowd cheers, "*Jai!*" (Hurrah!). Similar exclamations follow the calling out the names of some combination of famous patriots: Mahatma Gandhi, Jawaharlal Nehru, Indira Gandhi, Subhas Chandra Bose, and Bhagat Singh. Following the national anthem, sweets, *pān*, and cigarettes are distributed to the powerful, prominent, and wealthy, while one policeman distributes sweets to the quietly insistent children.

In conclusion to the last two chapters, I need to reemphasize my earlier point about exaggeration through examination. So as to highlight noncommunal identities, I have contrasted them with *Hindu* and *Muslim* identities, thus exaggerating the prominence of the latter. Also, I have purposely analyzed narratives that are either among the most common or the most communalist in order to draw two conclusions. First, narratives often express the group memories by which individuals define groups with which they associate themselves and others. Second, though an undercurrent of communalist narrative moves through the pool of Arampur social interaction, it would be a great mistake to overestimate it as always dominant and to underestimate or ignore the additional currents of territorial, caste, class, and familial memories organized around common group identities.

However, what cannot be overemphasized is the importance of narrative. The frequency with which Arampur residents answered questions about a local celebration, geographical feature, or piece of architecture with a story reflects the importance of the narrative strategies by which they emplot themselves not only on a map with spatial and temporal dimensions but also within a liquid world of constantly shifting social relations. Narratives operate in service of group memories, a crucial component within and between groups. The manner in which personal narrative strands shift in response to surface currents, crosscurrents, and countercurrents demonstrates the fluidity of the identities that often propel or are propelled by them. Individual residents of the Arampur area negotiate these currents according to the particular dimension of their complex identities (composed of multiple group affiliations) that they care to express at any particular moment in their lives in the ocean of the streams of memory.

Conclusion

The Well of Meanings

Arampur's busy main bazaar ends abruptly where it meets the eroding mound that was Raja Vicitra's fort. Beneath the stolid mass of the fort's gate, a road extends east and west toward other villages of the nexus. Not far from this normally well-trafficked intersection and just to the side of the Jama' Masjid and the attached Sufi shrine that houses the na 'l sahib, eight pillars stand above and surround an unusual large well. Its octagonal walls, lined with large blocks of the local sandstone, stand perhaps 6 meters opposite one another and disappear into scummy green water. A series of steps pierce one of the walls just above water level and climb to ground level after a 90-degree turn to the left. Forsaking entirely its exposed water in preference for government-installed tubewells, residents take advantage of the well only as a place to sit and socialize with neighbors and friends wandering the road to or from other villages.

By its name alone, however, this well has become a place of local contention. Some area residents, mostly Hindu, claim that the well's name is *hāthī kū'ā*, and others, mostly Muslim, call it *hāth kū'ā* [U].[1] The difference—the presence or absence of a final *ī* on one word—may seem minor to the outsider yet can indicate a world of difference to an area resident. Those who call it *hāthī kū'ā*, which means "elephant well," typically claim that Raja Vicitra built it to wash his elephants. Those who prefer *hāth kū'ā*, which means "hand well," say that the Delhi sultan who conquered the area built the well with the adjacent mosque so Muslims could performs their *wuzū* (ablutions) before their prayers.[2]

One might be tempted to seize on the well as a symbol of communal tension that divides even the most mundane facets of a shared environment. Hindus might be said to claim it for their own through the person of the Hindu

---

1. Other variants of these names replace *kū'ā* with the synonyms *kuṅwāṅ* and *nārā*.

2. Wendy Doniger has drawn to my attention that, ironically, the word *hāthī* is linked etymologically with *hāth* as derived from the Sanskrit *hasta* via *hastin* ("one with a hand," such as the elephant's trunk, apparently).

173

raja, while Muslims use the Muslim sultan. But this would oversimplify a situation that demands more nuanced analysis in scholarship. I would argue that the well finds its place on many of the maps by which nexus residents orient themselves relative to their time, space, and identity. And surely, some of these maps are communal and do attempt to label territory and communities as Hindu and Muslim.

But not all maps depict such an absolute polarity. Even those that distinguish between Hindu and Muslim need not necessarily assume the total, mutual exclusion of members of one group from the other. Many Hindus who identified the raja as Hindu and the sultan as Muslim declared the well the product of the latter, obviously not needing to force it onto Hindu territory. The fact that even the chauvinists on both sides claim the well for their groups according to the raja-*brahm*-sultan narrative upon which they largely agree (and which has contrasting versions that both sides know) demonstrates the tenacity of village and nexus group identity and the effectiveness of this memory to both express and perpetuate these identities. The well is meaningful not just for its depth or utility but also for the significance that the raja-*brahm*-sultan narrative lends it as a meaningful place on individuals' mnemonic maps of everyday life. It finds its way into many of the multiple pasts by which individuals construct their multiple identities.

This book has endeavored to demonstrate that group memories reflect the dynamic by which individuals in the Arampur nexus maintain a set of group identities, including, but not exclusively, religious identities. I hope it contributes to the current scholarly conversation regarding communalism in India by exploring the broad social context of identity formation and expression within the narrow area of a single group of villages. The focus on narrative permits us to listen to local discourses, hear the various concerns that they voice, and explore the different identities from which they speak. Not eschewing my role as interpreter and analyst, I have sought to write in such a way that Indians are the subjects of their own narratives while they are the objects of this study.

Previous scholarship has too often either unrealistically reified religion or ignored its unique social aspects. Works that have focused on religion to the exclusion of larger social issues often project onto Indians religious identities (with particular focus on *Hindu* and *Muslim*) that appear internally singular and absolutely exclusive. Although some authors have challenged such monolithic portrayals, they often note only the internal schisms that divide a group into smaller groups and fail to consider the identities by which individuals can claim membership in multiple religious and other social groups. This tendency, coupled with the long-standing, predominant interest of Western scholarship in Indian religiosity, has mistakenly led some to overemphasize the considerable importance of religious belief, practice, and institutions in India at the expense of other important social factors. This has resulted in the bifurcated characterization of time, space, and society in India as simply Hindu and Muslim.

Conscious of these tendencies among some, other scholars have overcompensated with an effort to depict religion as merely one ideology among many in the service of powerful political and economic interests. Some go so far as to portray Hindu and Muslim identities as primarily the construction of British agents. Too often this type of analysis impoverishes the agency of South Asians and/or focuses only on their subaltern resistance without appreciating their efforts to manage the perpetual and dynamic processes that negotiate tradition and change. South Asians have accomplished this through a variety of responses, including outright rejection, unconscious assimilation, grudging acceptance, and willful appropriation of Western influences (including epistemologies) by various segments of society. Furthermore, religion must be treated as more than an ideology because of the nonreflexive and habitual nature of many of its practices, which, through physical incorporating practices in meaningful places, help to define the identity of groups bodily.

Several examples of recent scholarship have aptly argued these points and deftly portrayed the impact of historical forces and social developments on long-standing issues of identity. Self-identified Muslims arrived in a country that they, and generations of West Asians before them, termed *al-Hind* long before any residents of the Subcontinent identified themselves with that particular name. Foreigners and natives recognized differences between one another, some of which they valorized and some which they disparaged. But as West Asian and Central Asian merchants, soldiers, and Sufis became permanent immigrants, parts of their identities also took root in South Asian soil, despite religious distinctions or cultural affiliations and family identifications with other places. While "Turks" and "Hindus," as they often labeled one another and increasingly themselves, began mutual participation in commerce, governance, land control, and certain religious practices, they started to develop shared identities that complemented identities they did not and could not share. In just this way, Urdu developed among Turkish Muslim soldiers as a linguistic identity that fostered interaction with the non-Muslims surrounding their encampments (*urdū* derives from the Turkish for "camp").

British hegemony thrust new cultural, political, and economic factors into this situation. Imperial efforts to define, maintain, and manage South Asian social and political formations, as well as the later introduction of representational politics, worked to alter, but not to construct ex nihilo, religious identities. To suggest otherwise would be to underrate the depth of these identities for and the self-awareness of so many South Asians. Contemporary Indian religious chauvinists have proven themselves as adept as many British and South Asians before them in the exploitation of these and other identities for their political ends.

The Arampur nexus acts as a setting in which local residents, self-consciously and otherwise, integrate and exclude themselves or are excluded from groups that surround them. These groups often identify themselves with the territory with which they associate. So, for instance, a girl identifies with her natal family, with whom she lives in a house in a *muhalla* that includes other members of her family's caste. If her family can spare her from work, she studies in the village school and meets children of other *muhalla*s. If her family has enough wealth and interest, she may study in the high school and meet women from other nexus villages while also learning lessons in state and national identity. When she reaches puberty, her family may demonstrate its economic status by marrying her into another village area, perhaps in another state altogether. Although her caste identity does not change, her family, village, and nexus identity most probably will. Even though she will tell the census taker that she is Hindu, she will have had to alter somewhat her religious identity, in communion with her new family and village identity, in order to perform the expected rituals to a different household deity and village guardian spirit. Yet, if she visits her natal home, she may return to the shrine of Mubarak Shah and offer thanksgiving for his help in her bearing a son. In another case, a poor family may have the resources just to marry their daughter to a family in their own village, requiring a shift in family identity only—onerous as this must be. All the while, the village nexus works as a useful setting for us to examine the interconnection and interplay between various group identities, whether based in family, class, caste, gender, territory, language, or religion.

Because groups often express their common interests and, thus, define themselves through narratives of the past, these have served as the medium by which we have examined group identity. Narratives serve as a bridge by which individuals emplot themselves in time and space through the group, overcoming the finitude of lived time and the vastness of cosmic time, as well as the unbounded expanse of space. But what acts as one group's narrative of the past may appear to another as a story of fiction.

Noted essayist and travel writer V. S. Naipaul has opined, "Respect for the past is new in Europe; and it was Europe that revealed India's past to India and made its veneration part of Indian nationalism. It is still through European eyes that India looks at her ruins and her art."[3] The fact that some Indians accept this perspective may have been demonstrated one day when the shiftless Adit Singh implored me, even as I asked him about his village's past, "You must translate for us whatever you find about the history of Arampur! How else will we know about it!?!" Naipaul is right only to the degree that Indians have been convinced or convince themselves that European historiography alone "reveals" the past. The past of Raja Vicitra and Shastri Brahm, so often prompted in the minds of residents as they see or are asked about a specific ruined fort and active temple, finds no place in the Western-style historiography that undergirds the six-volume *Comprehensive History of Bihar*. Yet that past remains *vital* in the lives and identities of nexus members. Of course, Western and Westernized observers such as Naipaul might label such a narrative as "myth" because its oral transmission and nonhuman agents cannot be qualified by the tools of the historiographic paradigm. Too often this label works to dismiss the narrative, and sometimes the narrator, from serious consideration.

To sidestep such arguments of veracity, I have argued for these narratives to be considered as the group memories for those who believe them to depict actual

---

3. V. S. Naipaul, *An Area of Darkness*. New York: Macmillan, 1965, p. 217.

events. This notion aptly captures the dynamic nature of these narratives, their intersubjective construction and reconstruction, and their preservation and expression through bodily commemoration. Furthermore, discussing narratives of the past as memory finds resonance not only in the Hindi and Urdu of Bihar but also in the English of American culture. Because groups recognize the importance of their truth claims regarding past events, they develop specialized techniques of transmission, authorization, and verification for the narrative, whether it is the oral telling of an illiterate or the written historiography of an academic.

Our analysis of group memories from the Arampur area has portrayed an ocean not of disparate stories but of strands, streams, and currents of narratives, many of which run crosswise or counter to others, yet all of which are propelled by shared group interests. Powerful regional or national narrative currents may coopt local narratives altogether. In this way, an individual can narrate the memory of an ancient raja as either the expression of a common village identity including Hindus and Muslims or as a depiction of an exclusive religious identity used to define a nation. Those who remember the cremation site of a *brahm* need not, by doing so, necessarily express an identity of religious devotion so much as one of village affiliation, should that *brahm* and his worship represent a unique and, thus, defining dimension of the village. At one moment, individuals may remember certain events that demonstrate their solidarity as a particular group while, at another moment and in a different context, the same people may recall other incidents that portray them at odds with one another as members of other, separate groups. In this way, residents of a *camṭol* may show themselves as Hindus through one story and as non-Hindus through another. Despite the inherent inertia of these narrative streams and their associated identities, some memories more than others are vulnerable to manipulation. Recognizing the motivational and emotional energy locked in such narratives, various political and religious leaders have attempted to manipulate group memories through tellings and interpretations remade in order to align group interests with their agendas. These are not merely political constructions but the effective, if often tragic, exploitation of pre-existing worldviews and sentiments. Yet, it would be naive to expect that these narratives can ever exist unchanged. As surely as historiography has reinterpreted even the best documented event to suit new social contexts, so all other forms of group memory operate within an intersubjective dynamic of confirmation and challenge motivated by the interests of asymmetrically empowered agents.

Through this complex and public interplay of memories, residents create a mnemonic map of the territory in which they live their lives. Narratives make certain places more meaningful than others, reflecting the social interrelations and tensions that color the map. But, because no individual belongs to only one group, each individual emplots herself or himself through a variety of maps, sorting through a mental map case and advancing one over others in response to the demands of the social context of the moment.

This dynamic of multiple identities could be further explored in any number of ways. First, as described in the introduction, another project might examine the unique features of women's narratives and identities in greater detail than I have been able to do here. Yet another project might focus more concertedly on individuals. Observing how the language, posture, and behavior of an individual shifts in everyday life according to social context and how these changes reflect the variety of group identities with which the person associates would offer valuable insights into multiple facets of any individual's public associations. Research in a better documented area might contrast local memories to historiographic memories and attempt to account for the differences in the representations of the past. Travelers' accounts, court records, government reports, and other resources might offer insightful contrasts to local narratives and outline changes in group definitions and interrelations. Although I have referred to these sources, limited as they are, for the Arampur nexus, I have deliberately left them out of the narrative analysis so as not to confuse what a foreign researcher can discover with what residents remember and, thus, remove the emphasis from them as agents of their own remembering.

Finally, scholarship would benefit from a reconsideration of how practices and beliefs become defined as belonging to one specific tradition *and* how a particular tradition becomes identified with certain practices and beliefs. To what degree can Sufi shrine veneration be accurately described as "Islamic" when so many non-Muslims participate and so many Muslims disparage such activities? When I identify Shastri Brahm's temple as "Hindu," don't I establish expectations as to whom its clientele includes and does not include? Without asking her, how do I religiously identify the woman who prays both there and at Asta Auliya's tomb? Not all researchers have the opportunity (albeit seldom taken) I did of simply asking the people I worked with, "What is your religion?" Yet, of course, just that question immediately limits the response. Such concerns should be of interest to scholars of other religions as well and to all of us who teach. It becomes all too easy, particularly in the undergraduate classroom, to simplify the portrayal of a religious tradition to the point that social contexts shared with members of other traditions disappear. In this common situation, Hinduism, Islam, or whatever religion is on the introductory syllabus becomes defined according to the *unique* features that *distinguish* it from other traditions. It would be worthwhile to consider how to make this necessary point without overlooking the interactive cultural milieu in which most religions develop and exist.

Overall, more projects of this sort are increasingly necessary to problematize the polarized paradigms of Indian societies that have dominated Western scholarship for so long. In any field, knowledge evolves from the simple toward the complex, and so it should not surprise us that many of our earlier models no longer satisfactorily answer the questions we ask now about South Asia. Maps are not territory, nor should we expect them to be. But, because they *are* all we have, we must take care to refine them.

We have come to realize how tentative and subjective all knowledge is. Some scholars despair of the impossibility of drawing anything but 1:1 scale maps and, so, mercilessly criticize those who try for leaving anything out. Others simply abandon the task of mapmaking, fearful of the necessary act of reduction. But, we still need to find our ways across the all-too-real landscape of cultural interactions. Although we need not take them as our own, we must not dismiss others' memories because they do not conform to our ways of remembering. Alternately, we cannot minimize the importance of historiography to our own memory making by enlarging that term to enfold all group mnemonic practices. Instead, we can hew to a middle course, aware of the dynamics of memory that bind us so powerfully, yet mutably, with one another and against one another, in time and space.

Most of the time, people rest easily against the moldy walls of the *hāthlī kū'ā* without feeling compelled to claim publicly a religious identity for themselves or the well. Although no one drinks its water or even washes (either hands or elephants) with it, the well remains a familiar part of the landscape, and people relax around it in casual conversation. However, in times of communal tension, residents fit the well into the familiar narrative of raja-*brahm*-sultan to suit their agendas of religious identities. Contemporarily, as communalists increasingly attempt to divide shared memories, it has become more important to recognize that there are more than two maps in India—Hindu and Muslim—and that this particular well exists as a place to relax in a shared place and time on many maps, as well as a place of contention on others. Residents—and visiting scholars—need to step cautiously because the stairs have become increasingly slippery and the well's depth is uncertain.

Appendix

*Indices of Bihar Government Textbooks
for Social Studies and History
(Standards II and IV to X)*
Translated from Hindi

नूतन बाल समाज—A Young Person's Society (Standard II)

Society

1. One's own family (p. 3)
2. Our neighborhood (p. 4)
3. School (p. 5)
4. Youth assembly (p. 6)
5. The hospital (p. 7)
6. The post office (p. 8)
7. The police (p. 9)
8. The bazaar (p. 10)
9. Neighboring people (p. 11)
10. Transportation (p. 14)
11. Means of entertainment, festivals & celebrations, and places of worship (p. 16)
12. The library (p. 19)
13. The village assembly (p. 20)
14. The city council (p. 21)

Natural History

15. Weather (p. 22)
16. Knowledge of direction and time (p. 24)
17. Our universe (p. 25)
18. Our Earth (p. 28)
19. Our country (*Bhārat*) (p. 30)
20. Gautam Buddha (p. 32)
21. Mahatma Gandhi (p. 33)
22. Jawaharlal Nehru (p. 34)
23. Lal Bahadur Shastri (p. 35)

हमारा देश भारत—Our Country India (Standard IV)

First Unit: India's Natural Divisions

Second Unit: Natural Resources

Third Unit: Human Resources

Fourth Unit: Transportation and Means of Communication

Fifth Unit: Our Lifestyle

Sixth Unit: Things That Make Our Lives Beautiful

Seventh Unit: We and Our Government

Eighth Unit: Primary Leaders of India's Independence Movement

हम और हमारी दुनिया—We and Our World (Standard V)

One: Maps of Our Globe and World

Two: Various Ways of Passing Life

(g) Attainment of independence and building a new India (p. 213)

प्राचीन भारत—Ancient India (Standard VI)

1. Resources for the study of Indian history (p. 1)
2. Prehistory (p. 10)
   Primitive phase
   Human food gatherer forms
   Invention and use of metals
   Invention of the wheel
   Beginning of agriculture
3. Harappan civilization (p. 25)
   City, occupations, religion
   Expansion of writing
   End of Harappan civilization
4. Life in the Vedic Age (p. 41)
   Arrival of the Aryans
   Institutions of economic and political life
   Vedic religion
5. Rise of Magadh (p. 51)
   Ancient Indian monarchies and republics
   Rise of cities
   Jainism and Buddhism
6. Invasions by Iran and Greece: impact (p. 68)
7. Maurya empire (p. 72)
   Chandragupt Maurya
   Ashok
   Maurya period administration and common life
8. India from 200 B.C. to 300 A.D. (p. 84)
   The Satvahans
   The Kushan empire
   Kingdoms of the South
   Chol, Pandey, and Cher
9. Gupt period (p. 104)
   Administration
   Business
   Religion
   Arts and sciences
10. India from 500 A.D. to 800 A.D. (p. 118)
    Harshvardhan
    Pallav and Chalukya
    Arts and culture

11. India's connections with the outside world (p. 129)
   Conquest
   India's connection with Southeast Asian countries
   Connections with Sri Lanka, Tibet, and China
   The rise of Islam
   The Arabs' conquest of Sind

मध्य कालीन भारत—Middle Period India (Standard VII)

1. The world and India of the Middle Period (p. 1)
   (a) Division of time
   (b) Study sources
   (c) The Middle Period in Western Asia
   (d) The Middle Period in Europe
   (e) Eminence of the Turks
   (f) Religious wars
   (g) The Mongol Empire
2. India (from 800 A.D. to 1200 A.D.) (Pratihar, Pal, and Rashtraku (p. 20)
   (a) Kannauj struggle
   (b) Kingdoms of the Far South
   (c) Establishment of Rajput kingdoms
   (d) The Turk invasion
3. The social and cultural situation of early Middle Period India (p. 48)
   Caste arrangements: various religions, construction of temples, Shankar-charya, Ramanuj, development of schools of thought *Economic situation*: villages, feudalism, condition of farmers, organizations of business and craftwork, education, development of new languages, regional writing, literature, development of new art styles
4. The Delhi Sultanate (from 1206 A.D. to 1526 A.D. (p. 63)
   The Slave Dynasty, the Khilji Dynasty, Tuglak Dynasty, Saiyyad Dynasty, Lodi Dynasty, methods of the Sultanate's administration, economic life
5. Independent kingdoms of the Sultanate Period (1335 A.D.–1526 A.D.: Disintegration of the Sultanate rule (p. 79)
   Vijaynagar, Bahamani, Jaunpur, Bengal, Kashmir, Rajputana, Malwa, Gujarat, Sindh, Kamrup, Orissa, Nepal, Khandesh
6. The social, economic, and cultural life of the Sultanate Period: Arab-India relations, Turk-Arab relations (p. 88)
   Society, aristocrat class, priest class, urban residents, lower classes, change in social life, condition of women, economic life, industries, trade, cultural developments, Parsi literature, regional literature, arts of painting and music, architectural arts, the Sufi movement, the *bhakti* movement
7. The arrival of Europeans to India: Europe-India relations, Renaissance in Europe (p. 104)

Geographical discoveries, oceanic journeys, new avenues of research, the Portuguese arrival in India

8. The arrival of the Mughals in India: India's political situation (p. 112) Babar, Humayun, Sher Shah

9. Mughal Period India: Development of the Mughal Empire (p. 119) The Second Battle at Panipat, Akbar, Jahangir, Shah Jahan, Aurangzeb, the Sikhs, Mughal administration, economic life, social life, religious policy of the Mughals, literary and cultural developments, arts, architectural arts, painting arts, musical arts, development of traditions of national unity

10. Disintegration of the Mughal Empire (p. 140) Policies of Aurangzeb, problems of succession, faulty military organization, economic difficulties, Maratha rule, development of Jat power, the Sikhs, Hyderabad, Awadh, the separation of Bengal, Nadir Shah's invasion, and the Europeans' arrival

Appendix: Time periods in history (p. 150)

Important phases and themes, important individuals in Middle Period India history, important dates of Middle Period India

आधुनिक भारत—Modern India (Standard VIII)

1. India and the modern world (p. 1)
   (a) The beginning of the Modern Age in Europe (p. 3)
   (b) The rise of capitalism (p. 12)
   (c) The arrival of the Europeans in India (p. 19)
2. Establishment of British rule in India: development and influence
   (a) The rise of British power in Bengal (p. 30)
   (b) Expansion of the British Empire in India (p. 40)
   (c) The development and organization of the British Empire (p. 55)
3. Opposition to British rule
   (a) Rebellion against the British (p. 73)
   (b) Causes of rebellion (p. 76)
4. British policy and organization in India after 1858
   (a) Social and religious policies of the British government (p. 87)
   (b) Constitutional development (1858 A.D. to 1947 A.D. (p. 97)
   (c) Relations with other neighboring countries (p. 102)
5. Economic life and change in society (p. 109)
   (a) Religious and social reform movements (p. 120)
6. The rise of national identity in India and the independence struggle
   (a) The rise of nationalism in India (p. 138)
   (b) The national movement from 1905 to 1918 (p. 150)
   (c) The beginning of opposition to imperialism (p. 163)
7. Rebirth of the revolutionary movement (p. 175)
   (a) Revolutionary activity in Bengal (p. 177)

सभ्यता का इतिहास, भाग-१—History of Civilization, Part 1 (Standard IX)

सभ्यता का इतिहास, भाग-२—History of Civilization, Part 2 (Standard X)

Glossary

See the introduction for an explanation of diacritic usage.

Allah—the primary name for the One God of Islamic faith

Anṣārī—a Muslim caste of lower social status than Paṭhān and associated with weaving

āzādī—independence; (when capitalized) the Independence of India in 1947 from British rule; also known as *Svatantratā*

bhūt—the ghost of someone dead

BJP—Bhāratīya Janatā Party (Indian People's Party), political arm of Sangh Parivar

brahm—the ghost of a Brahman man who dies an unjust death

Brahman—the priest-teacher division or *varṇa* of the classical Indian social model

Camār—a Hindu caste associated with leather work; considered among the most ritually impure of Hindus

camṭol—the name for a Camār neighborhood or quarter

dargāh—"place within"; shrine or tomb to a Muslim saint or Sufi

dharm—religion; duty; destiny

duʿā—a form of personal prayer derived from Islamic traditions

gāzī—a Muslim warrior against infidels

Harijan—Gandhi's alternative name for "Untouchable," a member of the lowest status Hindu castes

itihās—history

jāgīrdār—the holder of a government grant to own land and villages

Jamaʿ Masjid—"mosque of the [Friday] gathering"

jāti—caste

jinn—entities mentioned in the Quran as created from fire, which become, in South Asia, synonymous at times with ghosts of the dead

Kṣatriya—the warrior-king division or *varṇa* of the classical Indian social model

mandir—temple

masjid–mosque

muhalla—neighborhood

mūrti—embodiment; image

namāz—(Arabic: *ṣalāh*) ritualized Muslim prayers performed five times daily

Paṭhān—a Muslim caste associated with the tribes of Afghanistan and the Hindu Kush

prasād—a gift empowered through proximity with a superhuman agent

pret, preta—the malicious ghost of someone dead

pūjā—a general term for Hindu worship ritual

purohit—sacrifier of a Hindu ritual

Rājpūt—a Hindu high caste associated with the Kṣatrya or warrior-king class of society

Ram—one of the avatars of Vishnu and celebrated as a human king in the Sanskrit *Rāmāyaṇa* and the Hindi *Rāmcaritmānas.*

RSS—Rāṣṭrīya Swayaṁsevak Saṅgh (Association of National Volunteers), central organization of the Sangh Parivar

sadhu—a Hindu renunciant who lives an ascetic life in pursuit of release from the cycle of rebirth

Sangh Parivar—("Family of Organizations"), the family of Hindu revivalist organizations that includes the RSS, BJP, and VHP

shahīd—a Muslim martyred in an Islamic cause

sīṛhī—generation

Śūdra—the lowest ranked of the four divisions or *varṇa*s in the classical Indian social model

Sufi—a Muslim mystic who may or may not belong to a lineage of spiritual teachers

tārikh—date, history

Ṭolī, ṭolā—quarter of a town or city

'ulamā—body of Muslim scholars

'urs—the annual celebration of a particular Sufi's death day

VHP—Viswa Hindū Pariṣad (World Hindu Council), cultural promotional arm of the Sangh Parivar

yād—memory

zamindar—a landlord

zikr—mention, remembrance

Bibliography

Unpublished Works

Burkhalter-Flueckiger, Joyce. "Religious Identity at the Crossroads of a Muslim Female Healer's Practice." Paper presented at the annual South Asian Studies Conference, Madison, October 1996.

Burkhalter-Flueckiger, Joyce. "The Word Ingested, Burned, Performed: A Healing Crossroads in South India." Paper presented at the annual American Academy of Religion Conference, San Francisco, November 1997.

Coccari, Diane. *The Bir Babas of Banaras: An Analysis of a Folk Deity in North Indian Hinduism*. Ph.D. dissertation, University of Wisconsin–Madison, 1986.

Gottschalk, Peter. *Multiple Pasts, Multiple Identities: The Role of Narrative among Hindus and Muslims in Some Villages in Bihar*. Ph.D. dissertation, University of Chicago, 1997.

Katten, Michael. *Category Creation in the Colonial Setting: Identity Formation in 19th Century Telugu-Speaking India*. Ph.D. dissertation, University of California, Berkeley, 1998.

Schmalz, Mathew N. "Sins and Somatologies: Sexual Transgression and the Body in Indian Charismatic Healing." Paper presented at the annual American Academy of Religion conference, San Francisco, November 1997.

Schmalz, Mathew N. "Slave of Christ: Portrait of an Indian Charismatic Healer." Paper presented at the annual Conference on South Asia, Madison, October 1996.

Government Publications

Ādhunik Bhārat. Patna: Bihar State Textbook Publishing, 1994.

Archæological Survey of India. *Annual Report, 1902–03*. Calcutta: Office of the Superintendent of Government Printing, India, 1904.

Askari, Syed Hasan, and Qeyamuddin Ahmad, eds. *Comprehensive History of Bihar*, 3 volumes in 6 parts. Patna: Kashi Prasad Jayaswal Research Institute, 1983.

Barrow, F. H. "Report on the Census of Shahabad," letter no. 103.C (18 June 1881) in *Census of Bengal, 1881, District Report, Patna Division*.

Buchanan, Francis. *Journal of Francis Buchanan*, C. E. A. W. Oldham, ed. Patna: Superintendent, Government Printing, 1926.

Census of Bengal, 1881, District Report, Patna Division. Census Library, New Delhi.
Census of India 1981, Series 4—Bihar, District Census Handbook—Rohtas District, Parts XIII—A & B, Village and Town Directory. Patna: Government of Bihar, 1985.
1991 Census of India: Compressed PCA for Bihar (01-09), diskette. New Delhi: Census Publications, 1991.
Census of India 1991, Series 1 India, Final Population Totals: Brief Analysis of Primary Census Abstract, Paper 2 of 1992. New Delhi: Government of India Press, 1993.
Census of India 1991, Series 1 India, Paper 1 of 1992, vol. 1, *Final Population Totals.* New Delhi: Government of India Press, 1993.
Census of India 1991, Series 5 Bihar, Paper 1 of 1991 Provisional Population Totals. Patna: Secretariat Press, 1991.
Census of India 1991, Paper 2 of 1992. New Delhi: Government of India Press, 1993.
Chaudhury, P. C. Roy. *Bihar District Gazetteers: Shahabad.* Patna: Superintendent Secretariat Press, 1966.
Ham aur Hamārī Duniyā. Patna: Bihar State Textbook Publishing, 1995 (1991).
Hamārā Deś Bhārat. Patna: Bihar State Textbook Publishing, 1994 (1990).
Imperial Gazetteer of India, Provincial Series: Bengal, vol. 2. New Delhi: Usha Publications, 1984 (1909).
Lacey, W. G. *Census of India, 1931,* vol. 7, *Bihar and Orissa, II—Tables.* New Delhi, Usha Publications, 1987 (1932).
Lal, B. B. *Census of India, 1981. Series 4: Bihar. Paper 1 of 1985: Household Population by Religion of Head of Household.* Patna: Bihar Secretariat Press, 1985.
Madhyakālīn Bhārat. Patna: Bihar State Textbook Publishing, 1994.
Madhyatā kā Itihās. Patna: Bihar State Textbook Publishing, 1986.
Marshall, John, ed. *Annual Report of the Archæological Survey of India, 1923–24.* Calcutta: Government of India Central Publication Branch, 1926.
Nūtan Bāl Samāj. Patna: Vinod Prakashan, 1995.
O'Malley, L. S. S. *Census of India, 1911,* vol. 5, *Bihar and Orissa, Part II—Tables.* Calcutta: Bengal Secretariat Book Depot, 1913.
Prācīn Bhārat. Patna: Bihar State Textbook Publishing, 1992 (1991).
Prasad, Ran Chandra. *Bihar.* New Delhi: National Book Trust, 1992 (1983).
Sabhyatā kā Itihās. Patna: Bihar State Textbook Publishing, 1994.

Books

Ali, A. Yusuf, trans. *The Holy Qur'ān: Text, Translation, and Commentary.* Brentwood, Md.: Amana, 1983.
Amin, Shahid. *Event, Metaphor, Memory: Chauri Chaura 1922–1992.* Delhi: Oxford University Press, 1995.
Anderson, Benedict. *Imagined Communities.* New York: Verso, 1991.
Anderson, Walter, and Shridhar Damle. *The Brotherhood in Saffron: The Rashtriya Swayamsevak Sangh and Hindu Revivalism.* New Delhi: Vistaar, 1987.
Ansari, Sarah. *Sufi Saints and State Power: The Pirs of Sind, 1843–1947.* Cambridge: Cambridge University Press, 1992.
Archer, Mildred. *Early Views of India: The Picturesque Journeys of Thomas and William Daniell, 1786–1794.* London: Thames and Hudson, 1980.
Asher, Frederick. *The Art of Eastern India: 300–800.* Minneapolis: University of Minneapolis Press, 1980.
Asiatic Researches; or, Transactions of the Society, Instituted in Bengal, for Inquiring into

the History and Antiquities, the Arts, Sciences, and Literature of Asia, vol. 1. Varanasi: Bharat-Bharati, 1972 (1884).

An Atlas of India. New York: Oxford University Press, 1990.

Basu, Tapan, Pradip Datta, et al., *Khaki Shorts and Saffron Flags: A Critique of the Hindu Right.* New Delhi: Orient Longman, 1993.

Battaglia, Debbora. *On the Bones of the Serpent: Person, Memory, and Mortality in Saharl Island Society.* Chicago: University of Chicago Press, 1990.

Bayly, C. A. *Origins of Nationality in South Asia: Patriotism and Ethical Government in the Making of Modern India.* Delhi: Oxford University Press, 1998.

Bayly, Susan. *Saints, Goddesses, and Kings: Muslims and Christians in South Indian Society, 1700–1900.* New York: Cambridge University Press, 1989.

Becker, Carl. *Everyman His Own Historian: Essays on History and Politics.* Chicago: Quadrangle, 1935.

Bhatia, Hansraj. *Agra Red Fort Is a Hindu Building.* Delhi: Surya Prakash, 1971.

Bhattacharya, Sachchidananda. *A Dictionary of Indian History.* Calcutta: University of Calcutta, 1972.

Blackburn, Stuart, Peter Claus, Joyce Flueckiger, and Susan Wadley, eds. *Oral Epics in India.* Berkeley: University of California Press, 1989.

Bloch, Maurice. *The Historian's Craft.* Manchester: Manchester University Press, 1954.

Blochmann, H. *Contributions to the Geography and History of Bengal (Muhammedan Period).* Calcutta: Asiatic Society, 1968 (1873).

Bowen, John. *Muslims through Discourse: Religion and Ritual in Gayo Society.* Princeton: Princeton University Press, 1993.

Brass, Paul. *Language, Religion and Politics in North India.* Delhi: Vikas, 1974.

———. *The Politics of India since Independence.* New Delhi: Cambridge University Press, 1994.

———. *Theft of an Idol: Text and Context in the Representation of Collective Violence.* Calcutta: Seagull, 1998.

Buehler, Arthur. *Sufi Heirs of the Prophet: The Indian Naqshbandiyya and the Rise of the Mediating Sufi Shaykh.* Columbia: University of South Carolina Press, 1998.

Burke, S. M., and Salim Al-Din Quraishi, *The British Raj in India: An Historical Review.* New York: Oxford University Press, 1996.

Carr, David. *Phenomenology and the Problem of History.* Evanston: Northwestern University Press, 1974.

Chandra, Bipan. *Communalism in Modern India.* New Delhi: Vikas, 1984.

Char, S. V. Desika. *Hinduism and Islam in India: Caste, Religion, and Society from Antiquity to Early Modern Times.* Princeton: Markus Wiener, 1997.

Chatterjee, Partha. *The Nation and Its Fragments: Colonial and Postcolonial Histories.* Delhi: Oxford University Press, 1995.

Cohn, Bernard. *An Anthropologist among the Historians and Other Essays.* New York: Oxford University Press, 1990.

Collingwood, R. G. *The Idea of History.* New York: Oxford University Press, 1956.

Connerton, Paul. *How Societies Remember.* New York: Cambridge University Press, 1991.

Crooke, William. *A Glossary of North Indian Peasant Life.* New York: Oxford University Press, 1989 (1879).

———. *The Popular Religion and Folklore of Northern India*, vol. 1. Delhi: Munshiram Manoharlal, 1968 (1896).

Dalmia, Vasudha. *The Nationalization of Hindu Traditions: Bhāratendu Harischandra and Nineteenth-Century Banaras.* Calcutta: Oxford University Press, 1997.

Das, Arvind. *The Republic of Bihar*. New Delhi: Penguin, 1992.

Das, Suranjan. *Communal Riots in Bengal: 1905–1947*. Delhi: Oxford University Press, 1991.

Das, Veena, ed. *Mirrors of Violence: Communities, Riots and Survivors in South Asia*. Oxford: Oxford University Press, 1990.

Dasgupta, Satadal. *Caste, Kinship and Community: Social System of a Bengali Caste*. Hyderabad: Universities Press, 1993.

Dass, Nirmal, trans. *Songs of Kabir from the Adi Granth*. Albany: State University of New York Press, 1991.

Death and Death Ceremonies. Karachi: Peermahomed Ebrahim Trust, 1972.

De Certeau, Michel. *The Practice of Everyday Life*, Steven Rendall, trans. Berkeley: University of California Press, 1988.

Diwakar, R. R. *Bihar through the Ages*. New Delhi: Orient Longmans, 1959.

Eaton, Richard. *The Rise of Islam and the Bengal Frontier, 1204–1760*. Delhi: Oxford University Press, 1994.

———. *Sufis of Bijapur, 1300–1700: Social Roles of Sufis in Medieval India*. Princeton: Princeton University Press, 1978.

Eck, Diana. *Banaras: City of Light*. New York: Penguin, 1983.

Embree, Ainslie, ed. *Alberuni's India*, Edward C. Sachau, trans. New York: W. W. Norton, 1971.

Engineer, Ashgar Ali. *Communal Riots in Post-Independence India*. New Delhi: Sangam, 1991.

———. *Communalism and Communal Violence in India: An Analytical Approach to Hindu-Muslim Conflict*. Delhi: Ajanta (India), 1989.

———. *Lifting the Veil: Communal Violence and Communal Harmony in Contemporary India*. New Delhi: Sangam, 1995.

Fertess, James, and Chris Wickham. *Social Memory*. Cambridge: Blackwell, 1992.

Foster, Stephen William. *The Past Is Another Country: Representation, Historical Consciousness, and Resistance in the Blue Ridge*. Berkeley: University of California Press, 1988.

Freitag, Sandria B. *Collective Action and Community: Public Arena and the Emergence of Communalism in North India*. New Delhi: Oxford University Press, 1984.

Geertz, Clifford. *Islam Observed: Religious Development in Morocco and Indonesia*. Chicago: University of Chicago Press, 1968.

Gilsenan, Michael. *Recognizing Islam*. New York: Pantheon, 1982.

Gold, Ann Grodzins. *Fruitful Journeys: The Ways of Rajasthani Pilgrims*. Berkeley: University of California Press, 1988.

Gopal, Sarvepalli, ed. *Anatomy of a Confrontation: The Babri Masjid–Ram Janmabhumi Issue*. New Delhi: Penguin, 1991.

Grierson, George Abraham. *Bihar Peasant Life, Being a Discursive Catalogue of the Surroundings of the People of that Province*. Delhi: Cosmo, 1975 (1885).

Hanson, Thomas Blom. *The Saffron Wave: Democracy and Hindu Nationalism in Modern India*. Princeton: Princeton University Press, 1999.

Halbwachs, Maurice. *Les cadres sociaux de la mémoire*. Paris: Librairie Félix Alcan, 1925.

———. *The Collective Memory*, Francis J. Ditter Jr. and Vida Yazdi Ditter, trans. New York: Harper Colophon, 1980.

———. *La Mémoire Collective*. Paris: Presses Universitaires de France, 1968 (1950).

———. *On Collective Memory*, Lewis A. Coser, trans. Chicago: University of Chicago Press, 1992.

————. *La Topographie légendaire des Évangiles en Terre Sainte*. Paris: Presses Universitaires de France, 1971 (1941).

Hardy, Peter. *The Muslims of British India*. Cambridge: Cambridge University Press, 1972.

Harlan, Lindsey, and Paul Courtright, eds. *From the Margins of Hindu Marriage: Essays on Gender, Religion, and Culture*. New York: Oxford University Press, 1995.

Hasan, Mushirul. *Legacy of a Divided Nation: India's Muslims since Independence*. Boulder: Westview, 1997.

————. *Nationalism and Communal Politics in India, 1885–1930*. New Delhi: Manohar, 1991.

Hess, Linda, trans. *The Bījak of Kabir*. Delhi: Motilal Banarsidass, 1986.

Hobsbawn, E., and T. Rangers, eds. *The Invention of Tradition*. New York: Cambridge University Press, 1983.

Inden, Ronald. *Imagining India*. Oxford: Blackwell, 1990.

Jaffrelot, Christophe. *The Hindu Nationalist Movement in India*. New York: Columbia University Press, 1996.

Jain, S. P. *The Social Structure of Hindu-Muslim Community*. Delhi: National Publishing House, 1975.

Jalal, Ayesha. *Democracy and Authoritarianism in South Asia: A Comparative and Historical Perspective*. New York: Cambridge University Press, 1995.

————. *The Sole Spokesman: Jinnah, the Muslim League and the Demand for Pakistan*. Cambridge: Cambridge University Press, 1985.

Jeffery, Patricia, and Roger Jeffery. *Don't Marry Me to a Plowman! Women's Everyday Lives in Rural North India*. Boulder, Colo.: Westview, 1996.

Justice, Christopher, *Dying the Good Death: The Pilgrimage to Die in India's Holy City*. Albany: State University of New York Press, 1997.

Kakar, Sudhir. *The Colors of Violence: Cultural Identities, Religion, and Conflict*. Chicago: University of Chicago Press, 1996.

————. *Shamans, Mystics, and Doctors: A Psychological Inquiry into India and Its Healing Traditions*. Delhi: Oxford University Press, 1994.

Kalhana. *Rājataraṅgiṇī: The Saga of the Kings of Kaśmīr*, Ranjit Sitaram Pandit, trans. New Delhi: Sahitya Akademi, 1990 (1935).

Keen, Sam. *Faces of the Enemy: Reflections of the Hostile Imagination*. San Francisco: Harper, 1991.

Khan, Dominique-Sila. *Conversions and Shifting Identities: Ramdev Pir and the Ismailis in Rajasthan*. New Delhi: Manohar, 1997.

Khomeini, Imam. *Islam and Revolution*, Hamid Algar, trans. Berkeley: Mizab, 1981.

Khubchandani, Lachman M. *Plural Languages, Plural Cultures: Communication, Identity, and Sociopolitical Change in Contemporary India*. Honolulu: University of Hawaii Press, 1983.

Kumar, Nita. *The Artisans of Banaras: Popular Culture and Identity, 1880–1986*. New Delhi: Orient Longman, 1995.

Lahiri, Manosi. *The Bihar Geographic Information System*. Bombay: Popular Prakashan, 1993.

Larson, Gerald James. *India's Agony over Religion*. Albany: State University of New York Press, 1995.

Le Goff, Jacques. *History and Memory*, Steven Rendall and Elizabeth Claman, trans. New York: Columbia University Press, 1992.

Lelyveld, David. *Aligarh's First Generation: Muslim Solidarity in British India*. Delhi: Oxford University Press, 1996 (1978).

Lewis, P. *Pirs, Shrines and Pakistani Islam*. Rawalpindi: Christian Study Centre, 1985.

Lincoln, Bruce. *Discourse and the Construction of Society: Comparative Studies of Myth, Ritual, and Classification*. Oxford: Oxford University Press, 1989.

Lipsitz, George. *Time Passages: Collective Memory and American Popular Culture*. Minneapolis: University of Minneapolis Press, 1990.

Lorenzen, David N. *Kabir Legends and Ananta-das's Kabir Parachai*. Albany: State University of New York Press, 1991.

Lowenthal, David. *The Past Is a Foreign Country*. New York: Cambridge University Press, 1990.

Ludden, David, ed. *Contesting the Nation: Religion, Community, and the Politics of Democracy in India*. Philadelphia: University of Pennsylvania Press, 1996.

Lutgendorf, Philip. *The Life of a Text: Performing the Rāmcaritmānas of Tulsidas*. Berkeley: University of California Press, 1991.

Mann, E. A. *Boundaries and Identities: Muslims, Work and Status in Aligarh*. New Delhi: Sage, 1992.

Marshall, P. J., and Glyndwr Williams. *The Great Map of Mankind: British Perceptions of the World in the Age of Enlightenment*. Toronto: J. M. Dent, 1982.

McGregor, R. S., ed. *The Oxford Hindi-English Dictionary*. Delhi: Oxford University Press, 1993.

McKean, Lise. *Divine Enterprise: Gurus and the Hindu Nationalist Movement*. Chicago: University of Chicago Press, 1996.

McLeod, W. H. *Gurū Nānak and the Sikh Religion*. Delhi: Oxford University Press, 1996.

Mill, James. *The History of British India*. Chicago: University of Chicago Press, 1975.

Mines, Mattison. *Public Faces, Private Voices: Community and Individuality in South India*. Berkeley: University of California Press, 1994.

Munn, Nancy. *The Fame of Gawa*. New York: Cambridge University Press, 1989.

Naipaul, V. S. *An Area of Darkness*. New York: Macmillan, 1965.

Narayan, Kirin. *Storytellers, Saints, and Scoundrels: Folk Narrative in Hindu Religious Teaching*. Philadelphia: University of Pennsylvania Press, 1989.

O'Flaherty, Wendy Doniger. *Other People's Myths: The Cave of Echoes*. Chicago: University of Chicago Press, 1988.

Pandey, Gyanendra. *The Construction of Communalism in Colonial North India*. Delhi: Oxford University Press, 1990.

Parry, Jonathan P. *Death in Banaras*. Cambridge: Cambridge University Press, 1994.

Platts, John T. *A Dictionary of Urdū, Classical Hindī and English*. New Delhi, Munshiram Manoharlal, 1988 (1884).

Pouchepadass, Jacques, James Walker, trans. *Champaran and Gandhi: Planters, Peasants and Gandhian Politics*. New Delhi: Oxford University Press, 1999.

Qureshi, Regula Burckhardt. *Sufi Music of India and Pakistan: Sound, Context and Meaning in Qawwali*. Chicago: University of Chicago Press, 1995.

Rahman, Fariq. *Language and Politics in Pakistan*. Karachi: Oxford University Press, 1996.

Rai, Amrit. *A House Divided: The Origin and Development of Hindi/Hindavi*. Delhi: Oxford University Press, 1984.

Rakshasa, Mudra. *The Hunted*, Robert A. Hueckstedt, trans. New Delhi: Penguin, 1992.

Read, Peter. *Returning to Nothing: The Meaning of Lost Places*. Melbourne: Cambridge University Press, 1996.

Ricoeur, Paul. *History and Truth*, Charles A. Kelbley, trans. Evanston: Northwestern University Press, 1965.

————. *Time and Narrative*, volume 1, Kathleen Blamey and David Pellauer, trans. Chicago: University of Chicago Press, 1984.

————. *Time and Narrative*, volume 3, Kathleen Blamey and David Pellauer, trans. Chicago: University of Chicago Press, 1988.

Roy, Asim. *The Islamic Syncretistic Tradition in Bengal*. Princeton: Princeton University Press, 1983.

Rushdie, Salman. *Haroun and the Sea of Stories*. New York: Penguin, 1990.

Sahlins, Marshall. *Islands of History*. Chicago: University of Chicago Press, 1987.

Said, Edward. *Orientalism*. New York: Vintage, 1978.

Schwartzberg, Joseph E. *A Historical Atlas of South Asia*. New York: Oxford University Press, 1992.

Shrivastav, Ravindra Kumar. *Śrī Muṇḍeśvarī Maṅdīr: Smārikā 1994*. Bhabua, Bihar: Shri Mundeshvari Paryatan evam Sanskritik Vikas Parishad, 1994.

Seneviratne, H. L., ed. *Identity, Consciousness and the Past: Forging of Caste and Community in India and Sri Lanka*. Delhi: Oxford University Press, 1997.

Singh, S. B. *Fairs and Festivals in Rural India: A Geospatial Study of Belief Systems*. Varanasi: Tara Book Agency, 1989.

Smith, Jane Idleman, and Yvonne Yazbeck Haddad, *The Islamic Understanding of Death and Resurrection*. Albany: State University of New York Press, 1981.

Smith, Jonathan Z. *Map Is Not Territory*. Chicago: University of Chicago Press, 1978.

Smith, Vincent. *The Oxford History of India*. Karachi: Oxford University Press, 1981 (1919).

Tavernier, Jean-Baptiste. *Travels in India*, V. Ball, trans. Delhi: Oriental Books Reprint, 1977.

Tholfsen, Trygive R. *Historical Thinking: An Introduction*. New York: Harper and Row, 1967.

Tod, James. *Annals and Antiquities of Rajasthan or the Central and Western Rajput States of India*, William Crooke, ed. London: Oxford University Press, 1920 (1829–32).

Tripathi, L. *Brahmprakāś*. Bhabhua, Bihar: Ruchika, 1995.

Van der Veer, Peter. *Gods on Earth: The Management of Religious Experience and Identity in a North Indian Pilgrimage Centre*. London: Athlone, 1988.

————. *Religious Nationalism: Hindus and Muslims in India*. Berkeley: University of California Press, 1994.

Vansina, Jan. *Oral Tradition as History*. Madison: University of Wisconsin Press, 1985.

Vaudeville, Charlotte. *A Weaver Called Kabir: Selected Verses with a Detailed Biographical and Historical Introduction*. Delhi: Oxford University Press, 1997.

Veyne, Paul. *Did the Greeks Believe in Their Myths? An Essay on the Constitutive Imagination*. Paula Wissing, trans. Chicago: University of Chicago Press, 1988.

Wadley, Susan. *Struggling with Destiny in Karimpur, 1925–1984*. Berkeley: University of California Press, 1994.

Weiss, Anita. *Walls within Walls: Life Histories of Working Women in the Old City of Lahore*. Boulder, Colo.: Westview, 1992.

Weissman, Steve, and Herbert Krosney. *The Islamic Bomb: The Nuclear Threat to Israel and the Middle East*. New York: Times Books, 1981.

White, Hayden. *Metahistory: The Historical Imagination in Nineteenth-Century Europe*. Baltimore: Johns Hopkins University Press, 1973.

Wink, André. *Al-Hind: The Making of the Indo-Islamic World*, vol. 1. Delhi: Oxford University Press, 1990.

X, Malcolm. *The Autobiography of Malcolm X*. New York: Ballantine, 1993 (1964).

Yang, Anand A. *Bazaar India: Markets, Society, and the Colonial State in Bihar*. Berkeley: University of California Press, 1998.

Ziring, Lawrence. *Pakistan in the Twentieth Century: A Political History*. New York: Oxford University Press, 1997.

Contributions to Books

Amin, Shahid. "Gandhi as Mahatma: Gorakhpur District, Eastern U.P., 1921–2" in *Subaltern Studies III: Writings on South Asian History and Society*, Ranajit Guha, ed. New York: Oxford University Press, 1984, pp. 1–59.

Ansari, Hasan Nishat. "Early Muslim Contact with Bihar and Invasion of Bakhtiyār Khaljī" in *Comprehensive History of Bihar*, vol. 2, Part 1, Syed Hasan Askari and Qeyamuddin Ahmad, eds. Patna: Kashi Prasad Jayaswal Research Institute, 1983, pp. 29–54.

Appadurai, Arjun. "Number in Colonial Imagination" in *Modernity at Large: Cultural Dimensions of Globalization*, Arjun Appadura, ed. Minneapolis: University of Minnesota Press, 1996, pp. 114–135.

Basham, A. L. "Modern Historians of Ancient India" in *Historians of India, Pakistan and Ceylon*, C. H. Philips, ed. New York: Oxford University Press, 1962, pp. 260–293.

Bilgrami, Akeel. "What Is a Muslim? Fundamental Commitment and Cultural Identity" in *Hindus and Others: The Question of Identity in India Today*, Gyanendra Pandey, ed. New York: Viking, 1993, pp. 273–299.

Bloch, Maurice, and Jonathan Parry. "Introduction" in *Death and the Regeneration of Life*, Maurice Bloch and Jonathan Parry, eds. New York: Cambridge University Press, 1982, pp. 1–44.

Brow, James. "Nationalist Rhetoric and the Local Practice: The Fate of the Village Community of Kukulewa" in *Sri Lanka: History and the Roots of Conflict*, Jonathan Spenser, ed. New York: Routledge, 1990.

Chatterjee, Partha. "Agrarian Relations and Communalism in Bengal, 1926–1935" in *Subaltern Studies I: Writings on South Asian History and Society*, Ranajit Guha, ed. New York: Oxford University Press, 1982, pp. 9–38.

Coccari, Diane. "The Bir Babas and the Deified Dead" in *Criminal Gods and Demon Devotees: Essays on the Guardians of Popular Hinduism*, Alf Hiltebeitel, ed. Albany: State University of New York Press, 1989, pp. 251–270.

———. "Protection and Identity: Banaras's Bīr Babas as Neighborhood Guardian Deities" in *Culture and Power in Banaras: Community, Performance, and Environment, 1800–1980*, Sandria Freitag, ed. Berkeley: University of California Press, 1992 (1989), pp. 130–146.

Courtright, Paul. "The Iconographies of Sati" in *Sati, the Blessing and the Curse: The Burning of Wives in India*, John Stratton Hawley, ed. New York: Oxford University Press, 1994, pp. 27–48.

Devalle, Susana C. C. "Social Identities, Hindu Fundamentalism, and Politics in India" in *Bhakti Religion in North India: Community Identity and Political Action*, David Lorenzen, ed. Albany: State University of New York Press, 1995, pp. 306–322.

Freitag, Sandria B. "Introduction: The History and Political Economy of Banaras" in *Culture and Power in Banaras: Community, Performance, and Environment, 1800–1980*, Sandria Freitag, ed. Berkeley: University of California Press, 1992, pp. 1–22.

Gold, Daniel. "Clan and Lineage among the Sants: Seed, Service, Substance" in *The Sants: Studies in a Devotional Tradition*, Karine Schomer and W. H. McLeod, eds. Delhi: Motilal Banarsidass, 1987, pp. 305–328.

Guha, Ranajit. "On Some Aspects of the Historiography of Colonial India" in *Selected Subaltern Studies*, Ranajit Guha and Gayatri Chakravorty Spivak, eds. New York: Oxford University Press, 1988, pp. 37–44.

Knipe, David. "Night of the Growing Dead: A Cult of Vīrabhadra in Coastal Andra" in *Criminal Gods and Demon Devotees: Essays on the Guardians of Popular Hinduism*, Alf Hiltebeitel, ed. Albany: State University of New York Press, 1989, pp. 123–156.

———. "*Sapindikarana*: The Hindu Rite of Entry into Heaven" in *Religious Encounters with Death: Insights from the History and Anthropology of Religion*, E. Reynolds and E. Waugh, eds. University Park: Pennsylvania State University Press, 1977, pp. 111–124.

Kumar, Nita. "Work and Leisure in the Formation of Identity: Muslim Weavers in a Hindu City" in *Culture and Power in Banaras: Community, Performance, and Environment, 1800–1980*, Sandria Freitag, ed. Berkeley: University of California Press, 1992, pp. 147–170.

Lorenzen, David N. "Introduction: The Historical Vicissitudes of Bhakti Religion" in *Bhakti Religion in North India: Community Identity and Political Action*, David Lorenzen, ed. Albany: State University of New York Press, 1995, pp. 1–32.

Lutgendorf, Philip. "Interpreting Ramraj: Reflections on the *Ramayana*, Bhakti, and Hindu Nationalism" in *Bhakti Religion in North India: Community Identity and Political Action*, David Lorenzen, ed. Albany: State University of New York Press, 1995, pp. 253–287.

Manto, Saadat Hasan. "Toba Tek Singh" in *Kingdom's End and Other Stories*, Khalid Hasan, trans. New York: Verso, 1987, pp. 11–18.

Marriott, McKim. "Constructing an Indian Ethnosociology" in *India through Hindu Categories*, McKim Marriott, ed. London: SAGE, 1990, pp. 1–40.

Mines, Mattison. "Islamicization and Muslim Ethnicity in South India" in *Ritual and Religion among Muslims of the Sub-continent*, Imtiaz Ahmed, ed. Lahore: Vanguard, 1985.

Nandy, Ashis. "The Politics of Secularism and the Recovery of Religious Tolerance" in *Mirrors of Violence: Communities, Riots and Survivors in South Asia*, Veena Das, ed. Oxford: Oxford University Press, 1990, pp. 69–93.

Pandey, Gyanendra. "The Civilized and the Barbarian: The 'New' Politics of Late Twentieth Century India and the World" in *Hindus and Others: The Question of Identity in India Today*, Gyanendra Pandey, ed. New York: Viking, 1993, pp. 1–23.

———. "Which of Us Are Hindus?" in *Hindus and Others: The Question of Identity in India Today*, Gyanendra Pandey, ed. New York: Viking, 1993, pp. 238–272.

Philips, C. H. "James Mill, Mounstuart Elphinstone, and the History of India" in *Historians of India, Pakistan and Ceylon*, C. H. Philips, ed. New York: Oxford University Press, 1962, pp. 217–229.

Saheb, S. A. A. "A 'Festival of Flags': Hindu-Muslim Devotion and the Sacralising of Localism at the Shrine of Nagore-e-Sharif in Tamil Nadu" in *Embodying Charisma: Modernity, Locality, and the Performance of Emotion in Sufi Cults*, Pnina Werbner and Helene Basu, eds. New York: Routledge, 1998, pp. 55–76.

Selbin, Eric. "Revolution in the Real World: Bringing Agency Back In" in *Theorizing Revolutions*, John Foran, ed. New York: Routledge, 1997, pp. 123–136.

Journal Articles

Ahmed, Samina. "Pakistan's Nuclear Weapons Program: Turning Points and Nuclear Choices" in *International Security*, vol. 23, no. 4 (1999), pp. 178–204.

Asher, Catherine B. "Sub-imperial Palaces: Power and Authority in Mughal India" in *Ars Orientalis*, vol. 23 (1993), pp. 281–302.

Bayly, C. A. "The Pre-history of 'Communalism'? Religious Conflict in India, 1700–1860" in *Modern Asian Studies*, vol. 19, no. 2 (1985), pp. 177–203.

Blackburn, Stuart. "Death and Deification: Folk Cults in Hinduism" in *History of Religions*, vol. 24, no. 3 (1985), pp. 255–274.

Chakrabarty, Dipesh. "Class Consciousness and the Indian Working Class: *Dilemmas of Marxist Historiography*" in *Journal of Asian and African Studies*, vol. 23 (1988), pp. 21–31.

———. "Postcoloniality and the Artifice of History: Who Speaks for the Indian Pasts?" in *Representations*, no. 37 (1992), pp. 1–26.

Davis, Natalie Zemon, and Randolph Starn. "Introduction" to the special issue on "Memory and Counter-Memory" in *Representations*, no. 26 (1989), pp. 1–6.

Ganguly, Sumit. "India's Pathway to Pokhran II: The Prospects and Sources of New Delhi's Nuclear Weapons Program" in *International Security*, vol. 23, no. 4 (1999), pp. 148–177.

Knapp, Steven. "Collective Memory and the Actual Past" in *Representations*, no. 26 (1989), pp. 123–149.

Lutgendorf, Philip. "Monkey in the Middle: The Status of Hanuman in Popular Hinduism" in *Religion*, vol. 27 (1997), pp. 311–332.

———. "My Hanuman Is Bigger Than Yours" in *History of Religions*, vol. 33, no. 3 (1994), pp. 211–245.

Miller, Eric J. "Caste and Territory in Malabar" in *American Anthropologist*, vol. 56, no. 3 (1954), pp. 410–420.

Nora, Pierre. "Between Memory and History: *Las Lieux de Mémoire*" in *Representations*, no. 26 (1989), pp. 7–25.

Pandey, Gyanendra. "In Defense of the Fragment: Writing about Hindu-Muslim Riots in India Today" in *Representations*, no. 37 (1992), pp. 27–55.

Pollock, Sheldon. "Ramayana and Political Imagination in India" in *Journal of Asian Studies*, vol. 52, no. 2 (1993), pp. 261–297.

Roth, Michael. "Remembering Forgetting: *Maladies de la Mémoire* in Nineteenth-Century France." *Representations*, vol. 26 (1989), pp. 49–68.

Rudolf, Susanne Hoeber, and Lloyd Rudolf. "Modern Hate." *New Republic* (22 March 1993), pp. 24–29.

Talbot, Cynthia. "Inscribing the Other, Inscribing the Self: Hindu-Muslim Identities in Pre-Colonial India" in *Society for Comparative Study of Society and History*, vol. 37, no. 4 (1995), pp. 692–722.

Newspapers and Magazines

Dawn (Karachi, 1998).

Hindustan Times (New Delhi, 1998).

India Today International (1998).

New York Times (New York, 1996–1998).

New York Times Magazine (1991).

Times of India (Mumbai, 1998).
Times of India (Lucknow, 1994–1995).
Times of India (New Delhi, 1994–1995).
U.S. News & World Report (1998).

Other Publications

Kumar, Nita. "Children and Partition: History for Citizenship," Occasional Paper No. 167 (February 1998), Centre for Studies in Social Sciences, Calcutta.

Websites

http://forums.nytimes.com/webin/WebX?14@^894343@.eeccc3a (August 29, 1998).

Index

Page references in **bold** indicate where the description of a term or person can be found.

9 780195 189155